Aid, NGOs and the Realities of Women's Lives

Praise for this book

'Finally, here is a book which discusses openly concerns about the growing negative trends in the management of development aid. The corporatization, bureaucratization and top-down management of aid is discussed by people who have an intimate knowledge from the inside. The book documents how the language of rights and the need to address structural inequality is being eroded, and how donor requirements are going against the principles of people-centred and people-led work for sustainable livelihoods and development.

'Thankfully, the book also contains the experience of sensitive, innovative and people-centred initiatives in different parts of the world. This book is a must-read for concerned and committed policymakers and practitioners of development work.'
Kamla Bhasin, Adviser, Sangat, and Co-Chair of Peace Women Across the World

'Raising funds for creating change in women's lives in a way that respects women and is grounded in their realities is not easy, linear or the norm. But if this is something you are aspiring to, and you are on a journey of challenge and exploration away from rigid logframes and linear change maps, then this is the book for you. Wallace and Porter are leading the way by bringing together work on the mechanics and ideology of aid and research of women as recipients of aid today. They acknowledge that there are no easy answers and that perhaps the most important element is to root the way we raise funds and channel funds in the realities of lived experience. This places the greatest importance on learning from the work we do and listening to the recipients of aid as their voices need to not only influence what we raise the funds for, but also how we raise those funds.'
Brita Fernandez Schmidt, Executive Director, Women for Women International

'The increasingly positivist, normative and fatuous managerialism that governs the passage of resources from the centre to NGOs on the margins insidiously outlaws the most human of social endeavours. What a glorious gang of outlaws, then, is here arrayed, riding in response.'
Allan Kaplan, Founder of CDRA, South Africa, author of
The Development Practitioner's Handbook

'Managerialism within aid is creating new markets, bureaucracies and tools but ignoring the grounded realities of people's lives. This book forcefully describes this "perfect storm" and why it is women and girls who pay the greatest price. It is far more than a critique. The authors also offer positive examples from around the world about how conversations, evidence and relationships can be approached completely differently. If people working in donor agencies, governments and NGOs wish to advance gender equality, and other development goals, they need to read this book.'
Emma Crewe, Visiting Reader and Research Associate, Department of Anthropology and Sociology, SOAS, University of London

'This collection of articles provides an important counter-narrative to the linear logic and search for predictability that currently dominates the international development community. It reminds us of what can be achieved when development practice evolves in response to the imperatives on the ground rather than to targets imposed by funding agencies.'

Professor Naila Kabeer, Department of Development Studies, SOAS,
University of London

'This book correctly diagnoses the malaise at the heart of today's development practice. It is a wake-up call to those in the development industry who are driving the current obsession with results. For all the talk about "empowering women and girls", ending discrimination on the basis of gender calls for a transformative approach that takes power, process and relationships seriously.'

Professor Andrea Cornwall, Department of Anthropology,
Sussex University

'I recommend this work without qualification for essential study and application by INGOs, which need to take the critique and the action suggestions very seriously as their very essence is being threatened by state and corporate interests that, more and more, see the INGOs as convenient agents of their interests and not those of either the INGOs as agents of equality or those suffering from a world of growing inequality. Furthermore the volume is a constructive message to academics regarding the focus and methodology of their research into development.'

Meyer Brownstone, Chair emeritus, Oxfam Canada, and
Professor emeritus political economy, University of Toronto

'I cannot imagine a more opportune time for this volume. The book speaks courageously and with authority about growing trends that are increasingly detrimental to women and to local communities. The global development agenda is largely oblivious of the real issues women and local communities face and is driven by donor requirements rather than by these realities. The book made me hopeful given the solid evidence it gathers and its in-depth analysis of these trends.'

Lina Abou-Habib, Executive Director of the Collective for Research and Training on
Development – Action, and a member of the Women Learning Partnership.
Former president of the Association for Women's Rights in Development

'One of the most frank and engaging collections on the dilemmas faced by NGOs – and the women, men and children they should be serving – as the principles and practices of development are increasingly dominated by the major donors on the international scene. While Wallace, Porter and their contributors eschew prescriptions, they offer a host of deeply reflected opinions on the importance of building dialogue at all levels and across different sets of stakeholders, as well as some inspiring examples of small-scale initiatives built with people, for people. Anyone with a personal or professional interest in development, let alone gender and development, should read this important book.'

Sylvia Chant, Professor of Development Geography, London School of Economics and Political Science

'Whether challenging the ahistorical interventions that ignore years of practice able to inform current projects, exploring the technocratic and managerial demands of donors, or interpreting some of the consequences of an increasing dependence on public–private partnerships that fail to account for the lived experiences of everyday life in recipient communities, this wide-ranging collection offers an evidence-based challenge to development business as usual. Drawing particular attention to how these concerns frame poverty and gender programmes, and combining conceptual and practical experience to inform cross regional analyses, the volume is a must-read for researchers, practitioners and donors alike, as well as those who seek to recuperate what is best about the NGO–Aid nexus.'

Professor Shelley Feldman, Director of Feminist, Gender and Sexuality Studies, Cornell University

'This book is a timely reappraisal of the "Women and Development industry" at a time when many of us are alarmed at the increasing drift of donor-led policy away from the original aspirations and enthusiasm of women-centred development cooperation. They bring together the voices of grass-roots and committed development organizations to reflect how to re-assert the principles of feminist and gender-aware solidarity that have motivated us over the last half decade. They urge us not to give in to managerialism or donor fatigue, or the challenges of economic and political crises, but to pursue a development agenda that puts the rights of women and girls first.'

Ruth Pearson, Emeritus Professor of International Development, University of Leeds

Aid, NGOs and the Realities of Women's Lives

A perfect storm

Edited by
Tina Wallace and Fenella Porter,
with Mark Ralph-Bowman

PRACTICAL ACTION
Publishing

JZ
4841
A28

Practical Action Publishing Ltd
The Schumacher Centre
Bourton on Dunsmore, Rugby,
Warwickshire CV23 9QZ, UK
www.practicalactionpublishing.org

ISBN 978 1 85339 778 3 Hardback
ISBN 978 1 85339 779 0 Paperback
ISBN 978 1 78044 778 0 Library Ebook
ISBN 978 1 78044 779 7 Ebook

Tina Wallace and Fenella Porter (eds) (2013) *Aid, NGOs and the Realities of
Women's Lives: A Perfect Storm*, Rugby: Practical Action Publishing.

Since 1974, Practical Action Publishing (formerly Intermediate Technology
Publications and ITDG Publishing) has published and disseminated
books and information in support of international development work
throughout the world. Practical Action Publishing is a trading name of
Practical Action Publishing Ltd (Company Reg. No. 1159018), the wholly
owned publishing company of Practical Action. Practical Action Publishing
trades only in support of its parent charity objectives and any profits
are covenanted back to Practical Action (Charity Reg. No. 247257,
Group VAT Registration No. 880 9924 76).

Cover design: Alice Marwick
Indexed by Liz Fawcett, Harrogate, UK
Typeset by SJI Services, New Delhi
Printed in India by Replika Press

Contents

Acknowledgements

There are so many amazing women throughout the world, who have inspired and energized us over many years, as we have met and talked with them through our research and work in development. These women keep raising their voices, even though what they say is often hard for decision-makers and those with power to hear. We so appreciate their persistence and strength and have learned so much from working with them, talking, arguing and debating together. Thanks for everything we have shared.

Thanks also to the men (fewer in number) who have supported the struggles and taken the debates forward in different ways, especially around the way development is undertaken, highlighting how it is increasingly hard for diverse voices to be heard because of the current structures and procedures of aid.

Many more would have liked to write for this book. There were many barriers for several of them including lack of time because of intensely heavy work and domestic responsibilities, lack of English which remains the dominant language of development, and a real fear of reprisals from organizations that see open debate of these issues as a form of disloyalty. On our side there was a lack of space and the inevitable need to work to a timetable, which some could not meet. Let's find other ways of speaking out in future.

Thanks go to the Development Studies Association Gender Policy and Practice Study Group, which provides a rare space for people from research, academia and development practice to come together, share concerns, and discuss cases with each other. The energy and passion that so many members have brought to the seminars and workshops over several years have shaped ideas; the frustrations expressed and the commitment to the issues facing poor and marginalized women provided much of the impetus for writing the book. We developed many of our ideas in these spaces, as well making lasting friendships. We would also like to thank Maria Jaschok at the International Gender Studies Centre (now at Lady Margaret Hall, University of Oxford) for her insight and encouragement as we planned the 2011 joint workshop. The participants at that workshop, some of whom have contributed chapters to this book, challenged us to say what we were planning to do to capture and address the multiple and growing concerns expressed about current aid realities and their impact on women. Our answer was to try and capture the voices and issues, and share them through this book.

And finally we want to turn to our Mothers, who have been rocks of support over many years, and who continue to inspire us with their knowledge and energy. To Tina's mother, now in her 90s, who was a lively participant at the Oxford workshop, and Fenella's mother, who continues to resist the very same forces that try to squeeze out her voice and others', many heartfelt thanks.

Abbreviations and acronyms

APPRO	Afghanistan Public Policy Research Organization
ANDS	Afghanistan National Development Strategy
BPO	business processing organization
CBO	community-based organization
CEDAW	Convention on the Elimination of Discrimination Against Women
COPA	Coalition for Peace in Africa
COWLHA	Coalition of Women Living with HIV/AIDS
CSO	civil society organization
CSR	corporate social responsibility
DfID	Department for International Development
DoWAs	Department of Women's Affairs
EVAW	Elimination of Violence Against Women
FAP	flood action plan
GBV	gender-based violence
GRI	global reporting initiative
HIV	human immunodeficiency virus
ICAI	Independent Commission for Aid Impact
IDS	Institute of Development Studies
IIED	International Institute for Education and Development
INGO	international non-government organization
IPPF	International Planned Parenthood Foundation
IPV	intimate partner violence
LPP	linking practice to policy
MoWA	Ministry of Women's Affairs
NAPWA	National Action Plan for the Women of Afghanistan
NGO	non-government organization
PEER	participatory ethnographic evaluation and research
PLA	participatory learning and action
RBM	results-based management
RCA	reality check approach
RCT	randomized control trial
RRA	rapid rural appraisal
RTC	responding to conflict
SHG	self-help groups
SIDA	Swedish International Development Corporation Agency
SWAP	sector-wide approach
WHO	World Health Organization
WTO	World Trade Organization

CHAPTER 1

Introduction
Aid, NGOs and the shrinking space for women: a perfect storm

Fenella Porter and Tina Wallace

This book represents the coming together of many different experiences of working with and researching non-government organizations (NGOs) and their role in aid. One strand of this experience has been the concern with how NGO relationships – with their donors, partners, the people they aim to support, and more recently the private sector – are changing in response to the rise in aid funding accompanied by the increasing conditionality of aid, growing competition for funding, reach and influence, and demands to show evidence of success. These have led broadly to a shift in focus away from the needs of the poor and vulnerable towards donor requirements and aid compliance (Vernon, 2010). These concerns have been reflected in a number of publications, including *Standardising Development* (Wallace et al., 1997) and *The Aid Chain* (Wallace et al., 2006). In one sense this book is the third in this sequence, highlighting the dangers of the way development is currently practised within the donor and NGO sectors, in Europe and the USA especially.[1]

A second strand is a series of seminar workshops held in Oxford and London by the Development Studies Association, Gender Policy and Practice Study Group. Deep concerns were shared in these workshops by women and men working on gender inequality, who are grappling with how to address the issues effectively in the current instrumentalist context of development practice. This agenda increasingly demands short-term interventions, narrowly focused on achieving technical results, and fails to adequately address the political and social barriers and inequalities that keep so many women marginalized within development programmes. The discussions brought out clearly the need to raise the issues openly and create a critical space in which to share concerns; many feel silenced within their organizations whether they are academics, consultants, or international non-government organization (INGO) staff. These seminars highlighted the importance of talking about how to do things differently.

The individual experience of the authors writing for this volume is a third strand. Each has their own motivation for joining this debate, but what they

http://dx.doi.org/10.3362/9781780447780/001

share are their concerns about the shifts they see in the role and behaviour of many NGOs working in the UK and in countries in Africa and Asia. Each contribution points to troubling trends around the way development is now conceptualized, the move away from real engagement with development practice where NGOs find their legitimacy, and their limited accountability to the people, especially women, in whose name funds are raised and spent. Several authors in this volume also share positive experiences of working differently to better enable women and their communities to bring about changes in their lives. These contributions show that while there are strong, dominating trends in development practice, largely driven by the funding imperatives dictated by a prevailing culture of targets in much of Europe and the USA, there are still, of course, many NGOs and staff within NGOs that think and work differently, albeit often on a small scale and against a background of organizational struggle. The experiences of these authors (and of many others working in and with NGOs), and the knowledge they produce, are important and this volume provides the 'critical space' for them to share them.

These authors come from diverse countries and walks of life. All have direct engagement with NGOs, at international, national, and local levels: as staff members (past and present), as researchers, as consultants, and as activists. Many come from a feminist tradition, and draw on the history of gender and development (GAD) analysis, as well as on their own experience and knowledge. Others are more familiar with a critique of the bureaucratization and managerialism of aid, and look more broadly at how this affects understanding, relationships, and development practice within aid. The book is ambitious in that it brings together work on the mechanics and ideology of aid today, and research on the experiences of women as recipients of (and occasionally participants in) aid.

Being ambitious it faces many possible pitfalls. For example, we are aware of the challenges of how to discuss NGOs as a sector, when they are highly diverse organizations in terms of structure, size, missions, and mandates, as well as where they are located and the focus of their work. We do not intend in this book to homogenize NGOs or the people who work in them.[2] When we refer to 'NGOs' or 'INGOs', we do not have individual organizations in focus, but rather the dominant systems and procedures that these organizations adhere to and the commonality of their experience when responding to the pressures that govern their practice. We want to open out for discussion the relationship that NGOs, INGOs, and other third sector organizations have with these dominant systems, and how that relationship influences their work and relationships with partners or other organizations.[3] We also want to show that there are choices to be made in response to tight conditionalities but that many have chosen growth and influence over the arguably more difficult paths of, for example, independence or building on past experience. We argue that the existing literature[4] supports the fact that strong identifiable trends shape organizational behaviour and responses, and enables a broad depiction of some core changes and their implications, while recognizing that there are always exceptions to every generalization. The literature is further supported by the lived experiences of those writing this book, and many others who contributed in seminars and discussion.

Another challenge in the current climate is what counts as valid evidence for what is happening. Generalizations are often dismissed as misleading, case studies as anecdotal. There are very clear parameters around what is currently accepted as 'evidence', determined by the governance structures of development. The dominant paradigms are creating a 'narrative' of aid (Mosse, 2005) that is based on tightly prescribed and controlled methods, reflecting a very particular form of knowledge and expertise. These paradigms are backed up by the way money is disbursed and the power and influence of discourse, which privileges notions of predictability, control, and measurable change. Figures, however limited in their meaning and interpretation, are seen as robust, and trump more nuanced (or sometimes even contradictory) analysis drawn from the lived experiences of the poor. These questions of knowledge have also been covered in other literature in development, and they are the subject of discussions in forums such as 'The Big Push Forward'.[5] Many of those contributing to this book use other methodologies and evidence to challenge these dominant norms and practices. The book reasserts the importance of using multiple methodologies for learning and accountability, many of which are rooted in lived experience.

A third challenge is that while many involved in NGOs – be they from large international UK-based NGOs, national field offices, or large and small NGO partner organizations – talk about the issues they are facing and that we are describing, there is a fear about speaking out openly.[6] This is seen in many forums and gatherings of NGO staff at all levels, from directors through to advisors, where confidentiality must be guaranteed and people ask not to be quoted. Debates undoubtedly go on behind closed doors in many NGOs, but, as a sector, publicly challenging or raising questions with donors, governments, and key private-sector players about current aid paradigms is strangely absent. Many similar issues (e.g., around contracts, the results focus, tight competition for tenders, and requirements for statistical measurable evidence of success in a short time) are also experienced by domestic NGOs in the UK where there has been more public debate. This debate has been characterized by energy and passion and many diverse opinions, and has covered issues around current funding, accountability, and how these affect the purpose, legitimacy, roles, and values of NGOs in the sector.[7]

What is the crisis? Introducing 'A perfect storm'

'A perfect storm': an especially bad situation caused by a combination of unfavourable circumstances.
– *Oxford English Dictionary*

We feel there is a crisis – or rather a series of crises – in development practice, brought about by a confluence of different pressures. International non-governmental organizations increasingly must operate in a culture of managerialism where change must first be envisaged, then detailed, described, and planned for. Once implemented, projects must demonstrate the achievement of pre-set results, which must be measured and reported on in quantitative terms. Change is understood as linear, logical, and controlled, following theories of change based on a cause-and-effect model. This way of working is passed directly to partners and staff in Africa, Asia, Latin America, and the Middle East, affecting the way people are expected to write proposals, deliver the work, and account for the use of the funding they receive. The work on the ground is thus skewed in many ways. The voices of the donor and the technical expert often outweigh the voice of programme staff, whether in Europe or the USA, or in the country receiving the aid. The bureaucratic demands of the managerial approach to controlling aid, and what Mosse describes as the story (or narrative) of aid,[8] leave little time or space for the voices of those most affected by aid interventions to shape the work. Visiting INGOs at the time of year when they are completing frameworks for donors – when proposals are being assessed and revised – is a strange experience. Everyone is sitting, staring into computers, trying to make complex realities fit into simple boxes, squares, or other computer-generated pictures and diagrams; the work is interspersed with hurried Skype calls to national offices or key partners for further data and information. Expected results, milestones to be achieved each year, can often be changed at the last minute and are put in place without any discussion with staff, partners, or the communities who are expected to make the required changes.

There is plenty of evidence within NGOs and donor organizations to support this brief characterization of some of the challenges facing international and in turn national and local NGOs. For example, a review by USAID for the US government (USG) about the way monitoring and evaluation is carried out to support the results agenda came to some worrying conclusions:

- The role of monitoring in the USG foreign assistance community has shifted dramatically in the last 15 years. The role of USG staff has shifted to primarily monitoring contractors and grantees. Because this distances USG staff from implementation of programmes, it has resulted within the Agencies in the loss of dialogue, debate and learning from monitoring.
- The myriad of foreign assistance objectives has led to onerous reporting requirements that try to cover all bases.
- There is an over-reliance on quantitative indicators and outputs, deliverables over which the project implementers have control (number of people trained) rather than qualitative indicators and outcomes, expected changes in attitudes, knowledge, and behaviours that would be the consequence of the outputs. (Blue et al., 2009: 2)[9]

From the INGO side, one example among many comes from a programme manager:

> Looking at aid mechanisms, we can see that they are mainly blunt instruments … As such they entail significant risks of preventing the kinds of changes needed if poverty is genuinely to be overcome. [They are] … Northern tools for Southern problems … The 'partnerships' … tend to be conversations taking place in two mutually unintelligible tongues. (Vernon, 2010)

As the funding from the UN, governments, and the World Bank has risen dramatically, the proportion of funds raised from the public has dropped[10]; the relative loss of unrestricted funding limits the freedom of NGOs to work in ways they choose. Large INGOs – and some national NGOs – are now able to access significant volumes of aid, but under terms and conditions tightly set by government, EU, UN, and other donor agencies. The stakes are high, for many significant sums of money are involved, as is reputation and profile, which in turn are important for raising funds from the public. In addition, NGOs find themselves increasingly competing with a growing number of private-sector providers who have entered the market to access this lucrative funding. These organizations, while relatively new to development work, are seen (by many decision-makers) to provide good value for money in project management because they prioritize norms of efficiency, effectiveness, and value for money. How well these concepts fit the realities of development and addressing poverty is the subject of several chapters in the book.

The fast-changing conditions attached to this funding increasingly shape what is to be achieved, how it is to be reported, and what constitutes success. As more and more organizations enter the field of evaluation – many from the private-sector world of auditing – the nature of evaluations is changing. They are more likely now to be undertaken within tight contracts with clear expectations, based on the logic models and results frameworks set at the start of the work. The drive is to show that the money has been used effectively and the expected results achieved. Unexpected results are often ignored, and analysing failure is not usually part of the process. The purpose is to fulfil the terms of reference (TOR) and meet the client's expectations in order to ensure further work from a sector hungry to show it is a valuable player in development. Critical evaluations, those that raise difficult questions, those discussing real problems and challenges, and those focused on participatory learning are often not appreciated and may well be 'edited' when they are received (Wallace, personal experience). This is because as Mosse argues the narrative of development is often as or more important than what is actually happening on the ground. Limited time is spent in the field, talking to those most affected by the aid, or even to the frontline staff, who often do not understand or relate well to the complex language, increasingly drawn from auditing, used in evaluations. Consequently, 'the evidence' produced in many evaluations is based more on paper trails, complex project documents, and scoring systems

designed in offices far from lived realities, and less on observation, participation, reflection, and discussion.[11] The focus on short-term, measurable
results is flawed in contexts where change will be a struggle, slow, and often
contradictory and usually hard to see until much later. In line with the
experiences of schools, the police, and medical practitioners in the UK, the
current measurement systems tend to measure what is measurable, not what
is important. While the talk is all about 'evidence', much of what is accepted
as evidence does not help donors, NGOs, or communities to understand what
happened during a project or programme, what worked, what did not, and
why or whether the approach was one that could actually enable long-term
sustainable change.

For the editors this complex situation amounts to a 'perfect storm' in which
donor language and thinking, the increased role and influence of the private
sector, and the desire of many INGOs to grow and become international
corporate players in development combine to exclude – in so many ways –
the participation of the poor, and of many NGO partners in Africa, Asia, and
Latin America. The involvement of those most affected by poverty as actors
in their own development is being eroded; increasingly they are becoming
'consumers' or 'customers' of services and ideas provided by an aid industry
that is remote and constantly changing.

A philosopher, Gadamer, wrote at the start of this century:

> The great challenge of the coming century, both for politics and social
> science, is that of understanding the other. The days are long gone when
> Europeans and other 'Westerners' could consider their experience and
> culture as the norm towards which the whole of humanity was headed,
> so that the other could be understood as an earlier stage on the same
> road we had trodden. (Gadamer in Dostal, 2002: 126)

While many working in development would share this view, the way funding is
now disbursed, and the conceptual thinking behind approaches to addressing
poverty, especially of poor women and girls, are at odds with such ideas. The
growing centralization and control of development deeply affects relationships with 'the other'. Poor women and men, those denied their rights, their
organizations, and local NGOs, have little space to critique or influence these
agendas or ways of working.

Chapters in Part I look at this crisis in a number of ways, and from different
perspectives. Stan Thekaekara starts off this section, looking at the history
of aid, particularly as practised by NGOs in India over the past 50 years. He
describes what the changes in development trends look like, what they mean
to those working 'at the coal face', and how the shifting paradigms have
turned poor people from subjects of their own story into passive recipients
of aid designed, managed, and monitored by hierarchies of often remote
gatekeepers, with no knowledge or experience of their realities.

Chris Mowles comes from a different perspective, bringing analysis from a
deep understanding of how knowledge is produced, and of how this affects

the way that we are able to engage with the lives of others. He contrasts the complexity of relationships and interventions in development, and their essential unpredictability, with the desire for planning and control, and shows how current ways of knowing and learning exclude the messiness of reality and attempt to smooth out erratic, non-linear, unexpected changes into clear narratives of what was planned for. Instead of imagining an ideal future, planning how to get there, relying heavily on systems thinking to control the behaviour of staff, and then showing that the aims have been achieved, his chapter shows how partners and community organizations need to learn how to work with emerging and unexpected change. Change is not predetermined and neither does it have an end state.

The chapters that explore the reality of working within the dominant paradigms of knowledge and evidence are also in this section. Suzanne Walker tackles head-on the impact that the desire for increased funding and growth has on the missions and work practices of many large Northern NGOs, locking them into these donor requirements to the detriment of their own knowledge, experience, partnerships, and value base. Her chapter is based on her own experience of working with INGOs, and echoes what is often heard within INGOs and those NGOs they fund but rarely put out for public discussion because of the fear in the sector about talking openly. Her argument is that while the drive for funding is necessary and legitimate, it risks much else that INGOs stand for when it becomes the dominant organizational force, especially when the conditions of aid cut across INGO principles and what they understand about good practice. Her challenging narrative is applicable across numerous agencies, including many NGOs in the South seeking large institutional funding.

Nikki van der Gaag and Kate Grosser come from a long experience of working on the needs and challenges facing girls in development, and in their chapter they examine the issues arising from the growing role of the private sector. They argue that while it is positive that powerful players in development are highlighting the intense needs of girls, the solutions being proposed exclude girls in the planning, and do not address the structural inequalities they face. They do not build on past NGO knowledge and practice, and pay little attention to the challenges of how best to work with some of the world's most vulnerable people. Instead, styles of working and metrics in common use in the private sector govern the way they work. This in turn influences how INGOs work with girls, many of whom have noticeably changed their communications and marketing, to stress what girls can achieve for the economy and wider society. The language of rights and the need to address structural inequality is being eroded, and the claims to be able to deliver change quickly and effectively are skewing the painstaking, political, and long-term work required to tackle girls' inequality.

Anastasiya Hozyainova follows the work on gender mainstreaming in Afghanistan, and highlights how far current realities are from the rhetoric that drove part of the rationale for the invasion of Afghanistan: that of increasing women's equality there. This study shows that despite good intentions and strong financing, there has been limited achievement because of a lack of understanding and communication with local people, cultures, and indigenous ways of knowing and being. Donors brought a range of externally generated concepts and ideas that did not fit easily with traditional norms, with embedded Soviet understandings of what promotes gender equality, or with the constraints of the government bureaucracies trying to implement gender policies. The clash of cultures and multiple understandings of what gender equality means meant that there was no real dialogue with government or women in the country. Her chapter shows, along with others in the volume, that without a real connection with the context, development risks 'doing harm',[12] something highlighted in other recent studies (e.g. Concern Worldwide and Oxfam GB, 2011).

Tom Scott-Smith speaks from his own experience of being an expatriate development worker, and reflects on that as a way to gain insight into how the practice of development 'insulates' development workers from the lives of the people they serve. He believes that most INGO staff are fully aware of the tensions and contradictions in the way much of development work is currently practised. He uses a modern definition of class to argue that while they have this knowledge they are cocooned by virtue of belonging to a 'developing class', protected by security, living-standard norms, lack of language, and a drive to meet organizational expectations. They justify their way of life and work by the belief that development is an ultimate good; it brings benefits to people and so more of it is important and will bring more benefits.

Finally in this section, David Lewis looks at the situation through the lens of someone who experiences the tendency for development work to live in the 'perpetual present', not learning from the past but responding to the ever-changing fashions of development thinking, which are increasingly large-scale, 'sector-wide' approaches. This chapter casts a wider net, looking broadly in one context (Bangladesh) at how the influences of development trends have affected the way that interventions are designed and implemented, and most importantly how they are experienced by people. Although his chapter does not specifically draw on NGO practice, often INGOs and local staff and partners designing development projects do not draw on what they know, preferring – or feeling compelled – to follow the trends. This chapter brings to light some of the dominant trends that are governing development work, and that contribute to the 'gap' between how development is conceived and planned and the realities of people's lives.

From different places within the aid context, these chapters form a strong critique of current trends in development management, and their influence in shaping the way development is being done. We see this as a system of governance in which processes are honed to meet agendas set by donors, trustees, and competitors, eroding INGOs' own experience and the engaged, grounded knowledge that they have gained over many years. INGOs often cannot express what they and their partners know in the face of coherent, logical, results-focused systems that fit well with the way work is currently funded, framed, and accounted for. This is the power of the dominant discourse that supports the system of governance in development.

Yet critiques exist. INGOs and national and local NGOs, both large and small, have concerns about the sharply rising conditionality of aid, the tight contracts, the massive amounts of paperwork required to prove effectiveness, and the short-term 'high impact' approach of donors and their private-sector competitors. There is evidence that both international and local NGOs know that this is risking both the independence of the voluntary sector, something intrinsic to their purpose (Baring Foundation, 2012) and the support of the wider public.[13,14] The negative impact on partners and their sense of losing voice and power in the 'aid chain' is encountered daily by many staff (see Wallace et al., 2006), and the expertise, engagement, and contribution of partner organizations often gets squeezed out. There is little room for manoeuvre within these funding regimes, and limited space for NGOs – North and South – to bring their own learning and experiences to the table. As INGOs work more closely with donors in designing projects and accountability systems, the voices of their partners and those most affected by poverty and marginalization, especially women, get fainter.

As many of the authors in this volume point out, reality is unpredictable, and often messy. Local knowledge is frequently strikingly at odds with well-crafted projects; what actually happens often falls far outside 'the scope' of planning documents. And yet what happens in 'real life' is what INGOs and their partners can build on to create better interventions, based on people's lives and priorities. In the second section of this volume, we seek to understand and give voice to these initiatives, and promote the need for 'changing conversations' in development work.

Changing conversations: the need for critical space

> A talent for speaking differently, rather than for arguing well, is the chief instrument of cultural change.
> —Rorty (1998: 7)

Rorty's analysis of the need for new language to allow us to think differently suggests a need to open up more challenging and discursive spaces, which move beyond the permitted areas for discussion to enable radically new thinking and ways of working to evolve. Rather than engaging endlessly in complying with externally imposed frames, INGOs and their partners can choose to work more closely with communities, social movements, and others for whom the current debates are irrelevant, and work in a language that better fits the experience of poverty and gender inequality. They can learn from feminist movements, community-based organizations, and activists to develop new, shared understandings, and build ways of working aligned more th those facing the negative effects of globalization, patriarchy, and increasing poverty and marginalization.

The chapters in the second section of this volume indicate ways in which the conversation can be changed, current thinking challenged, and practice better aligned with 'the other'. David Harding introduces this section, showing how deeply rooted the current paradigms are in ideas from the Enlightenment onwards and how hard they can be to confront. He challenges the whole basis of the logic model and linear concepts rooted in Western thinking, and stresses the need to grapple with the complexity of life as it actually happens. Agencies need to do far less planning and controlling and to learn much more about how to listen, to analyse, to judge situations, and to work with the unexpected challenges that any intervention brings. He argues that there are effective ways of starting to 'change the conversation' and opening up new ways of understanding and behaving that contrast with rational management thinking. Different ways of working can enable staff and partners to better understand 'is the work working?', to really learn from their own experiences, and to see how better to navigate uncertainty and change.

Some INGOs and local NGOs are able to provide space in which the values of gender equality and social justice can be promoted, and where players from both within and outside development organizations can have a voice and a role in critiquing and challenging dominant paradigms. It is in this space that we can hear the voices of those most affected by inequality and poverty. Meenu Vadera illustrates how an intricate understanding of women's lives and the constraints that surround them was vital to the design and implementation of a whole set of interventions that have enabled them to empower themselves at multiple levels. The Women on Wheels organization takes women from the slums of Delhi and enables them to become 'chauffeurs'. The process requires time, understanding, proper resources, multiple interventions, and the building of strong support networks. It cannot be done on the cheap or quickly, and many women drop out of the process. But it can and does lead to real change in individual women's lives, taking them into arenas previously undreamt of. However, donors often shy away from the investment of time and money required to bring about such transformatory change because 'value for money' so often equates to helping large numbers of people, and 'scaling up' has become an accepted part of the development narrative.

Seri Wendoh brings us the voices of girls who are excluded from 'universal access to health programmes' because they fall outside the scope of most projects, which are largely focused on girls in school or on adult women. Those that fall between the cracks are often those in greatest need, with few options, and little access to services, information, or support. This chapter brings us the words of these girls, living in post-conflict West Africa, far from the neat language of project management and hard to pigeonhole. Their deprivations are multiple and intertwined, and serve as a stark reminder of the challenges facing those at the bottom of the heap. Yet the cases show that listening and responding to the world as the girls experience it can lead to creative responses that enable them to make positive changes.

Kanwal Ahluwalia shows how small-scale, experimental projects based on in-depth research can take root in some circumstances, though they may fail in others. Even within one country, different approaches are needed because of the specific way gender relations are structured and understood by communities. Where the work takes off, it has created real opportunities for confronting and changing attitudes and behaviour around gender-based violence, in ways that women and communities feel comfortable with, and that differ from existing ideas about the best ways to work on violence. The evidence from work in selected villages can be used successfully to influence policy agendas and state responses, while creating interest in other villages, which could see real changes taking place. However, expansion of the project was hampered by donor demands for quantitative and 'robust' evidence. These demands defined as insufficient the feedback of communities and an impressive participatory evaluation undertaken with hundreds of women engaged in the programme.

The chapter by Alice Welbourn clearly illustrates how the current norms and rules of how to work, and how to create evidence that is considered legitimate, have prevented proper donor engagement in a living process for tackling HIV and AIDS that has grown over the past two decades. This has developed largely through voluntary action and the commitment of those who have experienced it, to a point where it is now possible to meet some of the 'evidence' criteria set by those who have become the arbiters of what is and what is not 'good evidence'. But this chapter argues forcefully that if the value of their approach had been recognized sooner, and on their own terms, they might have gained access to some of the enormous funds for HIV and AIDS. This would have allowed a better resourced 'community of practice' to develop, as practitioners all over the world adapted the manual to fit their own contexts, and local analyses of gender and age inequality – factors that are often a major cause of HIV and AIDS. The learning from Stepping Stones is spreading, but systems-thinking and external solutions based on tight planning and control still override the voices, ideas, and ownership of those most affected.

Bridget Walker's chapter brings in reflections from peace work, where a fundamental principle is that communities themselves are able to negotiate solutions. This work takes a very different approach requiring the building of trust (a quality emphasized in many of the chapters), an ability to live and work with tensions and contradictions, and a long timescale. Her chapter comes from long experience of working in this area, and is based largely on 'grey literature' and oral reports. This kind of practice-based, local knowledge is often discounted as it is not published or well recorded for an external audience. However, this form of local knowledge is critical to negotiating peace and reconciliation and is widely used in both conflict and development contexts in Africa. To ignore or reject this as a legitimate and important way of knowing excludes some of the most accurate and nuanced records of how people actually experience the practice of development.

Ashish Shah builds on the themes of listening and learning that are articulated in Harding's chapter at the beginning of the section. He writes powerfully of his own experience as a young development worker in confronting the truth that he knew and understood very little about the lives of the sugar farmers he had come to work with. The more time he spent with them, the more he learned how much 'he did not know'. This chapter calls for humility, and a recognition of how little we as outsiders know and understand about the realities of other people's lives, particularly those women who live in rural poverty, whose voices are so rarely properly heard or engaged with. Rather than seeing external agents as driving change that has been designed elsewhere and is to be delivered by technical experts, development is about listening, learning, and finding ways of supporting the ideas, process, and aspirations of those most affected by poverty and injustice. They contrast strongly with current development norms, and this contrast illustrates clearly what needs to change if people are to become agents of their own development.

Deepa Joshi closes the section by analysing – from a theoretical and practical perspective – the assumptions that current sanitation programmes aimed at women are based on, and how far the resulting approaches are from women's lived realities. This chapter shows how simplistic and superficial understandings of poverty and gender lead to poorly designed projects for the poorest. They also reinforce the gendered nature of cleanliness and hygiene and do nothing to challenge or change women's unequal status and position. Women's roles in ensuring health and hygiene for the family are taken for granted, as is the shame they often feel around their bodies. Programmes designed to meet sanitation targets focus solely on the disposal of faeces and hand-washing, ignoring the lack of dignity, and the appalling reality of much sanitation provision for the poor. She argues that the poor, like all of us, want to be clean, respected, and treated with dignity. It is in her chapter that the effects of defining 'the other' as so different and needing far less than 'us' comes through so clearly.

The contributions to this volume show how the current configuration of players and approaches to development have major implications for the way INGOs conceptualize their work, their identity, legitimacy, and independence, and their relationships. As donors and the private sector increasingly become key players, certain kinds of quantifiable and replicable knowledge and measure are validated. Other forms of understanding rooted in relationships with partners such as small, local NGOs, women's organizations, or trade unions are now downgraded, resulting in a loss of critical space in which many NGOs, both North and South, can discuss and challenge dominant norms and practices.

Development agencies appear, at times, to have lost the understanding of people as citizens in their own countries, with relationships with their own governments, and embedded in their own cultures. Despite all that is known and understood about power and dominance in the aid industry, there is evidence that current procedures and ways of working do not accept that their languages, values, and ways of working are as valid as 'ours'. Yet this understanding needs to be at the centre of relationships with partners and other collaborative organizations. Increasingly NGO narratives are about *their* power and the way that *they* are changing the world; these narratives are now deeply embedded in the development discourse and governance. We see this as a structural problem – not just a problem of individual agencies working in inappropriate ways. It is in understanding this structure of power and governance that we can uncover and see clearly the vital role NGOs can potentially play in providing the space for resistance to the dominant discourse, and for the voices of 'the other'.

Understanding development governance, and the search for a critical space

The chapters in this volume illustrate very clearly the crisis that we see in development, and how this has affected the ways that NGOs relate to and behave in their partnerships with other organizations. However, they also illustrate the knowledge and understanding that exists within development organizations, about the complex realities that affect how people – particularly women – experience and deal with situations of poverty and inequality. As we discussed these issues in the workshops that preceded this book, we felt that the space to talk about and challenge NGO responses to the crisis had been increasingly dominated by norms accompanying the prevailing discourse, and that the opportunity to support and communicate the nuanced and relevant work being undertaken with women in different contexts had been diminished. In this introduction, we want to set out a framework for helping to understand how this space has been squeezed, and what we see as having been lost.

There have been many useful publications that have debated ideas of discourse and governmentality in development, many of which are rooted in Foucault's analysis of power (Crush, 1995; Li, 1999; Mosse, 2005; Shore and Wright, 1997). Although Foucault's ideas have been much criticized (including by feminists) for being overly structural in their understanding of power, we have found that these ideas do give a useful framework within which to understand how power is negotiated and maintained in development. We see 'governmentality' as a way of describing an overall system of power and control that operates through the 'Aid Chain', and how NGOs and their relationships with other organizations (other NGOs, donors, partners, social movements, trade unions) are structured within that system.

The most useful aspect of Foucault's analysis is in explaining how this system of power and control also operates discursively, defining what is 'normal', and how this definition changes according to the influences that are most powerful at any one time. However, we acknowledge and agree with the critics of Foucault who reject the overly structural interpretation of power it represents. We do not understand governmentality (the system of power and control in aid and development) to be a fixed or unchangeable structure – on the contrary, we see it as being constantly renegotiated, often according to the latest policy environment. We use the idea of 'governmentality' to see how the different spheres of development and aid policy and practice are linked, and how the influences of, for example, managerialism or private-sector norms of efficiency and effectiveness have spread throughout the Aid Chain.

But perhaps more important than describing existing structures of power, we wanted to find a way of understanding the role of challenge and dissent in development discourse that we now see being squeezed out. Over the past decades, development has been constructed from both neoliberal and capitalist norms and challenges to those norms. Initially these challenges were rooted in socialism and anti-colonial struggles (Fanon, 1963; Rodney, 1973), and over the years we have seen different challenges to development, both from within the industry (for example, 'alternative' approaches to development such as participation, rights-based approach) and from movements such as feminist and environmental movements. The discursive space of development, therefore, has been one in which the dominant capitalist norms and values have existed *in a relationship* with the values and principles of equality and social justice that are core concerns of participatory approaches, human rights, feminism, and environmentalism. It is a relationship in which different sets of values exist in tension with each other.

This is a defining feature of development, and it has over many years allowed a healthy debate to exist, in which the voices of different players have been heard. These different voices may not be of equal power and influence, but their presence is necessary in order for the discourse of development to grow and change. For example, in the negotiations that took place in the run-up to all the UN conferences in the 1990s, the voices and influences of NGO participants (often given a formal role through the accreditation system of ECOSOC, which itself illustrates a recognition of the need for different voices to be allowed) played an important and acknowledged part in the negotiation of the documents that were ultimately agreed by the government representatives at the conferences.

In fact we can see this understanding of power in Foucault's analysis, in which power exists *only as a relationship*, in which different interests and ideas react to each other in a continual tension. This relationship is essential for the discursive spaces to continue to evolve (Foucault, 1994).

> I would like to suggest another way to go further toward a new economy of power relations, a way that is more empirical, more directly related to our present situation, and one that implies more relations between theory and practice. It consists in taking the forms of resistance against different forms of power as a starting point ... Rather than analysing power from the point of view of its internal rationality, it consists

of analysing power *relations* through the antagonism of strategies. (Foucault, 1994: 327, emphasis added)

However, in the current context of development practice, the norms of predictability and control have become so dominant that they now permeate all systems, and this is squeezing out other ways of thinking and working. There is increasing exclusion of the more political approaches that have operated in a relationship with neoliberalism, and which have provided space for more politicized, alternative norms and values.[15] We do not want to overemphasize Foucault's ideas, as they are heavily contested in development thought; we only use them here as a way of opening out an understanding of power that *includes* a way to challenge dominant norms, and resist what is being presented as 'normal' through planning frameworks, and the ideals of measurement and evidence that permeate the development practice. Mosse (2005) also discusses the need to bridge the tension between the critical analysis of development policy that tends towards the structural and the more instrumental, engaged analysis that 'directly shapes the way that development is done' (Mosse, 2005: 2). His approach shows how power operates in a negotiated way in development, through the interpretation of events and the incorporation of various interests in that interpretation.

In the context of this volume, we think that the idea of power as a relationship, and the need for resistance to exist in a relationship with the dominant forces of power, can help to understand and assert the vital role of critical spaces in development that have been (and are still) occupied by gender analysts, participatory practitioners, and others in NGOs and in communities, social movements, trade unions, and other organizations. The role of resistance is, in the first instance, to challenge and de-stabilize what Mosse analyses as the dominant narratives of development. But these spaces are being squeezed, and people in NGOs and outside them are finding it increasingly difficult to articulate challenges and assert the value of politics and alternative approaches.

These critical spaces were – in the past – particularly important for improving how gender was understood in development work. For example, intricate negotiation of the ideas of gender justice and sexual and reproductive rights took place in the lead-up to the 1995 4th World Conference on Women, in Beijing (Baden and Goetz, 1998), and documents such as the Beijing Platform for Action (United Nations, 1995), and the earlier Convention on the Elimination of All Forms of Discrimination Against Women (United Nations, 1979), for all their weaknesses, reflected jointly crafted and long-term commitments to understanding and addressing the interrelated issues around gender inequality. Furthermore, gender equality and women's rights have been openly debated, contested, and pursued within INGOs and with partners and policymakers challenging existing development paradigms and opening out new understandings of development work and how to go about it (Porter et al., 1999). This space, in which gender can be understood as a political concept, involving deeply embedded and complex power relations, is now being bypassed in favour of simplified and ultimately instrumentalist agendas for women and girls represented in development discourse by the influence of the Nike Foundation's 'The Girl Effect' and Department for International Development's (DfID) SMART economics (Chant, 2012; Cornwall, 2012).

Listening, promoting local ownership, participatory planning, and monitoring are being squeezed as power shifts firmly back to the hands of external planners, strategists, and evaluators. The spaces in which INGOs are able to reflect on their position in relation to wider civil society action and their values of equality and social justice, and how far their ways of working are 'fit for purpose' in meeting the aspirations of the poor have shrunk; the room for meaningful participation and partnership is at risk (Chambers, 2005; Groves and Hinton, 2004).

What has been lost? The changing position of international development NGOs

The history of INGOs in development practice, and the unique role of 'not for profit' organizations, has been traced and critiqued by many (Bebbington et al., 2008; Dar and Cooke, 2008; Kothari, 2005; Lewis and Kanji, 2009; Lewis and Wallace, 2000; Wallace et al., 1997; Wallace et al., 2006), and we do not seek to repeat their arguments here. It is important, however, to highlight key shifts in INGOs, especially in relation to funding, their use of images, and their work on women and girls in order to illustrate how the growing pressures have affected their ability to understand and relate to the lives of the people they work with and on behalf of. Only dominant changes are highlighted, and always while recognizing there is great diversity amongst INGOs.

INGOs started out, in the main, as independent players in development and humanitarian aid, working with local partners and communities or as direct suppliers of services and sponsorship, especially for children. Money was raised from the public, and the sums were (in today's terms) relatively small. While some focused only on service provision, others were rooted in concepts of social justice, and consciously took little or no money from government, preferring to keep an independent voice able to speak out on behalf of the poor and marginalized. The debates about the ethics and implications of taking government money were strong, as were concerns with images of poor people, and how women and children were portrayed for fundraising purposes.[16] Concepts such as 'solidarity' and 'accompaniment' were common in many organizations, and the space for critiquing and challenging dominant norms existed, though it was often not a comfortable space to occupy, something experienced by many gender staff, for example. Gender work was starting, and gender units and focal points were set up, although often criticized and marginalized within INGOs (Porter et al., 1999). This was not a 'golden age' for NGOs; there was much that was criticized during those years, and has changed for the better. But for us what is important is that there was *space* for discussion; in many INGOs debates were fierce and long, critiques existed, and people were not afraid to speak. This contrasts with the fear of openly questioning strongly presented narratives of aid that exists in many organizations now.

Since then the sector has diverged, with many multi-million pound agencies emerging while the majority have remained relatively small with incomes of under £10 million. Many new players have entered the sector, which is now dominated by the largest INGOs – the 'opinion leaders'. Strategies focus on growth and, for many, accessing official funding is a good source despite the requirements for aid compliance; only a few are significantly diversifying their fundraising strategies, and income streams such as child sponsorship are becoming less significant in some agencies. Debates about the role and purpose of the third sector, the ethics of fundraising, the use of images for communications and marketing, and how funding is changing relationships appear subsidiary.[17] While these issues are contested internally, the time and energy now needed to meet donor requirements often overshadows time for these discussions, and they are not often publicly aired across the sector. It can appear that much of what has been learned (often painfully) has been forgotten, or there is a lack of confidence to put this learning forward as a basis for challenging inappropriate donor demands.

In relation to gender the way INGOs have incorporated the space for the issues is less uniform. On international aid agendas the issue of women and girls has risen, fallen, and is now rising again. When INGOs first took on issues of gender equality, often in response to women from programme offices concerned about the exclusion of women from development projects, their concerns were discussed in numerous meetings and workshops about how to include women in development interventions. This initial work on gender equality and women's rights was political, often radical, and not easy for bureaucratic organizations to respond to at times. During the 1980s, it was challenging, as indeed were ideas around people's participation and 'putting the last first' (Chambers, 1983). Over time the thrust became the need to 'mainstream gender' and enable everyone to work with a gender lens. The validity and history of this process is highly contested (Oxfam, 2012), with some seeing gains for gender mainstreaming reflected in the current promotion of aid for women and girls, while others feel it has been reduced to a technical, tick-box exercise, far from the urgency of addressing women's lack of rights and resources – reinforced by laws, religion, and tradition. Splits around the wisdom of trying 'to mainstream gender' and the risks to the political agenda of challenging deep-rooted inequality were evident soon after Beijing, with many women, in the South especially, questioning the approach of making gender equality 'fit' bureaucratic systems. These splits continue, with post-colonial feminist writing reminding us of the dangers of working to agendas that 'make sense' in Western contexts and to bureaucratic institutions, but which belie the diversity, struggles, and understanding of women from very different histories and geographies.

Gender staff have ebbed and flowed in INGOs; the centrality of women's inequality as a core cause and symptom of development has come and gone. Today the focus on women and girls is renewed by the interest from government and private sector, and more funding is available. But the dominant trend to which NGOs of all sizes and scope are responding is one of instrumentalizing women as key providers of development for their families, communities, and countries, as epitomized by the funding provided by Nike's 'Girl Effect' Foundation.

This view serves as a crude guide to locate INGOs in relation to the poor they work with and their major institutional donors over time. From the perspective of partners in the South, Everjoice Win, a prominent women's rights activist, captures some of these shifts in an 'Open Letter to My Donor Friend', in which she shows how these trends affect the *quality* of relationships in development:

> We first met when you came to my country as a young university graduate. They called you a 'volunteer', coming to us to learn about 'Africa', and to 'help us' where possible. You were a lovely person then – full of enthusiasm, reading books, asking questions. [...]
>
> In your next incarnation you became a donor! ... You recently came to show us your new proposal and reporting format ... you have developed your own 'template' ... We have to fit our visions, our way of thinking into your template. Gone are our free expression, our long paragraphs and our way of seeing and interpreting our reality. We are now forced to express ourselves in a way you understand and want. (Win, 2005: 124–5)

Most recently, INGOs are learning to position themselves vis-à-vis private-sector companies, in order to compete with them for major funding, and to work with them in multiple ways: both as contracted agents for project management systems support and in corporate social responsibility (CSR) partnerships. These relationships and positioning have a profound effect on the way INGOs understand their work, whose knowledge they value, to whom they listen and what kind of evidence they see as useful.[18]

The effect of the closing spaces on gender analysis

Gender analysis – much of it in the gender and development literature – has, over many years, challenged the norms of neoliberalism, pointing to the fundamental constraints on women's and girls' participation in the economy and polity, because of embedded gender inequalities at every level of their lives. We now understand how institutionalized structures of gender inequality shape women's lives – from the family and community, to the market and the public sphere, to their relationship with the state and systems of government (Chant, 2007; Jackson and Pearson, 1998; Kabeer, 1994; Tinker, 1990). These structures position women differently, according to other aspects of their identities. Gender analysts now understand that gender inequality is not uniform and all women are not the same; they are divided by wealth and status, education, location, and class, and any gender analysis must also include an understanding of these intersectional differences. The different ways that women experience and privilege different parts of their identities, such as age, ability, ethnicity, caste, or culture explain the many and varied constraints experienced by women, and the equally many and varied responses of women to situations of poverty and marginality.

The 'persistent inequalities' embedded in development assumptions have been studied and discussed over many years, developing and extending how we understand women's productive and reproductive roles, and the gender bias in the relationship that women have with government and the public sector (Jaquette and Summerfield, 2006; Rai, 2008). In the economic sphere, the gender bias of the market and macro-economic policies in development has been understood and analysed, leading to a far greater understanding of women's unpaid labour in the care economy (Folbre, 1994), how the exclusion of women's unpaid care work distorts understandings of the economy, and who is bearing the real costs of reproduction (Elson, 1991). Other writers, such as Sylvia Chant (2007, 2012), have enabled us to understand how development has become characterized by 'hand-me-down wisdoms' about women and poverty, particularly at the level of the household. Chant's analysis showed how female-headed households are not necessarily the 'poorest of the poor', and how women can experience poverty and marginalization even when living within households with higher levels of income, because of their unequal position within the household. Furthermore, writers in the gender and development literature understand how women's participation is constrained and structured, and how women's organizations and movements have responded to the challenges, often only to be undermined by international development efforts (Kandiyoti, 2007).

It is in the gender and development literature that we see how norms in development have been confronted and challenged, and the discursive space has been opened out for an understanding of women's rights in development, and an examination of power – both between women and men, and between North and South. Post-colonial feminist studies have enabled us to question our own assumptions about family, the sexual division of labour, and the importance of cultural positioning in women's lives (Mama, 2007; Mohanty et al., 1991). Through this space we have come to a more nuanced and complex understanding of women's multiple identities and intersecting interests.

The literature also shows complex and contradictory relationships between feminists, women's organizations, and development INGOs. For example, in Latin America, feminists point to the structural disadvantage of women in the context of globalized capitalism, neoliberal economics, and the increasing and damaging encroachment of private-sector norms and values in their lives – indeed many Latin American feminists understand this as a new form of colonialism (Dixon, 2011). They argue that women's responses to the situation in which they find themselves have been undermined by assumptions within development interventions, about how they organize themselves, and how they understand their own disadvantage: 'Their [NGO] models are often disempowering because of being based on "need" – that is lack – rather than on the recognition of women's power and resources; and on external financing rather than the creation of solidarity value chains and economic networking based on what is already known and produced' (Dixon, 2011: 5).[19]

Elsewhere there are articulated concerns about the squeeze on funding for women's organizations and locally derived agendas around women's rights to land, gender-based violence, women's lack of voice and representation, and the lack of attention to women's agency and what women themselves want support for (AWID, 2008). Recent INGO project proposals around the Arab Spring, for example, focused on short-term training for selected women leaders, with the bulk of funding going to the external 'expert' organizations providing the training and very few resources reaching existing organizations, rooted in the context, already working on women's leadership, women's right to participate in public arenas, and women's rights to act as citizens.

Small women's organizations and social movements often find it hard to get their voices heard. They do not speak the language of the current development discourse, they lack resources, and the already limited spaces for discussing gender and women's issues are being filled by communications from highly professional international agencies. But their work continues, often in very difficult circumstances and usually unpaid, and their ideas and experiences continue to question and challenge the prevailing norms around 'what women need' in development.

Without challenging the dominant norms, addressing the underlying gender biases within their context, and the resulting constraints faced by women and girls, women will continue to be marginalized at every level. This is the reality that is experienced by poor women, yet the 'myth' of women's ability to seize opportunities, unencumbered by gender relations (Cornwall, 2012), is increasingly accepted as 'normal' in development. This is the instrumentalist agenda that gender analysts and practitioners are grappling with currently. Although these ideas have been, and continue to be, contested in the literature, this new 'normality' has reduced the critical space in which these voices can be heard.

A note on methodology: how we can value what we know

As we have already suggested, one of the ways that the neoliberal paradigm has come to dominate the discursive space in which development is practised is by reducing the way we understand 'knowledge'. Authors such as Crush (1995) have highlighted how power operates discursively in development to produce myths of development 'knowledge', which are based on 'a modernist regime of knowledge and disciplinary power' (ibid: xiii), and feed into the norms and assumptions of development practice. Within the current paradigms it is these myths that dominate; there is little room for complex, contextual historical learning and experience, and almost no space in which practitioners can assert their knowledge and their understanding of the context in which they are working.

Methodologies in development (and indeed in research more generally) are now predominantly required to measure and count things, and thereby prove results that can be offered up to the donors and the public who are demanding 'hard evidence', i.e., numbers and 'value for money'.[20] However, we have known for some time that approaches that reduce everything of value to indicators that can be measured miss much of what we know to be true. We have learned that in order to understand people's realities we need other ways of 'knowing'. In this volume, we assert the value of insight, and of connection; it is from an engaged, connected methodology that we are able to form a relationship with a context, and begin to understand the multiple and overlapping complexities that shape peoples' lives.

There are so many different ways of learning and knowing. Feminist methodologies are built on principles of equality and connectedness. They see change as a process of constant negotiation between different positions, and stress the need to ensure there is 'democratic deliberation' of these views. A change agent needs to be a mediator/facilitator helping people to engage in the conversation and negotiation, not a technocrat. Feminist methodologies demand that we reflect on our own power and are sensitive to power in all methods (Oakley, 2000). They teach that insightful knowledge can emerge from a relationship of political commitment and a sense of shared values and of the need to bring about changes in how people think and behave (Dixon, 2011; Fonow and Cook 1991). 'Conscious partiality' is a process by which knowledge is constructed, both within the context in which the experience takes place, and also by the interaction of the researcher or practitioner with that context (Schrivjers, 1995: 22–3). Feminist methodologies do not expect to 'find' objective reality or predict the outcome of an intervention. They acknowledge that reality is complicated, and in order to understand it, we must engage with it on a political, as well as an intellectual, level. This is a far cry from the ideas of knowledge demanded and produced by current development frameworks. But it is in valuing and legitimizing this knowledge and these different ways of knowing that we are able to resist and challenge, and ensure that critical space is maintained.

Robert Chambers reminds us how crucial it is that our knowledge and understanding of development is built on close and collaborative relationships with marginalized communities with his seminal ideas of 'putting the last first' and 'handing over the stick'. In his work, he has continually highlighted the importance of 'critical self-awareness, thinking through the effects of actions' (Chambers, 2007: 184). This type of self-reflection is relevant to development knowledge and has also been theorized by academics as 'auto-ethnography' (Chang, 2008; Ellis and Bochner, 2000). Auto-ethnography contains the notion of self-reflexivity (critical to feminists) that Chambers refers to, alongside the embedded analysis of ethnography, which has long been the methodology of choice for gaining insight into different cultures and societies. Auto-ethnography combines these ideas, using the experience of a member of that society or culture reflecting on and analysing her or his experience in order to give insight and in-depth knowledge.

In the context of this book, it is critical to understand the value of different ways of knowing. Many of the contributors were initially reluctant to present their own experiences as one source of 'knowledge', but what they say is valid, insightful, and powerful. Often auto-ethnographic,[21] it is also committed analysis, developed in the context of wanting to bring about changes to the way that people understand development practice. To date we still know so little about the problems faced by people in poverty, because this kind of knowledge is difficult to represent, let alone measure or count.[22] This kind of understanding can only be formed through an intimate connection with a place. In order to really learn and ensure that critical space in development discourse is kept open, we must be able to listen and hear other ways of knowing and understanding in order to gain real knowledge of the quality of what we do, however difficult this is to achieve in the current context.

Learning from this evidence

This book draws on a wide range of authors, some published and others new to writing for a wide audience, each of whom has a different starting point, experience, and understanding of development, aid, NGOs, and gender inequality. Whatever the starting point, some coherent, interwoven themes emerge: the narrowness of modern rational scientific thinking and its distorting effect on how development work is currently understood and measured, coupled with the deep-rooted nature of this approach in Western thinking; the growing centralization, and at times arrogance, of the aid industry that increasingly pays attention to demands for accountability and rigour from donors, and sets development targets and approaches far away from the grinding realities of the poor and marginalized. The risks of aligning with these approaches are clear, taking many INGOs further from listening to their partners and communities, often undermining the agency of women and limiting the building of alliances and relationships needed for 'talking (and so thinking) differently'. INGOs appear to downplay their power, position, and potential and shy away from open debates about the challenges, opportunities, and changing configurations of development aid. The chapters highlight the urgency of analysing what is happening, assessing alignments, and questioning orthodoxies, which are at risk of becoming so dominant that there is little room for critique; the need to keep open and expand the discursive space is clear.

The chapters also show the potential for thinking and working differently, sometimes radically and sometimes by making small shifts; and what women and girls can do for themselves if they set agendas, and build on their own experiences and needs, which may be different in every context. This has been known to INGOs and others for a long time. NGOs cannot 'develop' others; development comes from within. Development requires changes in confidence, attitudes, and behaviour, and questioning how to do the work and build partnerships. In many NGOs there exists real, connected knowledge about the communities and people that they work with. This knowledge is at risk, however, because the dominant development discourse, reproduced through governance systems, embeds notions of self/other that make it difficult for different voices to find the space to speak, and for development organizations to understand and address the lived realities of poor women and men, girls and boys.

The risks of one discourse dominating all others are high. The picture, however, is still mixed, with some players, North and South, thinking and talking differently and finding ways to reach out to and connect with the poor to co-create ways of working that make a positive difference. New players are entering the arena as both funders and development actors. While the agenda for women and girls is high in the rhetoric, the risks are that funding for organizations that work closely with them are bypassed, while the agencies scooping up the funding are those offering 'bigger, better, faster' change. The need for 'changing the conversation' and challenging the discourse is great.

Within what often feels a difficult reality, challenges are still being raised, and alternative approaches are being used. There are some that argue that INGOs always follow the dominant trends and will never be significant independent actors in development. Clearly we do not agree and believe that a critical element of their role in development is to continue to challenge a context that often stifles criticism, generates fear and competition, and excludes the voices and agency of women, in whose name a great deal of funding is currently raised:

> There is a constant risk in the current context of aid that the voices, ideas and perspectives produced by those engaged in social struggle are often ignored, rendered invisible or overwritten by accounts of professionalized and academic experts … we must learn the importance of being constantly vigilant and have the courage to 'speak out' when necessary to ensure that the ways of working are consistent with the organization's mission statement and value. (Pimbert, 2011: 159)

Notes

1. Examples of other publications to have reflected these concerns are Dar and Cooke (2008) and Bebbington et al. (2008).
2. Banks and Hulme (2012) have done a comprehensive review of NGO typologies for those who want to understand the range of non-government organizations involved in development. In this book we are focusing on international NGOs that take some or all of their funding from institutional

donors such as the UK government (DfID), EU, other governments, UN, and World Bank.

3.   These relationships have been characterized previously in *The Aid Chain* (Wallace et al., 2006), and in many ways this volume develops the analysis, looking at how the governing structures of development (predominantly, but not only, funding structures) affect the way that different organizations understand and carry out their work.

4.   In a thorough literature review, Banks and Hulme (2012) have outlined how NGOs have become increasingly professionalized and de-politicized, and distanced from the people in whose name they raise funds and implement programmes. Other literature, such as Haddad et al. (2011), has highlighted the need to rethink how we understand progress and development, and question some of the assumptions that underpin the industry and the organizations working within it. The issue of power relationships between development organizations and the communities and organizations they work with has been raised in other publications such as Groves and Hinton (2004), and broader questions about how we understand and work with other realities have been examined in publications such as Quarles Van Ufford and Kumar Giri (2003). Crewe and Harrison (1998) and Lewis and Mosse (2006) have taken an ethnographic approach to examining relationships within development, challenging some of the assumptions that more powerful partners in the North bring to discussions, and Mosse (2005) undertakes a thorough examination of some of these issues in a particular development context.

5.   The Big Push Forward is an initiative of the Institute of Development Studies, University of Sussex. It seeks to provide space for discussion and debate about what constitutes evidence in development:

> 'Hard evidence, rigorous data, conclusive proof, value for money, evidence-based policy are tantalising terms promising clarity about what works and what should be funded in international development. Yet behind these terms lie definitional tussles, vested interests and contested world views. For those who hold the purse strings certain ways of knowing and assessing impact are considered more legitimate than others. Yet increasingly people are recognising the need for multiple and mixed methods and approaches to better understand complex change and that, compared to imposed standards, are more likely to lead to fair assessments helping us learn how to support a fairer world' (Big Push Forward [website], <http://bigpushforward.net/about>).

6.   See Chris Roche, 'Fear, innovation and the results agenda' (3 September 2012), Big Push Forward [website], <http://bigpushforward.net>.

7.   See, for example, the discussions on the Voluntary Sector Studies Network (<www.vssn.org.uk/discussion>), 'Strategic debate: Third Sector Service Delivery – Marrying Scale and Responsiveness', and 'Being forced to change business model because of funding', March–July 2012.

8.   Which is reflected in their own documentation such as reports and evaluations:

'What is usually more urgent and more practical is the control over the *interpretation* of events. As the critical analysts of policy discourse rightly argue, power lies in the narratives that maintain an organization's own definition of the problem' (Mosse, 2005: 8).

9. See also reports from the National Audit Office (2010) and the Office of Internal Oversight (2009).

10. Over the past 30 years many INGOs have moved from taking none or only 10 per cent of their income from institutional donors, relying rather on donations from the public. Now many draw heavily on institutional funding and the ratios have changed significantly. While each NGO has different funding streams many large INGOs now raise over 50% of their funding this way, with a few rising to 80–90%. Many small and medium NGOs are heavily reliant on funding from DfID as well as Comic Relief and the Big Lottery Fund, which share many of the same systems and requirements as DfID. Other government programmes such as Irish Aid have similar aid management systems.

11. It is well recognized that evaluations and learning have always been an Achilles' heel in the NGO sector, although there were improvements in recent years, especially around participatory approaches. The concern here is not the focus on evaluation but the way they are increasingly being undertaken and the tight focus on only narrow forms of evidence, which are defined as 'robust'. See also Guijt (2008).

12. The principle of 'do no harm' was long seen as the minimum standard for INGO work, and though it often fell short, was often discussed. It is now referred to much less often.

13. 'Conversely, enhancing the status of Northern 'givers' relative to Southern 'receivers', and delivering messages focused on giving money or taking easy actions will only discourage people from following more altruistic and intrinsic motivations in future' (Darton and Kirk, 2011, *Finding Frames*, The Report, <http://findingframes.org/report2.htm>, p. 2).

14. Blame for the decline in support for aid is partly put at the door of the way aid is being promoted to the UK public by DfID and INGOs; see <www.guardian.co.uk/global-development/poverty-matters/2012/jun/25/aid-campaigns-alienate-public-development?intcmp=122>

15. See also Cornwall and Brock's discussion of Buzzwords (2005).

16. There were many debates in UK INGOs around the ethical use of images, for example Nikki van der Gaag and Cathy Nash (1997), Images of Africa, FAO and Oxfam; <www.imaging-famine.org/images_africa.htm>

17. There is clear concern about the ethics around current images being used; Concord has set up a code of conduct for INGOs, putting these issues back on the agenda: <www.concordeurope.org/115-code-of-conduct-on-images-and-messages>

18. The rise of private-sector players has increased dramatically over the past few years, with new players entering the arena and old players moving from roles such as audits and financial management into appraisal of government aid projects, project management of large government contracts, evaluators, and reviewers, as well as increasingly roles in providing services to INGOs. This has been poorly researched to date. It

is an area greatly in need of analysis but it is hard to accurately describe at present. There is little transparency about the amount of government or INGOs' aid money being spent through the private sector and to date questions through freedom-of-information channels have yielded no data. The ICAI, the new watchdog body on aid, needs to start examining this area of government, INGO–private sector funding relationships and how they influence the way aid is being used.

19. An example from Dixon of how women's movements have created alternatives is also worth quoting:

> One of the most marvellous shifts in the paradigm of the 'office-based' movement occurred for me when I met Ana Milena Gonzales, one of the leaders of the Ruta Pacifica de Mujeres from Colombia (the Peaceful Route of Women). The central identity and action of the Rita Pacífica, as Ana Milena described it to us, was to mobilise women in peaceful protest, often across immense distances in Colombia to accompany women and their communities where massacres had occurred, as well as in national mobilisations in the capital city. (Dixon 2011: 12)

20. As illustrated in the debates aired on The Big Push Forward website (http://bigpushforward.net).
21. The importance of auto-ethnographic methodology for those of us involved in theorizing development practice was discussed in conversation with Tom Scott-Smith, who develops the idea in his chapter.
22. Mike Edwards rightly notes that we have not yet mastered the art of understanding or measuring poverty (Edwards, 2010).

References

AWID, (2008) 'Where is the money for women's rights? Survey results, 2008', AWID, New York [webpage] <www.awid.org/AWID-s-Publications/Funding-for-Women-s-Rights>

Baden, S. and Goetz, A.M. (1998) 'Who needs [sex] when you can have [gender]? Conflicting discourses on gender at Beijing' in C. Jackson and R. Pearson (eds) *Feminist Visions of Development: Gender Analysis and Policy*, Routledge, London.

Banks, N. and Hulme, D. (2012) 'The role of NGOs and civil society in development and poverty reduction', Brooks World Poverty Institute Working Paper 171, University of Manchester.

Baring Foundation, (2012). 'Protecting independence: The voluntary sector in 2012', Panel on the Independence of the Voluntary Sector, 2012, Baring Foundation, London.

Bebbington, A. J., Hickey, S and Mitlin, D.C. (2008) *Can NGOs Make a Difference? The Challenge of Development Alternatives*, Zed Books, London and New York

Blue, R., Clapp-Wincek, C. and Benner, H. (2009) 'Beyond success stories: monitoring and evaluation for foreign assistance results', report for US Government by independent consultants, USAID [PDF] <http://pdf.usaid.gov/pdf_docs/PCAAB890.pdf>

Chambers, R. (1983) *Rural Development: Putting the Last First*, Longman Scientific and Technical, Harlow.

Chambers, R. (2005) *Ideas for Development*, Earthscan, London and Washington, DC.

Chang, H. (2008) *Autoethnography as Method*, Left Coast Press, Walnut Creek, CA.

Chant, S. (2007) Gender, Generation and Poverty: Exploring the 'Feminisation of Poverty' in Africa, Asia, and Latin America, Edward Elgar, Cheltenham and Northampton MA.

Chant, S. (2012) 'The feminisation of Poverty as a global concept: Critical reflections from the Gambia, the Philippines, and Costa Rica', Phyllis Kaberry Commemorative Lecture, International Gender Studies at Lady Margaret Hall (IGS @ LMH), Oxford, 30 May 2012.

Concern Worldwide and Oxfam GB (2011) 'Walking the talk: cash transfers and gender dynamics', Research carried out by Tina Wallace and Jenny Chapman for this joint report, Oxfam, Oxford.

Cornwall, A. (2012) 'Framing women in international development', presentation at Development Studies Association (Gender policy and practice study group) and Gender and Development Network meeting, London, November 2011.

Cornwall, A. and Brock, K. (2005) 'What do Buzzwords do for Development Policy? A critical look at "participation", "empowerment" and "poverty reduction"', *Third World Quarterly*, 26(7): 1043–60.

Cornwall, A., Harrison, E. and Whitehead, A. (eds) (2007) *Feminisms in Development: Contradictions, Contestations and Challenges*, Zed Books, London and New York.

Crewe, E. and Harrison, E. (1998) *Whose Development? An Ethnography of Aid*, Zed Books, London and New York.

Crush, J. (1995) 'Introduction: Imagining development', in J. Crush (ed.), *Power of Development*, pp. 1–23, Routledge, London and New York.

Dar, S and Cooke, B. (eds) (2008) *The New Development Management*, Zed Books, London.

Darnton, A., and Kirk, M. (2011) *Finding Frames: New Ways to Engage the UK Public in Global Poverty* (website), <http://findingframes.org>

Denzin, N. K. and Lincoln, Y. S. (eds) (2000) *Handbook of Qualitative Research*, Sage, London.

Dixon, H. (2011) 'Feminism and the organized subjectivity of change', paper presented at the Development Studies Association (Gender policy and practice study group) and Gender and Development Network meeting, London, November 2011.

Dostal, R. (2002) *The Cambridge Companion to Gadamer*, Cambridge University Press, Cambridge.

Edwards, M. (2010) 'Reducing global poverty – back to the future?', *openDemocracy* [webpage] <www.opendemocracy.net/michael-edwards/reducing-global-poverty-back-to-future>

Ellis, C. And Bochner, A. (2000) 'Autoethnography, personal narrative, reflexivity: researcher as subject', in N. K. Denzin and Y. S. Lincoln (eds), *Handbook of Qualitative Research*, pp. 733–68, Sage, London.

Elson, D. (1991) *Male Bias in the Development Process*, Manchester University Press, Manchester.

Fanon, F. (1963) *The Wretched of the Earth*, Grove Press, New York.

Folbre, N. (1994) *Who Pays for the Kids? Gender and the Structures of Constraint*, Routledge, London and New York.

Fonow, M. and Cook, J. (1991) 'Back to the future: A look at the second wave of feminist epistemology and methodology', in M. M. Fonow and J. A. Cook (eds), *Beyond Methodology: Feminist Scholarship as Lived Research*, pp. 1–34, Indiana University Press, Bloomington.

Foucault, M. (1994) 'Governmentality', and 'The subject and power', in *James Faubion Michel Foucault – Power: Essential Works of Foucault 1954–1984*, pp. 201–22, 326–48, Penguin Books, London.

Groves, L. and Hinton, R. (eds) (2004) *Inclusive Aid: Changing Power and Relationships in international Development*, Earthscan, London and Sterling, VA.

Guijt, I. (2008) 'Seeking surprise: rethinking monitoring for collective learning in rural resource management', PhD thesis, Holland, Wageningen University,

Haddad, L., Hossein, N., McGregor, J. A. and Mehta, L. (eds) (2011) 'Time to reimagine development?', *IDS Bulletin* 42:5, IDS, Brighton.

IDS, *The Big Push Forward* [website] <www.bigpushforward.net>

Jackson, C. and Pearson, R. (eds) (1998) *Feminist Visions of Development: Gender Analysis and Policy*, Routledge, London and New York.

Jaquette, J S. and Summerfield, G. (eds) (2006) *Women and Gender Equity in Development Theory and Practice: Institutions, Resources, and Mobilization*, Duke University Press, Durham, NC, and London.

Kabeer, N. (1994) *Reversed Realities: Gender Hierarchies in Development Thought*, Verso, London.

Kandiyoti, D. (2007) 'Between the hammer and the anvil: post-conflict reconstruction, Islam and women's rights', *Third World Quarterly*, 28(3): 503–17.

Kothari, U. (2005) *A Radical History of Development Studies: Individuals, Institutions, Ideologies*, Zed Books, London and New York.

Lewis, D. (2001) *The Management of Non-Governmental Development Organizations*, Routledge, London.

Lewis, D. and Mosse, D. (eds) (2006) *Development Brokers and Translators: The Ethnography of Aid and Agencies*, Kumarian Press, Bloomfield, CT.

Lewis, D. and Kanji, N. (2009) *Non-Governmental Organizations and Development*, Routledge Perspectives on Development, London.

Lewis, D. and Wallace, T. (eds) (2000) *New Roles and Relevance: Development NGOs and the Challenge of Change*, Kumarian Press, Bloomfield, CT.

Li, T. M. (1999) 'Compromising power: development, culture and rule in Indonesia', *Cultural Anthropology* 14(3): 295–322.

Mama, A. (2007) 'Critical connections: feminist studies in African contexts', in A. Cornwall, E. Harrison, and A. Whitehead (eds), *Feminisms in Development: Contradictions, Contestations and Challenges*, pp. 150–60, Zed Books, London and New York.

Mohanty, C., Russo, A. and Torres, L. (eds) (1991) *Third World Women and the Politics of Feminism*, Indiana University Press, Bloomington and Indianapolis.

Mosse, D. (2005) *Cultivating Development: An Ethnography of Aid Policy and Practice*, Pluto Press, London and New York.

National Audit Office (NAO) (2010) Department for International Development: bi-lateral support to primary education, House of Commons 69 session, 2010–2011.

Oakley, A. (2000) *Experiments in Knowing: Gender and Method in the Social Sciences*, Polity Press, Cambridge.

Office of Internal Oversight Services (OIOS) (2009) 'Review of results based management at the UN', OIOS, Washington, DC.

Oxfam (2012) Special issue on gender mainstreaming to be published in gender and development, late 2012.

Pimbert, M. (2011) 'Learning from the IKM emergent project', PLA notes 63, IIED, London.

Porter, F., Smyth, I. and Sweetman, C. (eds) (1999) *Gender Works: Oxfam Experience in Policy and Practice*, Oxfam, Oxford.

Quarles van Ufford, P. and Kumar Giri, A. (eds) (2003) *A Moral Critique of Development: In Search of Global Responsibilities*, Routledge, London and New York.

Rai, S. (2008) *The Gender Politics of Development*, Zed Books, London and Zubaan, New Delhi.

Rodney, W. (1973) *How Europe Underdeveloped Africa*, Bogle-L'Ouverture Publications, London.

Rorty, R. (1998) *Contingency, Irony and Solidarity*, Cambridge University Press, Cambridge.

Schrijvers, J. (1995) 'Participation and power: a transformative feminist research perspective', in N. Nelson and S. Wright (eds), *Power and Participatory Development: Theory and Practice*, pp. 19–29, IT Publications, London.

Shore, C. and Wright, S. (eds) (1997) *Anthropology of Policy: Critical Perspectives on Governance and Power*, Routledge, London and New York.

Tinker, I. (ed.) (1990) *Persistent Inequalities: Women and World Development*, Oxford University Press, Oxford.

United Nations (1995) 'The United Nations Fourth World Conference on Women: Action for Equality, Development and Peace – Declaration and Platform for Action', Beijing, China.

United Nations (1979) 'Convention on the elimination of all forms of discrimination against women', New York.

Vernon, P. (2010) 'Overseas development aid: is it working?', unpublished paper for International Alert, London.

Wallace, T., Shepherd, A. and Crowther, S. (1997) *Standardising Development: Influences on UK NGOs' Policies and Procedures*, Worldview Publishing, Oxford.

Wallace, T. with Bornstein, L. and Chapman, J. (2006) *The Aid Chain: Coercion and Commitment in Development NGOs*, Practical Action Publishing, Rugby.

Win, E. (2005) '"If it doesn't fit on the blue square it's out!" An open letter to my donor friend', in L. Groves and R. Hinton (eds), *Inclusive Aid: Changing Power and Relationships in International Development*, Earthscan, London and Sterling, VA.

About the authors

Fenella Porter was co-convenor of the DSA-IGS workshop of 'A Perfect Storm', which gave rise to this volume. She is a lecturer on the Development Studies masters course, at Birkbeck College, University of London. She undertakes occasional teaching on the MA in International Labour and Trade Union Studies, at Ruskin College, Oxford, and is a research associate of IGS at LMH, University of Oxford. Current research and teaching interests include the different and evolving identities of development NGOs, and their relationships with communities and social movements; and the shifting roles and relation-ships of NGOs and private-sector organizations in health-related development programmes, and the consequences for women's health. Previous work includes research and publishing for VSO and Oxfam and several years with Isis-Women's International Cross Cultural Exchange in Uganda. Her work has included writing, editing, and publishing chapters and articles both for practi-tioner and academic audiences.

Tina Wallace has worked in development for over 30 years, as a teacher and researcher in UK and Africa and with International NGOs. Her PhD was from Makerere University in Kampala; she taught for many years in Nigeria. She has extensive experience of field-based work in Africa and the Middle East (some in Asia), in both research and development practice. She has worked in INGOs such as Oxfam and World University Service, more recently working as a freelancer with a wide range of UK and African NGOs, especially on issues around gender, strategy, monitoring, and learning. She works from a gender perspective, recognizing inequality in gender relations as a driver for poverty and injustice. She is affiliated to International Gender Studies at Lady Margaret Hall, Oxford University. With INGO staff, she has researched relationships between INGOs and their southern partners and what shapes/inhibits the relationships between them. She has published widely on gender and the changing roles and purpose of development NGOs since the 1990s (including The Aid Chain, 2006), disseminating learning through workshops, seminars, and grey literature to try to reach development practitioners.

PART I

A perfect storm

CHAPTER 2

Development from the ground: a worm's eye view

Stan Thekaekara

This chapter traces the history of 'development' from the 1970s into the new millennium, the transitions from activism, to development, and more recently to social entrepreneurship. From the perspective of working on the ground it reflects on why these changes came about and what their impact has been. It examines the shift away from a political understanding of the causes of poverty to an apolitical approach rooted in a concept of managing resources. The chapter shows the impact of this shift on change agents and poor communities. It also shows its profound, problematic, and sometimes troubling effect on the approaches and culture of organizations working on issues of poverty.

The year was 1974. I was a young graduate in India, fired by the radicalism of the time. It was heady stuff to capture the imagination of an impressionable young man barely out of his teens. So at the ripe old age of 21, I marched into a small *adivasi* (indigenous) village in Bihar (now Jharkhand) armed with little more than a smattering of Marxian analysis and a hefty dose of liberation theology. But I had no shortage of passion, determination, and enthusiasm. I, like many others of my time, believed the revolution was just around the corner: a revolution that would create a new egalitarian society, where all human beings lived with dignity and pride, sharing all that the world had to offer.

It is nearly four decades since I walked into that village. The hype around the millennium has come and gone. But the revolution has not happened, and we are still fighting for the rights of one of the poorest, most marginalized, and exploited communities in the country: the *adivasis*. In these four decades, we have had many avatars of social change. We have seen governments, civil society, philanthropists, and even corporations investing huge amounts of money. But has anything changed for people living in poverty?

This chapter puts forward a history of the development sector in India from the 1970s to the new millennium, as viewed by one working on the ground to bring about change. It will examine the gradual and steady shift away from a political understanding of the causes of poverty, the shift from an understanding rooted in concepts of social justice, to a managerial understanding of poverty (not necessarily its causes) which is largely apolitical. It

http://dx.doi.org/10.3362/9781780447780/002

will argue that this had an impact not only on the understanding and analysis of poverty, but also on the approaches and culture of organizations working on issues of poverty. It concludes by outlining the challenges that face the development sector as the world becomes increasingly fractured and the positions of political left and political right, capitalism and communism, are difficult to defend.

Part I: an historical sweep

Early influences

The development sector has been referred to as the voluntary sector, the social sector, the NGO sector, and more recently civil society. Irrespective of nomenclature, it has grown to become a highly sophisticated and widely accepted sector shaping society today. Public perception of this as a homogeneous group of do-gooders, however, is largely misplaced. Different historical strands have contributed to and influenced the evolution of the sector, resulting in very different approaches, operational cultures, and management styles.

India has a long history of voluntary action based on the concepts of *seva* (service) and *dhana* (giving). During British rule, Christian missionaries worked extensively in the areas of health, education, and care for destitute communities. India passed an Act giving legal status to these bodies as early as 1860 (ADB NGO and Civil Society Center, 2009). During the second half of the nineteenth century, a number of secular organizations were established in response to growing nationalism and the desire for self-reliance. Inspired and led by Gandhi, a number of social welfare organizations, like the All India Spinners Association, All India Village Industries Association,[1] Charkha Sangh,[2] Harijan Sevak Sangh,[3] and the Leprosy Education Fund, were set up across the country (Pandey, 1998). These organizations were seen as supportive of and complementary to the state. The Gandhian concept of voluntarism was rooted in his vision of post-colonial India being a self-reliant country based on village republics, where power flowed from the village to parliament and not the other way around.

Later, the social upheaval across the globe of the 1960s and early 1970s also contributed to the character of voluntary action, shifting it away from charity and welfare, to challenging the socio-economic and political structures of society. This shift is also seen in the approach by leading Gandhians like Bahaguna Sunderlal, who led the *Chipko* movement,[4] and Baba Amte, who became a major campaigner of the *Narmada Bachao Andolan*.[5] The African American Civil Rights Movement (1955–68), the largest strike in history of students and workers in France (May 1968), the anti-Vietnam War protests of the 1960s in the USA, the global movement against apartheid in South Africa, the growing influence of Marxian analysis on the peasant movements of South America, and the upheaval caused by liberation theology within the orthodoxy of the Catholic Church were some of the social movements rejecting the established social order. These movements were captured in iconic images ranging from an iron hammer clutched in a fist, to the young woman putting a rose in the barrel of a policeman's gun at an anti-Vietnam War rally.

With independence, India opted for a mix of Western capitalism and Russian communism, perhaps accounting for a strong class consciousness in areas such as Kerala and West Bengal, which, along with Tripura, have repeatedly elected communist governments. West Bengal also saw the emergence of the violent uprisings of the Naxalites, far left radicals rooted in Maoist–Leninist ideologies.[6]

These were heady times if you were young and looking to create a new world order. India was no exception. Though the spirit of the independence movement of the 1940s was beginning to fade, the social, political, and economic radicalism of the 1960s and 1970s reignited the idealism of young people wanting to create a more just society. Universities became highly volatile and politically active centres. Student unions and student strikes were the order of the day, especially in states like West Bengal and Kerala. The phrase 'status quo' became highly unpopular, while phrases such as 'social justice' and 'social change' became fashionable.

The emergence of social action groups

Student work camps organized by movements like the All India Catholic University Federation (AICUF), the National Service Scheme of the Government of India, and the Student Christian Movement exposed urban middle-class students to the realities of poverty in Indian villages and slums. In 1970, at a National Conference of the AICUF, students from all over the country signed the 'Poonamallee Declaration', stating 'we were born into an unjust world and we are determined not to leave it the way we found it'.

Many young people, inspired by left-wing movements, the Gandhian movement, and the radical liberation theology of the Catholic Church, made life-changing choices. Turning their backs on their middle-class and often privileged backgrounds, these young students opted to identify with the masses, by living with the poor in remote villages, and mobilizing people to resist exploitation and discrimination. Running adult literacy classes and non-formal education centres, they exhorted people to be aware of their rights and to assert them collectively. What they lacked in resources they made up for with zeal, passion, and a determination to initiate revolution and so usher in a more just society. Across the country, the poor and marginalized found new allies in the educated, middle-class young people willing to champion their cause no matter what the price. A new confidence and courage emerged, leading them to question age-old social hierarchies like caste, firmly entrenched economic structures like bonded labour and rural indebtedness, and exploitative employment practices in the industrial sector that blatantly violated the labour laws of the time.

While no evidence exists to evaluate the influence of these groups on social policy, it is interesting that much of India's pro-poor legislation was enacted during this period. The 20 Point Programme for the Eradication of Poverty, the Bonded Labour System Abolition Act of 1975, and the nationalization of banks in 1965 to ensure the extension of credit to marginalized people, especially in rural areas, were just some of the steps taken by the government of India and various state governments to fulfil their constitutional commitment to a socialist agenda.

The Emergency period and the Janata Party Movement

Ironically, this period that saw the emergence of some of India's most pro-poor legislation and policy was also one of the darkest periods of India's post-independence history. Prime Minister Indira Gandhi, faced with a conviction from the Allahabad High Court declaring her election to Parliament null and void, decided to invoke a constitutional provision to declare a 'state of internal emergency' that suspended democratic freedom and civil liberties. This unleashed a repressive regime that gave the government free rein to settle scores with all those who dared to question the established social order. Social activists were branded a threat to the nation, and scores were arrested and held without charge. Many were reported killed, and most were forced to go underground to stay alive. Dissent in any form was quickly and ruthlessly crushed. Press censorship was introduced, and forced sterilization under the guise of population control became rampant. A pall of gloom, fear, and hopelessness enveloped the idealism of the preceding years.

A single ray of hope during the period was the Janata Party (JP) Movement, led by Jayaprakash Narayan, a revered freedom fighter. The JP Movement demanded Indira Gandhi's resignation and called for a *sampoorna kranth* (total revolution). Thousands of students, especially in Bihar, responded to the call, and walked out of universities to join the fight against the Emergency. When the Emergency was finally withdrawn and elections announced, this cadre of young people were at the forefront. The JP Movement is credited with having brought the various non-Congress parties under the single banner of the Janata Party (People's Party), which defeated the Congress and gave India its first non-Congress government.

For many of the activists and for the JP Movement, this was the second freedom struggle. They saw it as a peaceful democratic revolution that overthrew an authoritarian regime. Sadly it was a short-lived victory as the Janata Party crumbled and Mrs. Gandhi and the Congress quickly returned to power. The activists responded to the disillusionment in a variety of ways. While some rode the wagon of power as elected members of Parliament or as active party workers, many opted out and wandered back into the establishment. Others remained lost, searching for alternatives. Significantly, however, this period introduced electoral politics as one of the means of social transformation and threw up a new cadre of political leaders (Thakur, 1976).

The 1977 Andhra cyclone and tidal wave

On 19 November 1977, a massive cyclone and tidal wave hit Andhra Pradesh on the east coast of India. This was the first time India had experienced a natural disaster of such magnitude. An army of young people from all over the country arrived to provide help. Many stayed on past the relief stage to set up rehabilitation projects. International aid organizations had already arrived in India in significant numbers by then – first in 1951, in response to the Bihar famine, and then between 1965 and 1967, in response to the widespread drought across the country. During these years, their approach was one of direct implementation through paid staff. Oxfam is often credited with having changed this approach during the Andhra cyclone by deciding not to work directly through paid staff but to fund local organizations and groups; an approach that subsequently became the norm.

During the Emergency the government of India had passed an Act to regulate the receipt of foreign donations. The Act stipulated that only registered charitable organizations could receive foreign funds and they should report the receipt and utilization of all funds received to the Home Ministry. Subsequently this was made more stringent and all organizations, although already registered as charities, were required to register also with the Home Ministry, or seek permission to receive foreign funds. Since Indian philanthropy of the time was largely for charity work and was funnelled through temples and churches, the social action groups of the 1970s depended more on Western philanthropy, commonly referred to as solidarity funding. This immediately brought them under the ambit of the Act. This meant that the more informal social-action groups and individuals of the early 1970s had to become formal and structured, and establish a legal identity by registering themselves as societies or trusts. They had to frame rules for their governance and management. Passion and commitment was no longer enough; there had to be a legal structure.

Coupled with the larger presence of international aid agencies and the new cadre of young people drawn into working for the poor through the cyclone, India saw the establishment of a number of small organizations working to bring about social change; and social change interventions became institutionalized as never before.

Integrated rural development of the 1980s and 1990s

One of the significant changes after the Andhra cyclone was that the new actors were driven by an apolitical view of poverty, which led to the notion of 'developed' and 'underdeveloped' nations. This notion frames the developed Western capitalist economy, based on growth, as the ideal model. In 1979, the Indian government launched the Integrated Rural Development Programme (IRDP; Mathur, 1995), which was influenced by the notion of underdevelopment. So through the 1980s the fight against exploitation and discrimination was relegated to the background, and energies and resources were focussed on income growth, health care, and education. In its seventh Five Year Plan (1985–9) the Planning Commission recognized voluntary organizations as allies in the development process and allocated resources to the sector. The NGO had finally arrived!

As part of this development agenda, the push was for 'holistic and integrated community development'. Small stand-alone interventions were no longer attractive. You could not just run a school or adult literacy classes; you also needed to think about income generation, health, etc. Around this time, the rupee started tumbling and by the early 1990s international aid agencies found themselves with larger budgets in rupee terms, and the government was financing NGOs through a myriad of different schemes, which led to a scramble to find NGOs to fund. A mushrooming of NGOs began.

The demand for integrated development, coupled with large resources, meant that NGOs were becoming increasingly complex organizations. The need to 'professionalize' the sector took centre stage. Social work schools started popping up across the country, and specialized business schools, like the Institute for Rural Management, Anand (IRMA), were set up. Its founder, Dr Kurien, believed the key to effective rural development was professional management and that professionalizing the management of rural organizations called for a matching of the specific but unmet needs of the sector with the formal techniques and skills of management professionals. Linking the two, he argued, would be the 'rural managers' prepared by IRMA through its two-year diploma (PRM) in rural management.

But these managers mostly came at a cost, and if organizations were to be able to afford them, they had to operate at a minimum scale. Donors found it easier and cheaper to deal with large NGOs rather than small scattered organizations. Scaling-up and measurable impact became the order of the day. NGOs, both local and international, began to look more like private-sector enterprises, and some even prided themselves on their corporate image. This made them an attractive option for official (governmental) assistance. Official Development Assistance, which used to be channelled only through bilateral agreements with other governments, was now channelled directly through NGOs.

With the collapse of the Soviet Union in 1991, Western capitalism gained an ascendancy that made poverty more a management issue than a social justice issue. Increasingly, the battle against poverty was about allocating greater resources and managing these resources effectively, rather than restructuring society. In 1991, India shed all pretence of being socialist, and threw open its economy to direct foreign investments under the catch-all of liberalization and globalization. And right through the 1990s, capitalism was no longer seen as the problem, but as a solution (Isserles 2003; Sriram, 2010). This view was bolstered by the much-acclaimed success of Mohammed Younis's Grameen Bank in Bangladesh. The first Microcredit Summit held in February 1998 in Washington, DC, gave birth to the Microcredit Campaign that sought 'to reach 100 million of the world's poorest families, especially the women of those families, with credit ... by the year 2005'.[7]

The new millennium

In India, as elsewhere, economic liberalization and globalization, which allowed the free flow of capital across the world, resulted in making trade the cornerstone of our economy. Production moved to poorer countries where input costs, especially labour, were far cheaper. Companies that were solely producers either gave up producing in favour of trading or diversified into trade. Smaller companies who could not survive in the now highly competitive and expensive marketplace were swallowed up through mergers and acquisitions.[8] Brands became more valuable than the product. The restructuring of the economy in India resulted in a growing middle class whose purchasing power had increased exponentially.

The voluntary sector was no exception. NGOs, at least those in the business of income generation, began targeting urban markets. Value addition, brand creation, and marketing became the mantras; many were successful, but they looked more like private companies than social change agents. On the other side of the fence, in the private sector, entrepreneurs such as Bill Gates, Richard Branson, and young people who became rich riding the information technology wave were seen as successes. And with their success came a new idea: can their approach be mimicked in the social sector? The model of an entrepreneurial individual creating social good became a very attractive proposition. And with strong backing from foundations like the Ashoka, Skoll, and Schwab Foundations, a new breed of change agent was born: the social entrepreneur. Notwithstanding the prefix 'social', these entrepreneurs and their enterprises skate dangerously close to being outright private-sector businesses. Interestingly, while this is a growing field (practically every school of social work and business management offers a course on social entrepreneurship) the idea does not seem to have found much traction with more traditional development actors but has attracted a new wave of practitioners, who otherwise might not have considered the social sector as a career option.

So, over the years, we have seen many avatars of social change strategies, from social justice, to development, to micro-finance, and finally now, the latest, social entrepreneurship. But what lies behind these changes? What has it meant to the organizations and people working for social change? Most importantly, what have these changing avatars meant to people on the ground: the proclaimed beneficiaries?

Part II: the view from the ground

These historical changes have resulted in the development sector now being anything but homogeneous. Some people have remained true to their initial political beliefs and continued their struggles with the poor. Others from the early years have morphed into managers of large organizations. For many, especially those who joined along the way, see it as a career, and pride themselves in being professional, it is simply a job. Some have jumped on the micro-finance bandwagon and are effectively moneylenders (although maybe not as exploitative as those they replaced). Some (the social entrepreneurs) appear to be very typical business people, but with a human face. And a few have merged these approaches in an attempt to respond to the challenges of an ever-changing society as effectively as possible and in a manner that ensures the protection of the rights of the people suffering in an unjust society.

The changing role of the community

To most of the activists of the 1970s, the 'people' were known as either the 'masses' or 'the community', depending on the political persuasion of the individual activist. But irrespective of the terminology, there was a clear sense of aligning with the poor; of becoming an ally. The community was central; everything began with an analysis of their situation, their needs, and an understanding of the changes required. Interventions were planned not so much to make life better for the poor, but to change the structures of society that kept them poor. It was less about poverty per se and more about the way society was structured.

This meant taking on the establishment, which often (especially during the Emergency) was a high-risk enterprise. While the activists may have had options such as going underground or simply withdrawing, poor people could not do that; and often they were the ones who paid the price. While little may have happened to improve the living conditions of the poor during this period, it did result in the politicization of large sections of the poor. People began to see for the first time that embedded exploitative social and economic hierarchies could and must be challenged. Overcoming their fear of the rich and powerful, they took direct action, violent and non-violent, to express their anger and to bring about change. This was epitomized in an incident when we were working with a group of *adivasis* to reclaim a piece of land that was their sacred grove, and which had been illegally appropriated by a non-tribal landlord. The landlord accused us of being troublemakers and claimed that the *adivasis* and the non-*adivasis* had always lived in peace until we came along. Vellutha, a Paniya tribal, looked up at the towering landlord who stood a foot taller, and declared, 'We never, ever lived in peace. For generations you have sat on our heads and so did not know our pain. Today we have put you down and disturbed your comfort so you feel the pain of being challenged'.

The approach of relief and rehabilitation that characterized the response to the 1977 tidal wave and cyclone saw a subtle shift away from changing society towards improving the lives of the poor who were seen as victims needing help rather than as a force for change. People tended to respond to this more easily as benefits were more immediate and tangible, unlike the earlier tilting at windmills in the hope of a promised land.

Sectoral approaches, such as ensuring better health care and education, and improving incomes, became the focus. People's status was not viewed from a power perspective but as providing statistics for baseline data. Measures of change were no longer based on land rights, freedom from bonded labour, or fighting against social discrimination. Numbers of children immunized, infant and maternal mortality rates, numbers of children enrolled in school, and increases in incomes were the new indicators of social change. From being centre stage and taking control over their own futures, poor people were slowly moved to the periphery, and seen as recipients of good intentions.

With increased funding came the emergence of a more 'professional' approach to tackling poverty. Integrated interventions, based on a needs assessment which was usually done through secondary data, shifted people even further to the periphery. Geographies rather than communities became more important. The attempt was to identify the poorest areas (as opposed to the poorest people) to define the gaps, and to try to fill them by ploughing in sufficient resources; what emerged were tools like Participatory Rural Appraisal (PRA) in an attempt to give people a role in the development process. People were now consulted but the power remained with the professionals.

The micro-finance movement brought about yet another shift in the role of the community. Women were organized into self-help groups (SHGs) and these were built into federations. While the language of community mobilization was still used, in effect this was nothing more than bringing together individual women to form small groups where the focus was not social change but self-interest; mainly quick and easy credit. While the SHG model has spread to every corner of the country, it is important to note that these groups are mobilized neither on the basis of class nor on the basis of being exploited communities like *dalits* and *adivasis*. From being viewed as socially and economically exploited communities who had to unite and fight unjust hierarchies, they became viewed as user groups, self-help groups, and, with the advent of the social entrepreneur, client groups. They are no longer communities but groups.

At another level the language moved away from injustice, exploitation, and social change, to development and poverty alleviation. The rhetoric often talked of shifting from top-down approaches to bottom-up approaches. Either way the language betrays how the community is perceived; they are the bottom.

In the past four decades, sadly, I have seen people's roles in shaping their own destinies steadily diminishing. Rather than challenging society, they are now required to acquiesce and strengthen the status quo in exchange for a few dollars more. Notwithstanding 'empowerment', 'rights-based approaches', and similar jargon liberally sprinkled through proposals for funding, poor people are no longer the drivers of social change: they are its recipients. These four decades have seen a shift from social movements to the creation of organizations, many so large that they resemble private-sector multinationals.

K. T. Subramanian, a Mullukurumba tribal who co-founded ACCORD with us, once declared at an anti-globalization forum, 'I am not so much concerned with the policy changes that take place at a global and national level, I am more concerned I am the last to know – and only after these changes have negatively affected me'.

The changing role of women

While the role of poor communities as a whole has steadily diminished, it is interesting to note that the role of women both within their own communities and within society has begun to see some changes for the better.

Women in India have always borne and continue to bear the burden of holding together both the family and the entire community. Not only are the daily chores of housekeeping and child rearing foisted on them, the back-breaking work around conducting community rituals of marriages, festivals, funerals, etc. is also the sole responsibility of women. But this important role, where they are the cornerstone of family and community, is not just taken for granted; it is seen as the male prerogative to demand their services, unacknowledged and unappreciated.

Despite this, throughout history, women have braved opposition from their husbands, community, and society at large to participate in freedom struggles, to charge male bastions of power, and to enforce their rights as equal partners. This has resulted in a rather skewed perception of the role of women in India. Many have broken glass ceilings to reach the top of the political, academic, and corporate ladders. CEOs, heads of universities, Prime Minister, and President of India, all of these have been women. But they are nowhere near an equitable representation of the female population. Furthermore, most of those who have broken through have been from the middle and upper classes of society.

For poor women, very little has changed. The daily grind of carrying their families and communities on their backs continues unabated. Worse, they face abuse of the worst possible kind. Dowry deaths, bride burning, and female infanticide are all everyday phrases in the Indian lexicon.

There have certainly been innumerable attempts and interventions to protect women. However, their position in society is little changed. Not being gender specific, much of the development aid has not reached women and, I would contend, has actually contributed to strengthening patriarchy.

It is often argued that the single most important factor in bringing about real changes in women's lives has been the micro-finance movement. It is beyond the scope of this paper to argue the merits or demerits of micro-finance. But even the critics of micro-finance (and I am one of them) must admit that women have now been given the opportunity to enter the public arena, no longer confined to household duties. However, their responsibilities and hard labour in running their homes has not decreased. The formation of women's SHGs to run micro-finance operations has led to women-only organizations being formed across the country; something unimaginable a few decades ago. I would argue that a capitalist solution to poverty – the provision of credit – has had more of a social impact than its intended economic impact. There is a growing awareness, even on the part of the state which is increasingly insisting on positive discrimination for women, that women's rights must be recognized.

But of course we are a long way from women asserting their rightful place in society. One can only hope that the glimmer of change witnessed through the women's self-help movement will be built upon, and through collective action by women we will arrive at a society where, along with other deprived and exploited communities like *adivasis* and *dalits*, women will be able to participate in society as equal partners.

The changing face of the donor

I remember in 1975 being visited by a friend from Holland. At the end of her one-week stay in my village she gave me an envelope of a few thousand rupees: enough to last me for a year. Years later, I met a woman in the UK who told me that she used to shut off her heating for a few hours every day and put the money she saved in a tin and when it reached a few pounds she gave it to Oxfam. That was the time of 'solidarity funding'. In 1977 during the Andhra cyclone after a village meeting with shepherds whose entire flock had been wiped out, people were adamant that they needed no charity, just a loan to buy more sheep and restart their lives. I went with them to the bank to negotiate a loan. The manager was more than sympathetic but needed some collateral. Oxfam was supporting the organization I had set up. I went to the nearest telephone booth (the era before cell phones) and called the Oxfam office 150 km away to ask whether Oxfam could keep a deposit in the local bank as guarantee. The Field Director of Oxfam immediately agreed and asked me to pick up the cheque. This was a Friday. I signed a receipt, and on Monday Oxfam's money was deposited. On Tuesday the shepherds got their loan to buy their sheep. Some days later when I visited Oxfam, I was given a proposal describing the project and asked to sign, and that was that.

Contrast that with today, where large proposals must be written with figures and charts (not possible without computers), passed back and forth between the NGO and donor a few times, followed by at least one if not more appraisal visits from donor consultants (and they do not come cheaply). Contractual agreements need to be signed by both parties, and money transferred in small tranches based on detailed reporting including logframes and pie charts; since 2000, two of our proposals, despite lightning-fast communication systems, have taken two and three years, respectively, to be completed.

Donors are often thrice removed. It is no longer uncommon for donors (especially official donors) to fund a large agency or consortium, which then funds a host organization in the 'developing' country, which in turn funds independent local NGOs. These chains create a huge managerial and financial bureaucracy, which means jobs. But these are not jobs for the people in poverty; rather they are jobs for the middle class. Who is counting the costs of such administrative machinery?

The modern obsession with numbers and measuring should make us pause. Is everything valued counted and is everything counted valued? We are not arguing for money in a brown envelope and a handshake, but somewhere along the line we seem to have lost our way and our sense of purpose. 'Accountability' has become less of a political term and more of a financial one. This is in keeping with the sector being more about money and less about justice and social change.

Where to from here?

The rural economy is collapsing and the rural poor increasingly depend on government help. Is this the solution? Most of us working with the poor will argue that this is not the way forward. What we are seeing is increasing gaps between the rich and the poor. The new wealth is not trickling down. This indicates a more fundamental problem of inequality, a problem that lies with the social and economic relationships between people.

The environment and climate change movement has also challenged the dominant economic model, not from a human rights or social justice perspective, but from a sustainability and ecological perspective. As we look to the future, it is important to recognize that the NGO/development/voluntary sector is not a homogeneous whole. It includes the *dalit* movement, the *adivasi* movement, the women's movement, the environment movement, and many others. We need to recognize that these movements have common cause: an unjust society that needs changing. These movements are a key arena in which inequalities can be challenged. They can reclaim some of the political space that characterized the early years described at the beginning of this chapter.

While there is a role for the larger, richer, and more dominant development actors, who seek to mitigate the pain of poverty through various developmental interventions, I would argue that these are not the solution. Instead of tinkering around the edges and trying to make life a little better for people; instead of alleviating poverty; instead of focusing on extending a development model that is gobbling up the Earth's resources at what is now accepted to be an unsustainable rate, it will help us if we go back to the basics. If we are to be a truly civilized society, one that believes in equality, fraternity, liberty, and justice for all, we should be looking to recreate the structures of our civilization on those lines. We should, in the words of the young students at Poonamallee, declare 'we were born into an unjust society and we are determined not to leave it the way we found it'.

Notes

1. In 1925 Gandhi founded the All-India Spinners Association and in 1935 he formed the All-India Village Industries Association. This was in keeping with his concept of *Swadeshi* (self-sufficiency) which aimed at creating self-reliant village economies.
2. *Charkha* – the spinning wheel. This was the symbol of Gandhian Swadeshi. In 1925 the Charkha Sangh (Association) was formed to popularize hand-spun yarn to be used for hand loom cloth called *khadhi*.
3. Harijan, or Children of God, was the name Gandhi applied to 'the untouchables' or lower castes, The HSS was set up to start a movement against untouchability in the country. The term *harijan* is no longer considered acceptable and *dalit* is now the term used.
4. The Chipko (literally translated as 'to stick to') Movement was launched in the early 1970s in the Garwhal region of the Himalayas where local villagers hugged trees to prevent their felling by loggers.
5. *Narmada Bachao Andolan*, or Save the Narmada Movement, is a social movement consisting of tribal people, *adivasis*, farmers, environmentalists, and human rights activists protesting the damming of the Narmada river, Gujarat, India.
6. The word 'Naxalites' comes from Naxalbari, a small West Bengalian village where a section of the Communist Party of India (Marxist) (CPM) began a violent uprising in 1967.
7. 'Declaration and Action Plan' of the Microcredit Summit 1997. <www.microcreditsummit.org/declaration.htm>
8. Hindustan Lever, the Indian arm of Unilever and Tata Tea – which bought up Tetley Tea to become the second biggest player in the tea industry – gave up all their plantations and now are mere traders of tea.

References

ADB Non Governmental Organisation and Civil Society Center (2009), 'Overview of civil society organisations: India' [PDF] <www.adb.org/sites/default/files/pub/2009/CSB-IND.pdf> [accessed 28 February 2012].
Isserles, R. G. (2003), 'Microcredit: the rhetoric of empowerment, the reality of "development as usual"', *Women's Studies Quarterly* 31 (3/4), Women and Development: Rethinking Policy and Reconceptualizing Practice, 38–57, <www.jstor.org/stable/40003319> [accessed 5 March 2012].
Mathur, K. (1995), 'Politics and Implementation of Integrated Rural Development Programme', *Economic and Political Weekly* 30: 2703–8 <www.jstor.org/stable/4403342> [accessed 5 March 2012].
Pandey, J. (ed.) (1998) *Gandhi and Voluntary Organisations*, M D Publications, New Delhi.
Sriram, M. S. (2010), 'A fairy tale turns into a nightmare', *Economic and Political Weekly*, 45: 10–13 <www.mssriram.in/sites/mssriram.in/files/epw-fairytalenightmare_0.pdf> [accessed 5 March, 2012].
Thakur, R. C. (1976), 'The Fate of India's Parliamentary Democracy', *Pacific Affairs* 49: 263–93 <www.jstor.org/stable/2756068> [accessed 5 March 2012].

About the author

Stan Thekaekara has worked for over 30 years in the field of human rights and development. Stan's activist life began in 1974 with *adivasis* in Bihar. In 1986, he co-founded ACCORD, to mobilize the *adivasis* of the Gudalur Valley, Tamilnadu to fight for their social, political, and human rights. In 2000, Stan founded Just Change, an international cooperative linking producers, investors, and consumers to rebuild the notion of community and regain power in the marketplace. Stan was a trustee of Oxfam GB and Visiting Fellow at the Skoll Centre for Social Entrepreneurship at the Said Business School, Oxford University. His numerous lectures include the Alternative Mansion House Speech in London and the Fourth Annual Feasta Lecture at Trinity College, Ireland. He's also written extensively on development issues. Outlook Business listed him among the top 50 social entrepreneurs of India, describing him as 'the man who delights in turning textbook theories on its head'.

CHAPTER 3

Evaluation, complexity, uncertainty – theories of change and some alternatives

Chris Mowles

Certain ways of planning and evaluating social development currently dominate in the international aid sector. Using abstract and simplified logical schemata, these methods simplify distant complexity to enable bureaucracies to 'see like a state'. Development interventions aligned with managerial requirements support the idea that social development can be engineered. Quantifiable techniques readily enable global aggregation and un-nuanced statements about the 'success' of interventions suiting a marketized development domain. Moral rhetoric about 'transparency', 'accountability', and 'value for money' often accompanies the appeal to rational abstraction and logical consistency. As an alternative I draw on the complexity sciences to explore why the future is radically unpredictable. I look at how insights from the complexity sciences are or are not taken up in evaluation methods. Without developing ways of engaging with the contextual, the particular, and the dynamic nature of social development, we risk covering over important relationships of power, compromising the ability to treat counterparts as moral equivalents.

In many ways there is nothing extraordinary about evaluating what we are engaged in, since we do it every day. We try to get things done with others, have ideas about how we would like to improve our own and other people's lives, try out new things, and reflect on what we have done together. We give accounts to each other about what we intended, how things did and didn't turn out as we expected, and narrate the reasons. Power (1997, 2007), who has written extensively about what he calls the 'audit explosion' and the modern tendency to evaluate, audit, and assess, has argued that it would be hard to take against the idea of auditing and evaluation per se, since it is such an ordinary activity without which social life would be impossible. What we might explore instead, however, is why there has been an audit and evaluation explosion, and what sorts of evaluations are favoured in order to better think through the consequences for development practice.

The political philosopher Hannah Arendt observed that one of the most important aspects of being human is this process of beginning things anew with others, something she termed 'natality', which involves the making and keeping of promises (1958/1998: 244–5). However, she also pointed

http://dx.doi.org/10.3362/9781780447780/003

paradoxically to the dangers of making collective agreements to dispose of the future as though it were the present. Throughout her work Arendt was very concerned about the potential for totalitarianism to suppress political engagement, pluralism, and thinking, which she considered necessary for sustaining human endeavour and freedom. For her, making plans with other people is both a danger and an opportunity. The opportunity lies in the fact that people acting in concert can achieve a lot more than they can alone. The danger arises from our repeated experience that when we act, we do so into a web of actions of other people who are our moral equals. The moment we think we can map out the whole of the future in every direction according to our intentions is the moment our plans become self-defeating, she argues, and potentially totalitarian. Instead, the best they can offer is 'limited independence from the incalculability of the future' (ibid.). The will to improve is a provisional activity and one that needs to embrace pluralism and the interweaving of intentions.

In this chapter I want to explore some aspects of current discussions about the evaluation of international development by drawing some broad distinctions between different ways of thinking about intervening in other people's societies and evaluating these interventions. One of the contrasts I will be making is between what I understand to be the current, dominant way of framing evaluative work, which draws on logic models and which assumes a predictable future, and some of the more radical insights from the complexity sciences, which stress the nonlinear and unpredictable nature of social life. The unpredictability arises from the interweaving of intentions of social actors mediated by power relationships, manifested as gender relations and themes of class, caste, and race. I will also reflect upon how ways of thinking about evaluating and assessing have emerged over time and are themselves a reflection of a particular configuration of current power relations and the dominance of particular ideologies. The current dominant discourse on evaluation comes wrapped in a moral discourse, which makes it very difficult to gainsay and to set out alternatives.

Making the argument for evaluation as a scientific and moral undertaking

In claiming that there is a dominant way of understanding evaluation of international development interventions, I do not intend to imply that there is just one way. I realize that the domain of evaluation is rich, contested, and nuanced, and ask forgiveness for some necessary simplifications. However, I am arguing that much contemporary discourse on the planning of development and its evaluation is based on the fallacy that the rational, autonomous individual is capable of designing predictable and successful futures for social interventions, and that 'success' can be measured by the extent to which these predictions have been realized. There is an assumption that other people's social development can be engineered. Increasingly INGOs are encouraged to adopt a 'theory of change' model, a concept developed by the Aspen Institute in the USA (1997). In theory of change logic models, an evaluation aims to test how far the project's hypothesis, the changes which are predicted and the causal processes to achieve them, is proven.

International development has long been dominated by the logical framework as a planning method, and the theory of change, though supposedly different in each particular project, is nonetheless predicated on the same kind of propositional if-then logic. The idea of proving or disproving a development hypothesis and the increasing experimentation with statistical methods in the sector for doing so draws on the language and methods employed in the natural sciences. Alongside is a moral argument that accompanies discussions of methods, particularly from donors, where the nuances and uncertainties of different approaches to development and evaluation can become lost. When discussion becomes wrapped up in both quasi-scientific and moral language, it becomes more difficult to engage in critique, a situation which threatens to cover over power relations. Who would want to be seen to be using methods which might be described as 'unscientific' or to be acting in a way which is considered not 'transparent' and 'accountable'?

As an example of the moral case for using particular methods it may be worthwhile noting the new UK Department for International Development (DfID) business plan and summary strategy document published a year after the coalition government came to power.

> In the current financial climate, we have a particular duty to show that we are achieving value for every pound of taxpayers' money that we spend on development. Results, transparency and accountability will be our watchwords and will guide everything we do.
>
> **Results and impact** – getting value for money from every pound of aid ...
>
> **Working with fewer international organisations** – putting more resources behind the most effective agencies to deliver better results on the ground. (DfID, 2011)

At the same time as espousing values of 'results, transparency and account-ability' and 'achieving value for every pound', DfID intends funding fewer organizations. How might INGOs show that they comply with the ministry's values? One suggestion comes from the Independent Commission for Aid Impact (ICAI), a body set up by the government and responsible for scrutinizing UK aid spend. The ICAI notes in its first report that effective organizations must have a clear plan: 'This clear plan is commonly referred to as a "theory of change". A theory of change defines the chain of activities required to bring about a given long-term goal' (ICAI, 2011: 1). Adopting a theory of change for development projects is not just a technical prerequisite, then, it is also a demonstration of commitment to DfID's values. Any INGO concerned about its long-term sustainability must take both phenomena seriously.

In the development domain the principle values are those of being 'effective and efficient', being 'accountable' and 'transparent', 'oriented towards results' and being in favour of 'good governance'. 'Good governance' is taken to mean adhering to all of the preceding values, thus completing a circularity of reasoning and creating a particular moral climate which constrains and shapes discussion and participation in international development. Of course, values are terribly important: they are a vital part of who we are, but whoever gets to decide what the values are and what they mean in practice is in a particularly powerful position.

In my experience as a trustee of INGOs, and as a consultant sometimes employed to participate in evaluative work, I have noticed an enhanced degree of anxiety amongst INGO staff about how they might demonstrate 'results', which is linked to fears about continuing to belong to a professional group which complies with the particular values set out above. Technical demands couched in moral vocabulary can lead to feelings of vulnerability, anxiety, and a preoccupation with organizational reputation, as Power (2007) has noted.

This is especially the case in highly marketized times where large numbers of INGOs have sometimes made quite grand claims for the impact of their work in order to generate funding. Donor pressure on intermediary organizations to 'deliver' creates pressure in turn from intermediary organizations on their Southern partners, and subsequently of Southern partners on their beneficiaries. In a recent article (Mowles, 2010) I gave an example, which I have experienced increasingly frequently in the sector, of joining a group of field-workers meeting to review their work together. Although promising to make time to discuss what they were actually doing, the difficulties, the complexities and uncertainties, in the morning-long presentations staff chose instead to gravitate anxiously around a series of dualisms as to whether a particular aspect of the programme had reached its targets, and whether it could be considered successful. A variety of other scholars (Gulrajani, 2011; Mosse, 2006; Wallace et al., 1997, 2006) have noted that a focus on the technical inhibits the ability of staff to engage critically with what is being asked of them, and significantly reduces the scope of discussions of development interventions. Discussion can revolve narrowly around the precise application of the planning and evaluation tools, displacing opportunities for wider exploration and understanding, and questions of power, judgement, and ethics.

Managerialism and public trust

At the beginning of the chapter I argued that giving accounts to each other of who we are and what we have been doing is a necessary part of human life. But there has been an intensification of demands for evaluation of a particular kind. No not-for-profit organization will have escaped both organizational and personal performance targets, and a host of other metrics for 'measuring success' in the workplace, often linked to rituals of public humiliation and shaming as encouragement to try harder and *pour encourager les autres*.

Ordering, regulating, controlling, and disciplining social activity is not new, but has arisen over many centuries and is a central concern of governments, leaders, and managers. The way we currently and predominantly try to exercise control of social activity is drawn from methods which have proven particularly successful in engineering and medical sciences: target-setting, parts and whole thinking, and logical disaggregation have been helpful in taming the natural world and understanding the human body, but the question remains as to how helpful they are in thinking about the social world.

James C. Scott (1998) noted how methods of measuring, inscribing, comparing, and mapping have developed coterminously with the flourishing of the Enlightenment and have enabled particular kinds of social control, through making phenomena abstract and thus more legible at a distance. In Scott's terms, using quantitative methods and 'thin simplifications', maps and schemata, have facilitated bureaucracies and governments to 'see like a state'. That is to say, in reduced, schematic terms, events happening at a distance are visible to legislators sitting in the capital as abstractions: one of the main functions of the logframe, for example, is to abstract away from the complex detail of development programming to present a simplified schematic. Scott argues that our highly differentiated societies would not have been possible without such abstract and systematic thinking, but he also points to the way that such techniques exert disciplinary power. They produce knowledge, at the same time as constraining what counts as knowledge; the way they operate does not just represent social reality, but also organizes and shapes it. What concerned Scott was modernizing regimes moving to suppress local improvisation around their abstract plans for improvement, which they mistake for opposition, but which are necessary for their implementation. Modernizing regimes are often disinterested in political contestation. However, without the opportunity for contestation, variation, and improvisation in the local context, he argues, grand schemes for human improvement often fail or become totalitarian; they are too abstract to make sense in a particular context.

International development is no exception for the use of abstract and logical methods for regulating social life. During the past 30 years every social domain has been affected by the ascendancy of certain ways of understanding the world. Accompanying the rise of economic neoliberalism, there has developed a particular ideology that managers and particular techniques of management have a privileged role in shaping social activity and organizational life. Where neoliberalism sets a premium on the operation of 'free' markets, the profit motive, and the shrinking of the welfare state by privatizing and contracting out, managers are considered to be a uniquely qualified cadre of professionals to promote the changes that neoliberalism espouses. This often involves introducing 'business-like' practices of discipline and control into not-for-profit organizations. Economic principles of getting more for less and setting a premium on efficiency, effectiveness, and economy, the three Es, have come to dominate. There has been a proliferation of abstract tools and techniques of management, based on assumptions of predictability and

d a burgeoning of management courses in business schools teaching
_ods. This doctrine privileging the role of managers has come to be
described as 'managerialism' (Clarke and Newman, 1997; Pollitt, 1990, 1997),
which Gulrajani (2011) describes as operating in the aid domain:

> Managerialism is an ideology that assumes corporate doctrines operate
> as a proven science that can objectively and causally steer changes
> in the foreign aid apparatus in an orderly manner ... The growth of
> performance measurement and management systems (PMMS) and of
> monitoring and evaluation professionals in aid agencies illustrates the
> widespread belief that abstract practices in aid are vehicles for enhanced
> results. 'Results-based management' is increasingly prevalent in the aid
> sector; some examples include targets like the Millennium Development
> Goals or Paris Declaration on Aid Effectiveness indicators, global
> rankings assessing everything from transparency, competitiveness and
> human development and intelligence-gathering activities to assess aid
> agency employee performance, project disbursements and value for
> money. (Gulrajani, 2011: 206–7)

One of the effects of the widespread take-up of managerialism in the aid
sector, then, is the development of many more apparatuses of scrutiny and
control, and a burgeoning in the numbers of people employed to measure
and ensure compliance. If more work is contracted out by donors and INGOs
and awarded on the basis of competitive tendering, as more and more INGOs
take a greater percentage of their income from government and large donors,
there is a much greater reliance on documentation, and the demonstration
of technical ability of a particular kind, and of reporting that conforms to
the requirements of bureaucracies which are trying to 'see like a state'. One
consequence of making development a more technical and document-based
undertaking is that this also describes a shift in power, which is now tilted
more towards donor agencies and managerial requirements. The ubiquitous
disciplinary techniques are also practised as self-discipline: it is interesting to
note how many INGOs develop targets and methods of scrutiny to discipline
themselves.

Trust in numbers

I want to say a bit more about the concept of accountability, often the most
cited reason for the adoption of logic models and quantitative evaluation
techniques. It turns on the supposed transparency of numbers, and ultimately
is concerned with ideas of trust. As Theodore Porter (1995) has argued, greater
reliance on quantitative methods, 'trust in numbers', arises in situations
where there is less trust in people, there is greater emphasis on imperson-
ality, discipline, and rules, and communities of experts have relatively weak
protection from outside criticism. Over the past period, leaders and managers
of INGOs have been called upon to demonstrate incontrovertibly that money

is well spent. This has led to demands for abstract forms of knowledge, which are supposed to be universally legible and are beyond the warranting of development 'experts'. Increasingly, development professionals are asked to demonstrate that their interventions 'work' objectively, that they 'are achieving value for every pound of taxpayers' money'.

However, the link between quantification and trust is not straightforward. For example, the moral philosopher Onora O'Neill (2002) has questioned whether producing league tables, performance metrics, and reams of 'transparent' data really does enhance public trust in government or organizations. Some high-profile examples in the public sector in the UK, where institutions seem to have hit their targets but missed the point, are good evidence of what she is talking about. For O'Neill there is no linear link between information, openness, and trust. She argues that trust develops as a process of active enquiry with those one is invited to trust, and is cultivated on the basis of good judgment, to which we will return later in the chapter. Nonetheless, the exploding audit and evaluation culture is the twin of the targets, milestones, and instrumental approaches to engineering social development which has come to dominate.

On the limitations of linear and logical approaches to social order: the complexity sciences

I mentioned earlier that logframes and theories of change are abstractions based on propositional logic, the logical disaggregation of a unified whole into nesting parts, and/or target setting or milestones. These ideas are borrowed from the engineering and medical sciences, and both these conceptualizations have powerful and intuitive appeal. It is very hard to conceive of doing things differently.

However, as an alternative in a variety of scientific disciplines and over the past 50 years, there has been a growing interest in the sciences of complexity. Scientists from different disciplines have demonstrated that Newton's ideas of efficient causality are only partially helpful for explaining how change occurs in both the natural and social worlds. I will investigate one branch of the complexity sciences which attempts to model complex behaviour on computers using agent-based simulations termed complex adaptive systems. I accept in advance the limitations of doing so: I do not believe that social life is programmable any more than it can be engineered, despite the best efforts of legislators and international development managers to make it so. Nonlinear agent-based models are an alternative heuristic to the notion of unified wholes, disaggregated parts, and logical causality and help to explain why, in Arendt's terms, the future is incalculable and not simply a logical progression from the present.

A complex adaptive system is a computer model comprising a large number of interacting entities called agents. These agents operate according to a set of algorithms, or rules, guiding their interactions with other agents. As the agents interact, the complex adaptive system begins to develop in ways which could not have been predicted in advance of running the programme, even though the local rules of engagement have been determined by the programmer. The system, which has no overall blueprint or plan, operates in a paradoxical dynamic of stability and instability at the same time. The novelty in the emerging global patterns arises only if the agents differ from each other: diversity is a prerequisite for novel forms to emerge as the interacting agents both constrain and enable each other in their interactions. The model produces a dynamic pattern that arises precisely as a result of what all the agents are doing and not doing in their interactions with each other, but is not logically reducible to it. It shows a qualitative development of patterning over time.

Why are these agent-based models important, and what challenges do they pose to the dominant orthodoxy that we can predict success for development interventions?

Firstly, over time the computer models take on a life of their own and evolve in ways that could not be predicted by the programmer: they are predictably unpredictable. Secondly, although the agents operate according to particular rules of interaction there is no blueprint or plan that guides the model's development: no one agent, or group of agents, is in control of how things evolve, which is not to deny that some agents have more influence over what happens than others. Thirdly, what agents can do is both constrained and enabled by what all the other agents are doing: individual agents and groups of agents shape the global while at the same time being shaped by what every other agent is doing. Fourthly, the model is never evolving towards equilibrium: in the language of the nonlinear sciences, it is far from equilibrium. The agents are constantly adapting to and learning from each other's behaviour and are never evolving towards an optimum state. This characteristic of complex adaptive systems makes the concepts of 'efficiency' and 'effectiveness' much more problematic. Indeed, it is possible to make a counter argument that to impose notions of effectiveness and efficiency could inhibit evolution: the model evolves with a certain degree of redundancy as the agents experiment, adapt, and learn and try out different 'strategies' with each other. Innovation often occurs through maverick or 'subversive' behaviour which turns out to be a successful adaptive behaviour, although there is no telling in advance whether it will be successful.

Taken seriously as an alternative scientific account of social stability and change, these models pose a direct challenge to the idea that development occurs because of INGO managers acting rationally using predictive grids and frameworks and proving or disproving their logical hypotheses. Instead they conjure a world which is both stable and unstable at the same time, is both constrained and enabled by relationships of power, and evolves towards an uncertain future.

There is no space to explore these ideas further, but during the twentieth century a number of theoretical sociologists (Bourdieu, 1977, 1990; Elias, 1991, 1939/2000; Giddens, 1993) have been working with similar analogies about the predictably unpredictable nature of social life and the paradoxical relationship between individuals and the society they form, and which in turn forms them. I explored some of the implications for development management in a previous article (Mowles et al., 2008).

How complexity is treated in current evaluation methods

I have been arguing that the contemporary development management depends to a large degree on notions of predictability and control, and assumes linear cause and effect. There is an accompanying moral and ideological discourse which can cover over questions of power and politics with appeals to values. Not left, not right, but what works, to paraphrase a famous politician.

I will now attempt a brief review of different approaches to evaluation as a way of differentiating some of their conceptual assumptions. I will explore the extent to which they do justice or not to what I see as the continuously evolving nature of social life, where notions of what is optimum, and for whom, is more problematic. I contend that the more static, abstract, and schematic the method, the more it facilitates 'seeing like a state', and the less discussable are detailed social phenomena which are in flux, such as questions of power (like gender relations, class, and race), context, and history. In drawing attention to some phenomena, i.e., difference expressed in quantitative terms, evaluative methods inevitably remain silent about others.

So at one end of a spectrum would be experimental (randomized control trials, or RCTs) or quasi-experimental methods of evaluation. Experimental evaluation design draws directly on techniques developed in medical research, and is the only method which produces what a purist would consider scientific evidence. It makes the greatest claim to being objective and value free. Development economists particularly favour this method and it usually requires large numbers in the research trial, or 'treatment' and 'non-treatment' groups, for the statistical techniques to demonstrate significance.

Experimental methods are the most likely to be viewed favourably by bureaucracies wanting to 'see like a state' since they produce answers of the proven/partially proven/unproven variety, although experimental researchers would complain that their methods are too little taken up by governments and donors. This is because RCTs can be expensive and take time. Experimental methods have little to say about how the intervention worked and why, what the variation was between different beneficiaries, or what the sponsoring organization should do next. Variation, self-organization, and the quality of patterning over time, the phenomena which I have been pointing to above in the complexity section, are averaged away as statistical noise. Experimentalists are generally disinterested in questions of causation, power, and what people are doing to make the project work. Nonetheless, quantification lends itself best to being aggregated into global indicators for those organizations wishing to claim that X per cent of their projects were 'successful'. They provide an explicit, but reduced way of speaking to the values of accountability and transparency understood in unproblematic terms.

Theory-based evaluations (Funnell and Rogers, 2011) are becoming the new orthodoxy. They may also draw on experimental methods, but are more likely to be methodologically pluralist. The process of developing a theory of change within a project sits well with many INGOs' emancipatory intent. Project stakeholders are usually co-opted using participative methods to develop a 'vision' of their ideal change state, and then are encouraged to work backwards, identifying milestones towards achieving it. Change comes about, then, because of people choosing it and designing a project which builds logically towards it. The idea is to test the durability of the logic model and in this way demonstrate orthodox thinking about development. Theory-based evaluators show little interest in power relations and present their theories as simply a choice between a wide variety of possible techniques, each with different technical merits.

A number of theory-based evaluators have become interested in the idea of complexity, but do so generally to subsume it within their logic models to make them more 'flexible' (Rogers, 2008). Either that or they argue for taking up ideas derived from the complexity sciences selectively. This is because the logic model is integral to theories of change.

Broadly speaking theories of change sit comfortably within the tradition of predictability and control in development management, and value 'trust in numbers'. These abstract, rational, and linear ways of representing development pose no challenge to the dominant discourse in development, that of engineering social change with or on behalf of others.

Towards the other end of the spectrum, so-called 'realist' evaluators (Callaghan, 2008; Pawson and Tilley, 1997; Pawson, 2006) are much more interested in how stakeholders in a project cooperate and compete to make it work. For example, Callaghan points to the importance of the reflexivity of agents who are both the subjects and objects of social development interventions. Particular actors negotiate the order which emerges in nonlinear fashion in specific contexts at a specific time. Evaluation, she argues, is best directed towards rich explanations of how a particular order has come to be in which power will figure as a determining factor. Pawson (2006) is particularly critical of experimental methods, pointing to the irony of squeezing out questions of human volition and intentionality, when this is at the heart of social development interventions.

Pawson and Callaghan are the scholars who, in my view, come closer to taking insights from the complexity sciences seriously from a starting position that social development interventions are always complex. Pawson argues that social interventions are always both successful and unsuccessful, depending on whom you ask, and findings are developed iteratively, if one takes an interest in what works for whom and in what circumstances. In this sense realist approaches are less amenable to simple dualisms such as successful/unsuccessful, and for global aggregation, and are hard to generalize and so, one might argue, much less likely to be taken up by bureaucracies. Their conclusions are much more provisional and fallible and as a consequence they are more sceptical of replicability, the tendency to think that programmes can be unproblematically 'scaled up'.

Realistic evaluation brings its own problems: interactions between human beings are still understood as 'mechanisms' that can be identified and potentially replicated; by no means all realistic evaluators address power relations, in the form of gender, class, or any other form of social relations; the role of the evaluator is relatively unproblematized. To gain further insight into these crucial aspects of social development it would be necessary to use methods which develop rich case studies and narratives about how the work is working and how global intentions are taken up in particular ways in specific contexts (Flyvbjerg, 2005; Greenhalgh et al., 2011). Case studies dealing with power relations, context, and history are the least likely to be valued by donor bureaucracies because they do not lend themselves to simplifications: they are specific, rather than abstract, are particular, rather than general, and require much more engagement from bureaucrats to render them useful for their purposes.

Concluding thoughts

This chapter pointed out that evaluating what we do and the commitments we make to each other are both an ordinary and a necessary part of everyday life. But by drawing on Hannah Arendt I pointed to the paradoxical nature of trying to dispose of the future as though it were the present: it is an important part of being human to begin things anew, but the moment we think we can map out the future in every direction our plans can become self-defeating and potentially totalitarian. This is a point on which both Arendt and James C. Scott agree. Trying to reduce complex social phenomena to simple abstractions enables us to 'see like a state' but at the same time suppresses the very conditions that will enable us to realize our objectives. Abstractions do not represent reality, but they do shape it, allowing and disallowing certain ways of seeing and knowing.

During the past two decades a particular understanding of how development professionals should plan and evaluate their development interventions has taken ideological hold coterminous with the ascendancy of neoliberalism and managerialism. Today, development professionals are invited to commit to moral idealizations of 'transparency', 'accountability, and 'value for money', which are paired with a commitment to the three Es of economic rationality: effectiveness, efficiency, and economy. Engineering or medical metaphors and methods dominate both the planning and evaluation of development. INGOs are encouraged to develop a 'theory of change' to be successful, and in effect every theory of change logic model assumes the same kind of linear cause and effect, assuming social development can be engineered. As with other parts of the not-for-profit sector, the production of quantitative indicators is assumed to cause greater public trust in INGO performance by proving incontrovertibly that particular development projects are successful. In this chapter I tried to show this is an illusory quest for certainty while exercising disciplinary power on those engaged in development.

Another analogy for social development, drawn from the non-linear sciences, gives a different account of how stability and change come about, through the interweaving of everyone's intentions as they compete and cooperate to get things done together. Social order is predictably unpredictable. Citizens in the developing world are not distant abstractions, or objects of our 'treatment', but are self-organizing, meaning-making animals, and our moral equals. They interact with each other and with us, enabling and constraining in relationships of power, as the future emerges in highly unpredictable ways and in response to our plans and actions as we differently construe them. Some social stabilities, such as continued inequalities between men and women, have a long contextual history which may be impervious to our 'theory of change'. Our successes are likely to be contested, provisional, and fallible. Our interactions with others are always dynamic and often unstable: they are 'far from equilibrium' in the parlance of the complexity sciences. In processes which are never in a state of equilibrium there is no way of knowing for certain what is optimal, so questions of effectiveness and efficiency are always contingent and subject to revision. The future is not contained in the present, and social development is not a 'problem' to be solved. There is always a variety of possible choices and each choice will lead to its own consequences, its own strengths and weaknesses, and its own successes and failures, depending on whom you ask. Very little of this thinking is currently represented in dominant theories of development planning and evaluation.

Evaluation, finding things of value, is not a simple choice between finding 'what works' and what does not in unproblematic terms. It requires, as O'Neill suggests, an active, enquiring trust, based on good judgment, discussion, and argumentation, and not just quantification or logic alone.

References

Arendt, H. (1958) *The Human Condition*, University of Chicago Press, Chicago (1998).

Aspen Institute (1997) *Voices from the Field: Learning from the Early Work of Comprehensive Community Initiatives*, Aspen Institute, Washington, DC.

Bourdieu, P. (1977) *Outline of a Theory of Practice*, Cambridge University Press, Cambridge.

Bourdieu, P. (1990) *The Logic of Practice*, Polity Press, Cambridge.

Callaghan, G. (2008) 'Evaluation and negotiated order developing the application of complexity theory', *Evaluation* 14: 399–411.

Clarke, J. and Newman, J. (1997) *The Managerial State*, Sage, London.

Department for International Development (DfID), Business Plan 2011–2015, <www.dfid.gov.uk> [accessed 9 January 2012].

DfID Strategy Summary Document: *Changing Lives, Delivering Results* <www.dfid.gov.uk> [accessed 9 January 2012].

Elias, N. (1991) *The Society of Individuals,* Blackwell, Oxford.

Elias, N (1939/2000) *The Civilising Process,* Blackwell, Oxford.

Flyvbjerg, B. (2001) *Making Social Science Matter: Why Social Enquiry Fails and How It Can Succeed Again,* Cambridge University Press, Cambridge.

Funnel, S. and Rogers, P. (2011) *Purposeful Program Theory: Effective Use of Theories of Change and Logic Models,* Jossey Bass, San Francisco.

Giddens, A. (1993) *New Rules of Sociological Method,* Stanford University Press, Stanford.

Greenhalgh, T., Russell, J., Ashcroft, R. and Parsons, W. (2011) 'Why national ehealth programs need dead philosophers: Wittgensteinian reflections on policymakers' reluctance to learn from history', *The Millbank Review* 89.

Gulrajani, N. (2011) 'Transcending the great foreign aid debate: managerialism, radicalism and the search for aid effectiveness', *Third World Quarterly* 32: 199–216.

Independent Commission for Aid Impact (ICAI) (2011) ICAI's Approach to Effectiveness and Value for Money, report 1. <http://icai.independent.gov.uk/wp-content/uploads/2010/11/ICAIs-Approach-to-Effectiveness-and-VFM.pdf>

Mosse D. (2006) 'Anti-social anthropology? Objectivity, objection, and the ethnography of public policy and professional communities', *Journal of the Royal Anthropological Institute* 12: 935–56.

Mowles, C., Stacey R. and Griffin, D. (2008) 'What contribution can insights from the complexity sciences make to the theory and practice of development management?', *Journal of International Development* 20: 804–20.

Mowles, C. (2010) 'Successful or not: evidence, emergence and development management', *Development in Practice* 20: 757–770.

O'Neill, O. (2002) *A Question of Trust, The BBC Reith Lectures 2002,* Cambridge University Press, Cambridge.

Pawson, R. (2006) *Evidence-Based Policy: A Realist Perspective,* Sage, London.

Pawson, R. and Tilley, N. (1997) *Realistic Evaluation,* Sage, London.

Pollitt, C. (1990) *Managerialism and the Public Service: The Anglo American Experience,* Basil Blackwell, Cambridge, MA.

Pollitt, C. (1997) 'Managerialism revisited', in B. G. Peters and D. Savoie (eds), *Taking Stock: Assessing Public Sector Reforms,* McGill-Queens University Press, Montreal.

Porter. T.M. (1995) *Trust in Numbers: The Pursuit of Objectivity in Science and Public Life,* Princeton University Press, Princeton, NJ.

Power, M. (1997) *The Audit Society: Rituals of Verification,* Oxford University Press, Oxford.

Power, M. (2007) *Organized Uncertainty: Designing a World of Risk Management,* Oxford University Press, Oxford.

Rogers, P. (2008) 'Using programme theory to evaluate complicated and complex aspects of interventions', *Evaluation* 14: 29–48.

Scott, J. C. (1998) *Seeing Like a State: How Certain Schemes to Improve the Human Condition Have Failed,* Yale University Press, New Haven, CT.

Wallace, T., Bornstein, L. and Chapman, J. (2006) *The Aid Chain: Commitment and Coercion in Development NGOs,* IT Publishing, London.

Wallace, T., Crowther, S. and Shepherd, A. (1997) *Standardising Development: Influences on UK NGOs' Policies and Procedures*, World View Publishing, Oxford.

About the author

Chris Mowles has been involved in international development for more than 30 years as a volunteer, as an employee, as a consultant, as a trustee, and latterly as an academic. He worked with VSO in Egypt, became a field officer in southern Lebanon, and subsequently became a desk officer for the Middle East, both for Oxfam GB. Latterly he became a community development worker in the UK, a senior manager in a Social Services Department, and then a consultant for the public and not-for-profit sectors. As a consultant he has worked for very many INGOs, large and small. He is currently Professor of Complexity and Management at the Business School, Hertfordshire University, where he is director of an innovative professional doctorate programme.

CHAPTER 4
Losing sight of our purpose?

Suzanne Walker

This chapter is concerned with how the funding imperative is taking over as the primary driving force behind decision-making in international non-governmental organizations (INGOs) and the detrimental consequences this trend is having on good practice and effectiveness. Based on the experiences and observations of the author, it explores various internal and external perverse incentives inherent to a fundraising-driven environment that constrain the ability of INGOs to put their values into practice, with particular reference to the challenges this approach creates for the promotion of gender equality and women's empowerment. It concludes with a short discussion of the internal culture shift required in order to bring the focus back to quality, and challenges INGOs to ensure that organizational missions and values remain at the core of what they do.

A quick scan of the websites of non-governmental development organizations will reveal the mission statements, core values, and principles of the organizations in question. More often than not, a strong commitment to human rights and the principles of equality, inclusion, and justice will be found. Beliefs in values and aspirations such as these are the reasons so many of us became involved in social justice and development, and why people give generously of their time and money to support our work. Values and principles constitute the foundation and legitimacy of development international non-governmental organizations (INGOs) and should remain firmly at the core of everything we do.

This may seem as though I am stating the obvious, but what I have observed in my time working in international development is that many INGOs are losing sight of their values and purpose. It seems that the pursuit of ever greater amounts of funding has taken over as the central focus and driving force behind decision-making. While fundraising is an inevitable necessity and it is increasingly challenging in the current financial climate, my concern is that many INGOs are allowing an overzealous pursuit of income to undermine good practice and the core principles of development work, with detrimental implications for effectiveness.

Alarmingly, the funding imperative seems to be dictating decisions relating to every facet of the work of INGOs, from programming to campaigning, communications, recruitment, even how to measure success. I will focus here

http://dx.doi.org/10.3362/9781780447780/004

on overseas programming, in particular the ways in which I have witnessed the primacy afforded to securing large grants from multilateral institutions negatively influencing the ability of INGOS to work strategically and in line with good practice. Of course INGOs vary significantly in terms of their approaches and the extent to which they put their values into practice, but I believe the challenges and constraints discussed here are faced by all of those actively pursuing large institutional grants. While the consequences for the achievement of human rights and development goals are far reaching, I will make specific reference to the implications for the promotion of women's rights and gender equality.

From the outset I wish to highlight that my analysis is based primarily on personal observations and experience as opposed to formal research, and while my analysis is critical, its intention is not to fuel cynicism or apathy but to spark reflection and debate that may lead to improved ways of working to bring about meaningful change.

The wrong starting point

Many INGOs are increasingly seeking out big grants, such as those available from multilateral institutions and philanthropic donors, to fund their programmes. The relatively large sums of money available render these opportunities hugely attractive to INGOs and whole teams may be employed with the primary purpose of securing and managing them.

While these grants represent exciting opportunities to achieve a significant impact, a grants-driven environment greatly constrains the ability of INGOs to work strategically or responsively. The starting point of decision-making processes tends to be 'what funding opportunities are available to us?', as opposed to 'what is the most critical or strategic issue we should tackle?' The availability and accessibility of funding become the primary determinants of what an organization chooses to work on.

The thematic area and priority issues to be addressed through many of these grants are set by the donors in advance of inviting applications and one of the criteria that applications are likely to be scored against is their fit with these priorities, which can be quite specific and inflexible. If the application does not align with these priorities it is highly unlikely to be funded, greatly squeezing the space for applicants to enable local partners and people to determine their priorities or set the agenda.

Not only must INGOs align to the thematic priorities of donors to access grants, the approach they are required to adopt has consequences for the issues they choose to work on and how they work. Responding to pressure for enhanced accountability through the demonstration of short-term results, 'value for money', and efficiency, institutional donors and INGOs are increasingly adopting a results-based management (RBM) approach. While greater accountability is to be welcomed and INGOs should be clear on what it is that they are aiming to achieve, a reliance on short-term funding contracts and a requirement to evidence results within two to four years can restrict organizations to working on programmes for which results are demonstrable and easily measured in the short term.

Yet the social issues that INGOs are grappling with are highly complex. They require a commitment to long-term thinking and approaches in order to achieve meaningful change, and it is not always possible to demonstrate results within relatively short time periods. As big grants assume greater priority, INGOs may find themselves limited to working only on the issues for which they can access grants and achieve easily measured 'quick wins', not on the critical issues as determined by those at the other end of the aid chain.

This is bad news for any organization attempting to promote gender equality and women's rights. Tackling gender inequality requires a long-term approach that attempts to change deeply entrenched attitudes, social norms, personal beliefs and behaviours. It is often sensitive, controversial, political, and difficult work, and the changes sought can be difficult to measure. Many organizations working for gender equality have expressed concern about the results agenda and the problematic need it creates to focus on narrow indicators that are easily measured (Collinson et al., 2008). INGOs themselves are keen to point out that supporting gender equality is essential for achieving their missions, yet the transformative approach required seems to be exactly that which grants-driven INGOs are in danger of moving away from.

Civil society organizations (CSOs), including INGOs and their partners, play an important role in ensuring that women's rights and gender equality are kept on the agenda. Given the concerns that overall funding for CSOs engaged in gender equality initiatives is declining and that the contemporary aid agenda does not explicitly support gender equality work, it is more important than ever that INGOs retain their independence and critical voice to ensure that gender equality remains a priority and that funding is made available for this work.

Quality programme design – a luxury INGOs cannot afford?

Not only does a central focus on securing grants constrain the ability of INGOs to determine what issues they work on, it also attracts attention and resources away from good practice and quality programming. I have found this particularly in relation to the quality and depth of planning and design processes for grant applications submitted to multilateral institutions.

Staff with the responsibility for leading on grant applications in INGOs face a range of perverse incentives internally and externally that inhibit the implementation of good practice. They can be under immense internal pressure to obtain income for their organization. Fundraising requirements are likely to form a core element of their job descriptions and they may be appraised against income-related targets. I have even come across an INGO where pay is linked to the achievement of organizational fundraising goals. Staff are keenly aware that salaries may depend on securing a certain level of income, possibly even their own.

In organizations that are increasingly concerned with income, staff are valued and rewarded primarily for the level of funding they secure as opposed to their contribution to good practice or effective programming. While ensuring quality programming is also likely to form a core element of job descriptions, staff are much less likely to be assessed formally or informally on this basis. Even if staff are highly committed to effectiveness, this kind of environment incentivizes staff to prioritize income over good practice.

Application processes for large grants can be greatly competitive and chances of success may be slim, even if an application receives a high score. I recently looked into one such funding opportunity for gender equality initiatives, only to discover that the success rate of the previous funding round was less than 1 per cent of total applications. This is an extreme example, but many organizations would have invested resources into developing applications. It is frightening to consider the huge amount of time and resources invested by INGOs, only to compete against each other for the same funds.

When it is very possible that an application will not succeed, it becomes extremely difficult for staff to justify investing resources in the design process that goes into the development of applications, such as an extensive, participatory analysis of the local context that ensures that local power and social dynamics are properly understood and taken into consideration. This is particularly the case if such investments are deemed unnecessary to secure the grant. Further compounding this issue is that, even if successful, donors rarely provide funding for the design or pre-application phase of a programme, and sourcing the resources required to develop applications is very challenging for INGOs.

The problem is that grant applications or proposals constitute much more than application forms; they contain detailed information on the rationale, strategy and design of the programme to be implemented and, once submitted, it is too late to go back and make significant changes to the programme design. The proposal document outlines the programme objectives and expected results which form part of the contract with the donor and the INGO must then implement what it has been funded to do.

A good quality programme design process is costly, but it is also crucial to ensure the effectiveness of the planned intervention. Yet INGOs seem to have convinced themselves that investing in a high-quality process is a luxury that they simply cannot afford, particularly when unnecessary to secure income. Unfortunately what *is* actually necessary to secure a grant often falls far short of what could be considered good development practice.

Ticking the boxes

Despite efforts by donors to promote and reward good practice through their assessment criteria and scoring methods, programme design and planning for grants is too often reduced to a superficial exercise in understanding the particular requirements of the donor and ticking all the right boxes. In the worst cases, programme design has become a largely desk-based process of filling in an application form or results framework, as opposed to a comprehensive and participatory process based on rigorous analysis and good practice principles. The central focus is placed firmly on understanding the donor as opposed to understanding the context or the issues to be tackled.

As corners are cut and attention is on donor requirements, key elements of good practice are implemented only to the levels that are necessary to secure funding. As we have seen from other contributions to this publication, an extensive and critical analysis of local contexts and of people's realities is crucial if we are to be effective in achieving meaningful change. Yet grant applications do not necessitate the in-depth analysis of social relationships and power dynamics necessary to understand the issues INGOs are attempting to address, particularly at the community level. Generally only a minimal and relatively shallow level is required.

The competitive nature of application processes and the huge pressure on staff to maximize application scores act as perverse incentives against presenting a full and critical analysis that would lead to a thorough understanding of the context. Programmes must be presented in the most positive light possible and there is great temptation to exaggerate what can be realistically achieved in the short time span of the funding cycle. I was involved in an application recently where it was required to describe how a two-year programme for promoting the participation of marginalized groups in local governance processes in a highly undemocratic society was going to be sustainable beyond the life of the programme. The conundrum in this situation is that it is unlikely that such a short intervention tackling deeply rooted and politically sensitive issues would be sustainable, unless efforts were continued beyond the initial funding cycle. Yet to imply that the intervention was in any way unsustainable would jeopardize the possibility of acquiring funding for a good initiative that a lot of resources had already been invested in. Similar difficulties are encountered when reporting to donors, as staff are under pressure to present the organization in the most positive way possible to maximize future funding opportunities.

Constraints on presenting an open and honest analysis prevent donors, INGOs, and their partners from deepening their understanding of complex issues and social change processes. This is further compounded by narrow requirements for presenting and reporting on results which overlook how and why the results were or were not achieved. It also creates unrealistic expectations from donors, placing great pressure on INGOs.

A core element of good practice, strongly espoused by the dominant development discourse articulated by institutional and non-governmental actors, is participation. There has been a lot of debate about what participation means in practice and in different contexts, which is beyond the scope of this chapter, but I would argue here that a crucial way in which participation should be practised is ensuring that the views and experiences of local people, including women and socially marginalized groups who are often unrepresented, inform programme design. Ideally this would involve providing space and time for various groups to critically reflect on and discuss their situations, a genuine attempt to listen to and understand their perspectives, and then to ensure those experiences inform decisions and shape programmes. Not only should this process contribute to ensuring that programmes are relevant, effective, and locally owned, but also that local people are viewed as active agents of change as opposed to passive recipients of aid.

This is in line with research commissioned by BOND (2006) into quality in NGOs, which strongly concluded that 'NGOs deliver quality when their work is based on a sensitive and dynamic understanding of beneficiaries' realities; responds to local priorities in a way that beneficiaries feel is appropriate; and is judged to be useful by beneficiaries' (BOND, 2006: v). This vision of quality seems far from current practice. Participation in programme design is frequently reduced to tokenistic measures, such as inviting a few partners or representatives of various target groups along to planning workshops, often quite far along in the planning process and too late to significantly influence the content of the programme. Such one-off consultations and planning workshops are rarely adequate to achieve a sufficient understanding of the perspective of different interests and social groups. The motivation seems to be to tick the participation box and ensure that these groups are on board with the programme, particularly as they are likely to be relied on to implement it. Staff who do attempt to facilitate more meaningful processes are further constrained by the top-down parameters of the funding opportunity to which they are bound.

Criticism in relation to how INGOs put participation into practice is not new, nor is the funding imperative entirely to blame, but clearly the extent and quality of participation in programme planning is constrained by the kind of grants-driven environment I have described. Ensuring meaningful participation of marginalized groups is a time and resource-intensive exercise (Bell, 2001), but sufficient time and resources are rarely allocated.

It is as though INGOs have become so consumed with fulfilling donor requirements and securing funding that we have forgotten the crucial importance of the process, the 'how' of what we do. We have forgotten that it is possible to have a positive impact by implementing planning and design processes that are participatory and empowering, even if the funding application is ultimately unsuccessful. Investing in these processes is not a waste of resources, but a valuable means to promote empowerment and effectiveness.

The implications for gender equality and women's empowerment are clearly evident. In the absence of a thorough and critical analysis of complex local realities, it is not possible to gain a comprehensive understanding of the situation of women and girls in specific contexts or to ensure that the root causes of inequality are being addressed. If we do not meaningfully consult with women and girls, how can we be sure that we are working on the issues most important to them? If they were provided with space to come together and discuss their situations and meaningfully contribute to programme design, not only would the design be more relevant, locally owned, and effective, but the very process of enabling women and girls to use their voice and to have influence could in itself be greatly empowering. Similarly, if spaces for discussing issues of gender equality were created for men and boys, simply the opportunity to encourage critical reflection and dialogue on these issues could encourage deeper understanding that might form a first step towards change.

Gender mainstreaming is another widely accepted element of good practice that has received a high level of attention and commitment as a development strategy across the sector. On the surface, gender mainstreaming appears to be very much at the forefront of priorities for INGOs and donors. However, as noted by Moser and Moser (2005), while most international institutions have adopted the terminology of gender equality and have put gender mainstreaming policies in place, commitments tend to evaporate during planning and implementation processes. Development actors have been widely criticized for poor implementation of gender mainstreaming despite high-level commitments, policies, and action plans.

While the debate on the effectiveness of gender mainstreaming is ongoing, there is clearly growing frustration with the phenomenon of policy evaporation and the gap between professed intention and actual practice (Cornwall et al., 2007). In my experience the criticisms seem justified. I have read countless proposals and reports from a wide range of development organizations in which gender mainstreaming has been reduced to ensuring that a sizeable percentage of target groups and participants at various workshops and training sessions are female. I have yet to come across a project or programme where I thought addressing gender inequalities had been well integrated.

The funding imperative is not the primary reason why gender equality has not been adequately mainstreamed. However, as with other elements of good practice that INGOs are under pressure from donors to take into consideration, it has been largely reduced to a technical checklist, where the boxes are easily ticked but unequal power relations remain unchallenged (Standing, 2006). Unfortunately such half-hearted and ad hoc measures to incorporate gender are frequently sufficient to satisfy INGOs and donors. Instead of setting their own minimum standards of good practice and ensuring a certain level of quality in their programming, INGOs are too often implementing just the minimum requirements to secure funding. This is unlikely to change as long as the primary motivation behind gender mainstreaming is to access funding, and donor requirements remain superficial.

Reducing the complex to the easily measured

In the design of grant-funded programmes, a large proportion of time and resources is invested in the development of logic models such as logframes and results frameworks. While the process may have some merit in supporting staff to think through what it is they are trying to achieve, it can also restrict thinking to what is reflected in the framework, which, as discussed above, tends to be only what can be easily measured and concisely communicated. The frameworks do not ensure that programmes are appropriate to their contexts, that they are responsive to local priorities, or that the most critical issues are being addressed in an effective way. They also ignore the quality of relationships; yet the central conclusion of BOND's research into quality in NGOs is that 'The quality of an NGO's work is primarily determined by the quality of its relationships with its intended beneficiaries' (BOND, 2006: vi). There is increasing recognition of the need to develop and monitor relationships in development practice (Jacobs, 2011). When you consider the complexity and the unpredictable nature of people's behaviour and social change, the level of specificity and precision required in predicting outcomes in advance of implementation that exists in results frameworks seems highly unrealistic.

It is difficult to ensure that the development of logic models is bottom-up and participatory. Generally the frameworks are filled in by head office staff, who understand the confusing jargon and what the donor wants, which poses an ethical dilemma for those who do not believe development work should be practised like this. Furthermore, the enormous amount of time and energy spent on developing results frameworks takes resources and attention away from ensuring effectiveness. Very frustratingly for staff involved, seemingly endless hours spent on fine-tuning the wording of outputs, outcomes, objectives, and indicators places huge demands on already overstretched workloads and leaves little time for processes that are more likely to ensure quality, such as analysing the social and political context, consulting with partners, facilitating participatory processes, or researching best practice and learning. Staff can be so caught up in meeting donor requirements that there is little time to stop and think, and if you do stop to think it can be hard to make the link between the long hours you are working and the effectiveness of the programme.

There is a growing body of literature and research that highlights the limitations of reductionist approaches to development such as RBM and the associated managerial tools including logical and results frameworks (for example, Wallace, 2006; Collinson et al., 2008; Mowles et al., 2008; UN, 2008; Ramalingam, 2011). The review of RBM at the UN (2008) found that the introduction of RBM to the UN is not only an addition to the existing myriad rules and procedures involved in development management but also stifles the innovation and flexibility required to achieve intended outcomes, overlooks the influence of external actors and risk-factors on outcomes, and makes virtually no contribution to strategic decision-making. In fact it concluded quite damningly that 'Results-based management at the United Nations has been an administrative chore of little value to accountability and decision-making' (ibid.: 1).

Despite extensive criticism and documentation of various shortcomings, however, the results agenda remains firmly in place. Ironically RBM itself does not appear to need to demonstrate results in terms of its effectiveness as a development tool in order to be promoted (Ramalingam, 2011). Clearly donors have a role to play in listening to and responding to these criticisms and creating a more favourable environment for effective programming.

However, the purpose of this chapter is not to discuss the limitations of RBM per se, but to highlight how prioritizing the acquisition of funding is undermining good practice. INGOs focused on securing funds are constrained by donor requirements. They seem increasingly unable to critically analyse the way they work or to have the courage to communicate their concerns to donors. INGOs must start redirecting some of their resources and energy into piloting and proposing alternative models.

The role of the private sector

This chapter does not attempt to provide an explanation as to why INGOs are allowing a preoccupation with generating income to undermine values and effectiveness, but the increasing influence of the private sector in development work does seem to be playing a significant role. Private-sector expertise has been brought into INGOs with the principal aim of securing greater levels of income. Individuals, often with little development experience and who may not necessarily buy into the ethos of the organization, have been placed in leadership positions with extensive decision-making power and influence. These individuals are assessed and rewarded according to the income they secure, and this concern dictates their decisions. Corporate organizations are also increasingly being contracted by donors and INGOs to conduct processes such as strategic planning, organizational appraisals, and evaluations, despite having little knowledge of development issues or social change.

While expertise from the corporate sector is sourced with the best of intentions, and this influence may be successfully generating greater funding, the corporate influence is undoubtedly changing the culture and ethos of INGOs. This change is reflected by the use of monetary targets to assess organizational and individual progress, top-down directives and approaches, and even the day-to-day language we use ('corporate plans', 'business cases', 'value for money', 'growth', 'competitors', etc.). The complexity and political nature of the issues that INGOs are grappling with are being undermined by a simplistic assumption that raising more money is the solution. Fundraising is fast becoming an end in itself as opposed to a means to an end, and some INGOs are beginning to more closely resemble businesses in pursuit of maximizing profit than non-profit organizations in pursuit of justice and equality.

The value placed on fundraising is further evident in how INGOs are increasingly looking to corporations as potential sources of funding without adequate consideration of what might be more effective engagement, such as influencing the practice of these organizations in developing countries. INGOs may argue that this kind of advocacy or lobbying is not within their remit, but if their mission is to tackle poverty and injustice, surely it is their respon-sibility to employ the most effective strategies for achieving this. Some INGOs are accepting funding from ethically dubious businesses, for example corporations involved in highly controversial extractives industries which operate in developing countries. Accepting funding from these corporations helps restore the tarnished public reputation of these organizations and attracts attention away from the myriad criticisms levied against them in relation to their human rights and environmental records, not to mention the low proportion of revenue that makes its way back into the local economy through taxes. Partnering with these corporations seriously compromises the values and ethical basis from which INGOs draw their credibility and legitimacy.

Culture shift

For me, the crux of the problem is the willingness of INGOs to allow quality and effectiveness to be compromised for the sake of acquiring funding. I have focused here on programming, but the phenomenon extends to other strategies employed by INGOs, such as campaigning and development education. These potentially highly effective initiatives sometimes seem to be more about promoting brand and visibility than opportunities to foster critical understanding and action on justice issues. The public in wealthy countries are treated simply as passive donors of charity, thereby missing the opportunity to engage them as active citizens with the consumer and political power to contribute to positive change.

There is great scope and potential to improve the way we work in INGOs to bring about meaningful and sustainable change. As the custodians of considerable resources we have the means and the responsibility to ensure that we are working as effectively as we possibly can and that we are not compromising on purpose and values, despite an inevitable and challenging dependency on funding.

I would argue strongly that it is simply not good enough to claim good intentions or to blame the difficult financial climate. I am fully aware that INGOs are dependent on funding in order to conduct their work and without income they would be paralysed. It should not, however, be the potential to raise funds that dictates our decisions. What may actually be the most critical or important issues for people experiencing poverty or injustice, or the most effective ways of working to tackle these, are not necessarily those for which large grants are available or accessible. If we are genuine in what we are trying to achieve, we must start by determining the most crucial or pressing issues and ways of working and then consider how funding can be accessed for these, even if this is a more difficult approach and potentially less financially rewarding. INGOs should also keep in mind that the most effective approaches are not necessarily the most expensive.

Neither is it good enough to blame donors. Of course donors have a respon-sibility to ensure that their resources are used effectively and to create an enabling environment for good quality programming. Furthermore, donors should recognize the inherent power imbalance in funding relationships and the genuine fears of INGOs about providing honest feedback. However, INGOs, as independent entities, must hold themselves accountable for their own actions and decisions. It is imperative that INGOs maintain their credibility and critical voice and that they put their knowledge and learning into practice. If it is the case that funding is not available for the initiatives and strategies that are known to be important and effective, then it is the responsibility of INGOs to lobby and advocate for donors to change their funding approach or to find other means to source funding, as opposed to abandoning the issues and the people experiencing them.

INGOs should be well placed to drive good practice, building on experience built up over many years, and to propose alternative and more effective ways of working to address injustice and inequality. Many organizations have the opportunity, through unrestricted sources of funding such as regular donations from the public, to pilot new ways of working and to use the evidence to influence others. More courage and backbone is needed, to be more open and honest internally and externally, to tackle difficult and complex issues, and to propose alternatives when current systems are not working effectively.

A culture shift is required. With all the focus on fundraising targets and deadlines, there is little time to stop and think, to take a step back and reflect on what we are doing, to look into alternative perspectives and ideas, or to engage in contemporary debates. Contradictions and hypocrisy abound in the sector, and debilitating cynicism is far more common than optimism or idealism. The fundamental ways in which we approach our work are rarely questioned internally, and questions are often met with frustration and viewed as obstructive. If it is the case that we are allowing a pursuit of funding to undermine effectiveness, we must ask serious questions as to why we exist and remind ourselves what our purpose actually is.

A new culture of critical reflection, analysis, and questioning should be fostered. This starts with exploring whether we are practising what we preach internally as well as externally, whether we are learning and building on what we know, and whether we are employing the most effective strategies available to us. This way of working requires strong leadership to ensure that the work of INGOs is driven by values and quality. If we can bring the central focus of our work back to our original purpose, and ensure that values are driving our decisions, I have no doubt that INGOs could be more effective in contributing towards meaningful change.

References

Bell, E. (2001) 'Coping with conflict: the case of Redd Barna Uganda', in *Development and Gender In Brief*, Issue 9: Gender and participation, BRIDGE [PDF], <www.bridge.ids.ac.uk/vfile/upload/4/document/1109/Participation_IB_English.pdf> [accessed 9 April 2012].

BOND (2006) 'A BOND approach to quality in non-governmental organizations: putting beneficiaries first', a report by Keystone and AccoutAbility for the British Overseas NGOs for Development (BOND) [PDF], <www.bond.org.uk/pages/report.html> [accessed 13 April 2012].

Collinson, H., Derbyshire, H., Fernandez Schmidt, B. and Wallace, T. (2008) 'Women's rights and gender equality, the new aid environment and civil society organisations: a research project of the UK Gender and Development Network', UK Gender and Development Network [PDF] <www.gadnetwork. org.uk/storage/gadn-publications/GAD%20Network%20Report%20-%20 New%20Aid%20Modalities.pdf> [accessed 14 April 2012].

Cornwall, A., Harrison, E. and Whitehead, A. (2007) *Feminisms in Development: Contradictions, Contestations and Challenges*, Zed Books, London.

Jacobs, A. (2011) 'Managing performance in NGOs: a 10 point agenda', *NGO Performance* [website], <www.ngoperformance.org/2011/01/11/ managing-performance-in-ngos/> [accessed 5 April 2012].

Moser, C. and Moser, A. (2005) 'Gender mainstreaming since Beijing: A review of success and limitations in international institutions', *Gender and Development*, 13: 11–22.

Mowles, C., Stacey, R. and Griffin, D. (2008) 'What contribution can insights from the complexity sciences make to the theory and practice of development management?', *Journal on International Development*, 20: 804–20 [PDF], <www.laics.net/LLD_Everest/Publications/BlackBoard/Module%202%20 x2D%202011/Seminar%202/20111122143312/CurrentVersion/7%20%20 Mowles%20et%20al%20-%20WHAT%20CONTRIBUTION%20CAN%20 INSIGHTS.pdf> [accessed 16 April 2012].

Ramalingam, B. (2011) 'Why the results agenda doesn't need results, and what to do about it', *Aid on the Edge of Chaos* [website], <http://aidontheedge. info/2011/01/31/why-the-results-agenda-doesnt-need-results-and-what-to-do-about-it> [accessed 6 April 2012].

Standing, H. (2006) 'Gender, myth and fable: the perils of mainstreaming in sector bureaucracies', in Cornwall, A., Harrison, E. and Whitehead, A. (eds.) *Feminisms in Development: Contradictions, Contestations and Challenges*, pp. 101–111, Zed Books, London.

UN (2008) 'Review of results-based management at the United Nations: report of the Office of Internal Oversight Services', Office of Internal Oversight Services.

Wallace, T., Bornstein, L. and Chapman, J. (2006) *The Aid Chain: Coercion and Commitment in Development NGOs*, Practical Action Publishing, Rugby.

About the author

Originally from Dublin, **Suzanne Walker** has experience volunteering and working for various Irish-based social justice and development organizations. This work has led her to various parts of the Horn and East of Africa, West Africa and India. She has an MSc in Development Studies from University College Dublin. She is particularly interested in programme effectiveness, accountability and gender equality.

CHAPTER 5
Can girls save the world?

Kate Grosser and Nikki van der Gaag

This chapter raises questions about how the discourse and practice of development has changed over the past half-decade in relation to girls. While we welcome the fact that girls and young women are gaining increasing visibility within the development agenda, we highlight a number of significant problems in the way that this agenda is currently being articulated by the private sector. We ask what the girl trend means for gender equality, and for girls themselves. Finally, we open a discussion about how the new focus on girls and development might be used to create opportunities for more positive practice.

Everyone is talking about girls. Almost all the major United Nations and multi-lateral development organizations, not to mention non-governmental organizations and the private sector, are setting up projects and programmes with a girl focus. So why is this? What has happened in the past few years to make girls such a popular focus of development rhetoric and funding? This chapter examines the rise of the 'Girl Effect' and its relationship with corporate social responsibility (CSR) in the private sector.

The fact that the world is turning its attention to girls should be a good thing. For many decades in development circles, 'girls' were a neglected sector of the population, often simply a category filed somewhere under 'women' or 'children'. Even organizations working specifically on children's issues often did not disaggregate data by sex, despite a focus on the 'girl child', particularly in Africa, during the 1990s.[1]

But today, the list of international development organizations involved in work on girls is a very long one, from the UN's Coalition for Adolescent Girls (in collaboration with the Nike Foundation and others), the World Bank Adolescent Girls Initiative, and the Girl Hub at the UK's Department for International Development (also a collaboration with the Nike Foundation). Many non-governmental organizations also now have girls' programmes.

The great and the good are interested too. When the World Economic Forum hosted a session on girls in 2009 it included Melinda Gates, Mohammed Yunus, Maria Eitel from the Nike Foundation, Ngozi Okonjo-Iweala, at that time Managing Director of World Bank, Ann Veneman from UNICEF, and Mari Pangestu, Indonesia's Minister of Trade. It was the fourth most popular

http://dx.doi.org/10.3362/9781780447780/005

session of the whole Forum. When asked why there had not been a focus on girls up until that point, Melinda Gates said:

> the issue wasn't brought to the forefront before, so when NGOs or foundations or civil society were developing their programs, they just weren't thinking that way. ... Part of it is just a mind shift. (Eitel, 2009)

Perhaps it is no coincidence that many of the voices at the World Economic Forum's girls' session were from private companies and foundations. So far, the Girl Effect remains largely driven by the rich world and in particular by the corporate sector. It coincides with a growing business focus on corporate social responsibility.

Going in the same direction? Girls, globalization, and corporate social responsibility

Over the past 20 years, privatization, liberalization, and globalization have led, among other things, to an increasing involvement of business in societal governance (Scholte, 2005; Scherer and Palazzo, 2007), including administering what were previously regarded as government responsibilities, such as delivering public goods, and citizenship rights (e.g., Crane et al., 2008). As a result of these changes, the issue of corporate responsibility and, in particular, corporate accountability for the social and environmental impacts of business has risen to the top of the social, political, and economic agenda (Matten et al., 2003; Bendell, 2004). The business community has responded, in turn, with a renewed focus on CSR, which has become a major trend in contemporary business over the past decade (Moon, 2004; Moon and Vogel, 2008).

There are many incentives for companies that address CSR. These include an attempt to avoid further regulation, and to maintain, or regain, legitimacy and the so-called 'license to operate'. While many of the resulting business programmes have been rhetorical in nature, some have involved significant changes, including the development of a well-grounded business case for addressing social and environmental issues more effectively.

There is a growing focus on metrics, and reporting of metrics, in CSR. For example, the global reporting initiative (GRI), which provides the most comprehensive and widely used sustainability reporting framework globally, asks companies to report not just on policies and programmes, but also on many quantitative indicators. This development is partly the result of an effort by NGOs to identify those companies seriously addressing the social and environmental externalities of their business, as opposed to those merely paying lip-service. The GRI includes a number of gender equality indicators, although none currently identify young women and girls specifically.[2]

So what does CSR have to do with girls and development? Those businesses that articulate the new girls and development agenda place it within their wider approach to CSR, where it is used to suggest that the company proactively addresses gender equality issues. The CSR agenda has increasingly incorporated at least a lip-service commitment to gender equality (Kilgour, 2007; GRI). Thus the new corporate focus on girls can be regarded in part as a legitimating device. The corporate world to date – including Nike in the past – has not had a wonderful record when it comes to its treatment of children, including girls, and young women in its supply chains (see, e.g., Oxfam, 2004).

The rationale for companies to address girls' issues may include a real interest in women and development, and Nike is certainly putting its money where its mouth is. However, as we argue below, in reality, less focus is being given to how this new agenda will benefit girls and young women themselves, and more to what it can achieve for the rest of us. Campaigns which suggest that girls can somehow 'save the world' ignore decades of research on women and development, and risk diverting us from the serious gender equality issues relating to young women in the global economy that still urgently need to be addressed more effectively by business.

The Girl Effect

This most recent major international interest in girls in development started in earnest with the launch of the Nike Foundation in 2004, but it was not until 2008 that the Foundation decided to focus exclusively on girls with the launch of the 'Girl Effect'. Its website notes: 'When the Nike Foundation started, we sought the best investment with the highest returns. We traced the symptoms of poverty back to their roots, and it led us to an unexpected solution and a catalyst for change: adolescent girls'.

The message from the Foundation about what it calls 'the Girl Effect' is very simple: invest in a girl and you can change the world. Its first short but powerful video begins almost like a poem, accompanied by dramatic music:

> The world is a mess. Poverty, AIDS, Hunger, War.
> So what else is new?
> What if there was an unexpected solution
> That could turn this sinking ship around?
> Would you even know it if you saw it?
> It's not the internet.
> It's not science.
> It's not the government.
> It's not money.
> It's ... a girl.[3]

The video goes on to explain that if we invest in a girl (a poor girl who would otherwise have a husband and a baby and go hungry), give her an education, and a loan for a cow, she will use the profits from the milk to help her family and soon she will be able to buy a herd and become a business owner who brings clean water to her village, which makes the men respect her and invite her to the village council, where she convinces everyone that all girls are valuable, and so the village thrives. The result is – food, peace, lower HIV, healthier babies, education and commerce, sanitation, and stability. Which means the economy of the entire country improves and the whole world is better off.

The animated clip is only 2.24 minutes long. It has no pictures or photos. And it is very powerful. To date it has had more than 3 million hits, a number that any development agency would die for.

From victim to saviour

So what messages are being given about girls in these campaigns? The story sounds like a fairy tale, and one wonders where it is taking place. The first message is girl as victim, with the focus on the plight of adolescent girls in particular. Global numbers quoted by different organizations vary from 250 to 600 million adolescent girls (which shows that even counting girls is not simple).

In the Girl Effect video, the viewer is told to 'imagine a girl living in poverty.' Then the word 'girl' is shown surrounded by buzzing flies, reminding us of the stereotype of a starving child in a famine somewhere in the developing world, and so reinforcing the division between 'us' in the rich world and 'them' in the poor one.

The second, more positive, message is the one that inspires people: if we 'invest' in girls, they can change the world. 'Because they are the women of the future, girls have the potential to influence their families and their communities and gain financial independence and become productive members of society' (The Adolescent Girls Initiative, 2010).

The Nike Foundation goes further:

> When a girl in the developing world realizes her potential, she isn't the only one who escapes poverty—she brings her family, community, and country with her. It's a leverage strategy that can't be beat. That's why adolescent girls are our exclusive focus. Investing in a girl stops poverty before it starts.

DfID's Girl Hub says it aims 'to inspire girls, amplify their voices and provide a platform from which they can demand change and participate in society'.

But we wonder how many people actually look beyond these first messages. Our analysis in this chapter reveals evidence that there is a real danger that the current girls' projects could potentially undermine more politically aware, and analytically accurate, approaches to work with girls, which were built upon decades of experience and expertise in the fields of gender equality and development.

Is a cow the answer? What's wrong with the new 'girls and development' agenda?

We argue that many of the new girls and development campaigns are limited and misleading in a number of important respects.[4] First, they focus on girls as individuals, ignoring the social and political environments in which they grow up, including the context of gender inequality, discrimination within households as well as the wider society, and poverty. Second, they ignore decades of wider research on women and development. Third, the campaigns can appear to reinforce gender stereotypes. Fourth, they attempt to instrumentalize girls and young women. Finally, they give confusing messages about girls' agency.

The focus on the individual girl

The language of the girls' campaigns is striking in its similarity. The same words are used by all the organizations involved: investing in girls, building their assets, supporting their agency, building their livelihoods. There is a strong emphasis on investment and economics rather than on the social and political. This fits well with the neoliberal context of contemporary Western capitalism, and the fact that the initial impetus for the focus on girls came from the private sector. The emphasis is on the girl as an individual. The impetus is laid clearly on the girl's power to change her own situation, and that of her family, community, and even her country, rather than the context in which she lives, or on social attitudes and power relationships that govern her life. To return to the Nike clip, the message explicitly denies the importance of structural factors. It says the world is in a mess not because of external or structural things like 'the internet, science, government' (Does that mean policies have no effect?) or 'money' (Does this contradict the next message about investment?) but because we are not 'investing' in the one solution – girls. This decontextualization fails to take account of the fact that girls are often disadvantaged by both age and sex and, especially if they are poor, unlikely to have the power or the ability to change very much at all.

This focus on the role of individual women or girls to overcome social and political discrimination and economic disadvantage is not new. Even a brief glance at the literature on gender equality in the workplace reveals that approaches to improving gender equality that focus on 'fixing individual women' (Martin, 2003), including education, training, creating women's networks, and mentoring, are insufficient because 'though responsible for important and often necessary change in organizations, [these strategies] are not sufficient to disrupt the pervasive and deeply entrenched imbalance of power in the social relations between men and women' (Ely and Meyerson, 2000: 590). A much more structural approach to the problem is necessary.

The girls' campaigns often emphasize the liberating force of education. Adolescent girls, goes the argument, are less likely than boys the same age to be in school and more likely to marry and have children (very) early.[5] It is essential that girls as well as boys get an education, and that this is of good quality. Poor education does little to improve the situation or employability of either girls or boys.

However, while education is vitally important, the evidence from many industrialized countries is that even when girls get access to excellent education and do better than boys (at school), this has not eliminated unequal pay or unequal burdens with respect to work in the home, or solved the problem of gender inequality. Even the most educated and skilled woman in New York or Sydney may find it hard to change her family and her community, let alone the world. In fact, some of the trends are going in the opposite direction. In 2012, there were only 21 women (out of 500) running Fortune 500 companies (Sellers, 2012). Only 19.8 per cent of Members of Parliament globally are women (InterParliamentary Union, 2011). These statistics reveal that improved education, although vital, cannot by itself enable girls to advance to positions of leadership within their communities, and gain influence and power to effect wider change.

Gender relations – stereotypes and discrimination

The message about girls and young women in the campaigns is steeped in stereotypes about their lives, and also strongly implies that girls are better than boys. The Girl Effect website notes:

> Why girls? They are uniquely capable of raising the standard of living in the developing world. It's been shown: she will reinvest her income and knowledge back into her family and her community. As an educated mother, an active citizen, an ambitious entrepreneur or prepared employee, a girl will break the cycle of intergenerational poverty.

Girls look after their families, go to work, change the world, while boys play and laze around. (There is even a spoof based on the Nike girls' video to that effect.) Evidence from many countries shows that women work much longer hours than men, including doing the majority of work in the home. It is good to have these facts recognized. However, while there are some footnotes about the critical role of boys in 'unleashing girls' ripple effect' (Girl Effect, 'Girl Effect Media Kit'), boys mostly feature in the girl story only as a negative factor.

It is refreshing to have the age and gender blindness of much development policy interrupted; however, the binary opposites presented here do not, we believe, help either girls or boys. Surely we should be working with boys as well (Barker, 2005; van der Gaag, 2011), encouraging them not to be violent, to care for their children, to challenge traditional stereotypes of what it means to be male? The impact of poverty on boys' sense of identity and value are important in the equation. While excellent programmes exist addressing these issues (e.g., Instituto Promundo[6]), they are small compared to the girl tide.

Without a focus on boys as well as girls, programmes may train girls, giving them skills and confidence, but this can in turn put them in danger of a backlash from those around them who see their new self-esteem as a threat. Building a better world involves working with the relatively powerful as well as the less powerful. This may be happening with girls' programmes on the ground, but it is not coming through from the way the campaign is described.

Overall, there is little mention of politics, or rights, or power, or feminism. Nor do we hear about stereotyping and the sexualization of young teenage women, including in the advertising campaigns of large corporations who claim to promote the advancement of girls and young women. There is no mention of pornography, or of corporate investment in the $100 billion global porn industry. More broadly, there is no discussion of the structures, attitudes, and policies that have ensured that for millennia girls and women in all countries have remained second-class citizens. For example, where are the links with all the excellent work being done all around the world on violence against women? What about initiatives from the South?

Lacking any serious contextualization or reference to gender discrimination in society, including within households, the girls and development agenda offers what seems to be a very simple solution. As Rosalind Eyben notes: 'Development is being communicated to taxpayers and supporters as simple and easy to do. Give a girl a cow and you will save a world' (Eyben, 2011). A critical assessment of the Girl Hub by the Independent Commission for Aid Impact (ICAI) notes that: '[The initiative] appears to have struggled ... to reconcile the power of a simple message with its efforts to tackle a complex social problem. This has contributed to a lack of clarity about Girl Hub's role and aims' (ICAI, 2012).

Development, like life in general, is complex. To continue the metaphor of the Girl Effect video, the girl's cow might die. Or the fact that she has been given a cow might make others jealous. Her husband might beat her. She might not be able to pay off the loan. And how does a herd of cows lead to clean water, or to respect from the whole village, especially the men?

The instrumentalist agenda ignores the realities of young women's lives

The girls and development agenda also often argues that girls are important because they are future mothers and workers, rather than for their own sake. It attempts to instrumentalize girls, arguing that they are 'an unrealized economic force, accelerating growth and progress in every sector' (Girl Effect, n.d.). Yet women already make up a large proportion of the workforce in many countries. Globally, women, including young women and girls, work long hours on domestic responsibilities, rearing and caring for the next generation, and for the elderly and sick. They do most subsistence farming globally, as well as collecting firewood and water for household purposes. This domestic work is necessary for the sustainability of families, communities, workplaces, and society generally. It is also indispensable for business (and the state), producing future workers and consumers upon which companies depend, and providing essential care for the current workforce. Yet this work is unpaid, rarely noted or valued in economic policymaking (Elson, 1991, 1994), or acknowledged in the discussion about girls and women in the business community. If the value of this work was counted in financial terms, global output would be 50 per cent higher (ILO, 2009). Without an understanding of the role girls are expected to play in the home in many countries, and the long hours of labour this involves, the girls' campaigns risk making young women's lives more difficult.[7]

Agency and voice

Our main argument in this section has been that by putting all the weight on a girl's power to change her own situation, and equipping her with some of the skills and knowledge needed to do this (leadership skills, etc.), the messages ignore the fact that most girls have little power to change their situation, and it is not because they are stupid or uneducated or lack skills. In fact, the assessment of the Girl Hub by ICAI (2012) notes that 'there is a risk that Girl Hub could end up initiating many individual projects that do not link together to bring real, substantial change for girls'.

This brings us to our final point in this section. While suggesting that girls can change the world, the campaigns invite Westerners to 'fix this picture', a message that gives more 'agency' (another popular word) to those watching campaign videos than to the girls they claim to be 'empowering'. It is not clear how much girls in developing countries have been consulted about the girls' campaigns, even when they are the beneficiaries of the funds that have been raised. Yet the history of development suggests that until girls and young women are consulted about development issues, and empowered to define the terms of their own engagement, their lives, needs, and hopes cannot be addressed effectively.

Gender equality as a resource for global capital

The girls' campaigns also need to be viewed within the wider context of women's roles in the global economy. There are some contradictions in relation to what is being said about girls and young women as part of the new agenda, and what is actually happening to them on the ground, particularly in the workplaces of corporate supply chains. Feminist scholars have, over many years, documented how gender inequality is used as a resource for global capital (Acker, 2004; Calas and Smircich, 2006). Issues include reproduction and equal pay, where women workers do lower paid jobs, and where companies relocate offshore in search of cheap labour, particularly that of young women in developing countries.

On its CSR website Nike states: 'It's not just about getting better at what we do – addressing impacts throughout our supply chain – it's about striving for the best, creating value for the business and innovating for a better world'.[8] Nike may now be a leader in terms of addressing social issues in its supply chain. However, there is an extensive gender and development literature which reveals that gender discrimination, particularly with regard to young women, is rife within corporate supply chains globally, and that the exploitation of young women lies at the heart of the contemporary capitalist project.

For example, why is it that women, and especially young women, form the vast majority of workers in many corporate supply chains globally (e.g., Barrientos et al., 2003; Barrientos and Smith, 2006)? Within the CSR agenda, Julia Hawkins of the Ethical Trading Initiative (ETI) has noted that 'the majority of people working in our members' supply chains are women, but gender inequality, sexual harassment and discrimination against women in recruitment, reward and promotion persist' (Hawkins, 2010). By creating jobs for women, businesses can help them earn a living and support their families. However, if companies, or their suppliers, employ large numbers of young women, but fail to provide working conditions that meet basic standards for decent work, to uphold human rights, or to pay a 'living wage', they have a negative impact upon young women's lives, and gender equality and poverty. Indeed the precarious nature of the employment provided, and the poor pay and conditions, often prevents these workers from lifting themselves out of poverty, and reinforces their subordinate position in society (Oxfam, 2010). The impact of such working conditions upon women's and children's poverty is significant (Acker, 2004), leading Oxfam (2004: 2) to conclude that 'women workers are systematically being denied their fair share of the benefits brought by globalization' (see Box 5.1).

Box 5.1 Young women in the private sector

- In China's Guangdong province, one of the world's fastest growing industrial areas, young women face 150 hours of overtime each month in the garment factories – but 60 per cent have no written contract and 90 per cent have no access to social insurance (Oxfam, 2004).

Young and older women are discriminated against in numerous other ways in supply chains, including:

- In Chile, 75 per cent of women in the agricultural sector are hired on temporary contracts picking fruit, and put in more than 60 hours a week during the season. But one in three still earns below the minimum wage (Oxfam 2004, p. 3).
- Fewer than half of the women employed in Bangladesh's textile and garment export sector have a contract, and the vast majority get no maternity or health coverage – but 80 per cent fear dismissal if they complain. (Oxfam, 2004)
- In the run up to the 2012 Olympics in London, UK, the organization War on Want found that in Bangladesh, five out of six factories making goods for Adidas, Nike, and Puma 'did not even pay their workers the Bangladeshi minimum wage, let alone a living wage that allows them to meet their basic needs.' The report noted that 'The burden of long hours falls especially hard on women workers, who make up the vast majority of the Bangladeshi clothing industry.'[1]

1   <www.waronwant.org/attachments/Race%20to%20the%20Bottom.pdf>

Moreover, access to education, particularly for girls, is often limited by the fact that they find themselves unable to reliably attend school because they are caring for younger siblings and have other family responsibilities while their mothers work long and unpredictable hours in corporate supply chains (Oxfam, 2010). When they do get to work, domestic responsibilities mean that young women often work in the informal sector where pay and conditions are worse than those in the formal economy (Barrientos et al., 2003).

The Nike Foundation says that the solution to the world's problems is not money, or government, but the girl. Are governments and the private sector prepared to pay the real costs of producing and raising the next generation, and sustaining the workforce through care, or is this labour going to continue to fall upon the shoulders of women, including young women? If so, how are long working hours with no pay going to be conducive to girls 'saving the world'?

Can we use the new rhetoric on girls in a positive way?

So how might women, and women's organizations, use the new rhetoric about girls and development to some advantage? Some socialist feminist approaches to changing gender relations within organizations have attempted to adopt a dual agenda approach, focusing on both instrumental and gender equality goals (e.g., Martin, 2003). Lessons from this work reveal the need for both a strong gender equality narrative, and specific gender-related indicators of progress, if this strategy is to prove useful (Coleman and Rippin, 2000). It seems that the girls and development campaigns have much to learn from this approach. For example, the new obsession with performance indicators in CSR might be used to suggest that companies claiming to be committed to helping girls and young women begin reporting against all the GRI gender indicators, providing specific information relating to young women in particular, and that they provide such data for their supply chain operations.

More importantly perhaps, transnational/(post)colonial feminist theory addresses the gendered aspects of globalization, regarding 'Transnational corporations/organizations [as the] primary actors in the perpetuation of race/gender/sex relations' (Calas and Smircich, 2006: 303). This analysis focuses in particular on ' "knowledge" as a system of power relations deployed by the "West" and "the rest" ' (Calas and Smircich, 2006: 302). Development and feminist scholars have highlighted the failure of much CSR practice to incorporate the voices and concerns of poorer and traditionally marginalized groups and stakeholders (Grosser, 2009; Grosser and Moon, 2005; Marshall, 2007; Newell, 2005). There is evidence that participation by women workers, and women's NGOs, can greatly enhance effective implementation of supply chain codes of conduct, to the benefit of both companies and women workers (Hale and Opondo, 2005). This perspective suggests that the voices of 'the rest', in this case young women and girls in developing countries, must now be included in shaping and evaluating the girls' campaigns if they are to achieve something other than business as usual (Coleman, 2002).

Conclusion

In communication and profiling terms, the campaigning and advocacy work on girls has been very successful. The press has covered the issue extensively, for example in *Time* magazine (Gibbs, 2011). It could be argued that the messages about girls need to be short and punchy in order to get people involved. They emerge in a context where everyone is communicating in sound-bites and 140 character tweets, and where governments feel the need to justify spending on overseas aid when they are cutting so much else by reaching for the lowest common denominator.

We welcome the fact that the international development world is finally talking about girls, beginning to work out how to disaggregate data by age and sex, and how to invest in programmes that support girls. Recently, the United Nations designated October 11 as 'International Day of the Girl Child'.

However, while we might expect the private sector to ignore social and political contexts, and decades of research on gender and development, why, we wonder, are governments and inter-governmental development agencies colluding with this ahistorical approach to girls? Are they just desperate for money? Or are they quietly attempting to use this agenda to fund more deep-rooted change? Our fear is that unless the girls campaign is underpinned by a deeper understanding and explanation of the causes of poverty, of power and justice and attitudinal change, and of gender discrimination and inequality, including the realities of rape and violence against girls and women, the Girl Effect will be ineffective, and perhaps even counter-productive. It may also become just one more fashion to be quietly dropped in a few years' time. And then what will happen to all those girls?

Notes

1. See www.girlchildnetwork.org/home.html [accessed 3 December 2012].
2. See www.globalreporting.org/reporting/latest-guidelines/g3-1-guidelines/Pages/default.aspx [accessed 3 December 2012].
3. Video available at www.girleffect.org/why-girls [accessed 3 December 2012].
4. Poststructuralist feminist analysis has deconstructed the discourses of the mainstream, in particular exploring key silences in corporate communications as well as academic texts (e.g., Martin, 1990, 2000).
5. This is true; however, the statistics are very nuanced globally, and in many countries it is in fact boys who are dropping out of school rather than girls.
6. www.promundo.org.br/en/ [accessed 3 December 2012].
7. Perhaps unsurprisingly, strategies that focus on women's difference as a resource for organizations (or development) frequently benefit those

organizations more than they do women themselves (Fletcher, 1994; Martin, 2003; Meyerson and Fletcher, 2000; Rutherford, 2001).

8. <http://nikeinc.com/pages/responsibility> [accessed 3 December 2012].

References

Acker, J. (2004) 'Gender, capitalism and globalization', *Critical Sociology* 30: 17–41.

Barker, G. T. (2005) *Dying to be Men: Youth Masculinity and Social Exclusion*, Routledge, London.

Barrientos, S, Dolan, C. and Tallontire, A. (2003) 'A gendered value chain approach to codes of conduct in African horticulture', *World Development* 31: 1511–26.

Barrientos, S. and Smith, S. (2006) 'Report on the ETI Impact Assessment 2006. The ETI code of labour practice: Do workers really benefit?', Institute of Development Studies, University of Sussex.

Bendell, J. (2004). 'Barricades and boardrooms. a contemporary history of the corporate accountability movement', UNRISD Technology, Business and Society Programme, Geneva.

Calas, M. B. and Smircich, L. (2006) 'From the "woman's point of view" ten years later: towards a feminist organization studies', in S. Clegg, C. Hardy, W. Nord, and T. Lawrence (eds), *Handbook of Organization Studies*, 2nd edn, Sage, London.

Coalition for Adolescent Girls [website] <www.coalitionforadolescentgirls.org> [accessed 3 December 2012).

Coleman, G. (2002) 'Gender, power and post-structuralism in corporate citizenship', *Journal of Corporate Citizenship* 5: 17–25.

Coleman, G. and Rippin, A. (2000) 'Putting feminist theory to work: collaboration as a means towards organizational change', *Organization* 7: 573–87.

Crane, A., Matten, D. and Moon, J. (2008) *Corporations and Citizenship*, Cambridge University Press, Cambridge.

Eitel, M. (2009) 'Girls session steals the show at Davos', *Huffington Post* [webpage], February 23 <www.huffingtonpost.com/maria-eitel/girls-session-steals-the_b_163633.html> [accessed 3 December 2012]

Elson, D. (1991) *Male Bias in the Development Process*, Manchester University Press, Manchester.

Elson, D. (1994) 'Micro, meso, macro: gender and economic analysis in the context of policy reform', in I. Bakker (ed.), *The Strategic Silence: Gender and Economic Policy*, Zed Books, London.

Ely, R. J. and Meyerson, D. E. (2000) 'Advancing gender equity in organizations: the challenge and importance of maintaining a gender narrative', *Organization* 7: 589–608.

Eyben, R. (2011), presentation at Women's Rights in the Current International Aid Environment: Challenges and Opportunities, Gender and Development Network Public Seminar, April.

Fletcher, J. K. (1994) 'Castrating the female advantage: feminist standpoint research and management science', *Journal of Management Inquiry* 3: 74–82.

Gibbs, N. (2011) 'To fight poverty, invest in girls', *Time*, February 14 <www.time.com/time/magazine/article/0,9171,2046045,00.html> [accessed 3 December 2012].

The Girl Hub [website] <www.girlhub.org> [accessed 3 December 2012].

Girl Effect (no date), 'The Girl Effect media kit' [PDF] <www.girleffect.org/uploads/documents/2/Girl_Effect_Media_Kit.pdf> [accessed 23 January 2012]

Grosser, K. (2009) 'CSR and gender equality: women as stakeholders and the EU sustainability strategy', *Business Ethics: A European Review* 18: 290–307.

Grosser, K. and Moon, J. (2005) 'The role of corporate social responsibility in gender mainstreaming', *International Feminist Journal of Politics* 7: 532–54.

Hale, A. and Opondo, M. (2005) 'Humanising the cut flower chain: confronting the realities of flower production for workers in Kenya', *Antipode* 37: 301–23.

Hawkins, J. (2010) 'The race is on to end poverty: can ethical trade contribute?', 17 September, *Ethical Trading Initiative* [webpage], <www.ethicaltrade.org/news-and-events/blog/julia-hawkins/the-race-is-on-to-end-poverty>

Independent Commission for Aid Impact (ICAI) (2012) 'Girl Hub: a DFID and Nike Foundation initiative' (PDF), <http://icai.independent.gov.uk/wp-content/uploads/2012/03/ICAI-Girl-Hub-Final-Report_P1-51.pdf>

ILO (2009) 'Global Employment Trends for Women', March 2009, United Nations, Geneva.

InterParliamentary Union (2011) <www.ipu.org/wmn-e/world.htm> [accessed 3 December 2012]

Kilgour, M. A. (2007) 'The UN Global Compact and substantive equality for women: revealing a "well hidden" mandate', *Third World Quarterly* 28: 751–73.

Marshall, J. (2007), 'The gendering of leadership in corporate social responsibility', *Journal of Organizational Change Management* 20: 165–81.

Martin, J. (1990) 'Deconstructing organizational taboos: the suppression of gender conflict in organizations', *Organization and Science* 1: 339–59.

Martin, J. (2000) 'Hidden gendered assumptions in mainstream organizational theory and research', *Journal of Management Inquiry* 9: 207.

Martin, J. (2003) 'Feminist theory and critical theory: unexplored synergies', in M. Alvesson and H. Willmott (eds), *Studying Management Critically*, Sage Publications, London.

Matten, D., Crane, A. and Chapple, W. (2003) 'Behind the mask: revealing the true face of corporate citizenship', *Journal of Business Ethics* 45: 109–20.

Meyerson, E. and Fletcher, K. (2000) 'A modest manifesto for shattering the glass ceiling', *Harvard Business Review* (January–February): 127–36.

Moon, J. (2004) 'CSR in the UK: an explicit model of business–society relations', in A. Habisch, J. Jonker, M. Wegner and R. Schmidpeter (eds), *CSR Across Europe*, Springer-Verlag, Berlin, New York.

Moon, J. and Vogel, D. (2008) 'Corporate social responsibility, government, and civil society', in A. Crane, A. McWilliams, D. Matten, J. Moon and D. Siegel (eds), *The Oxford Handbook of Corporate Social Responsibility*, Oxford University Press, Oxford.

Newell, P. (2005) 'Citizenship, accountability and community: the limits of the CSR agenda', *International Affairs* 81: 541–57.

Nike Foundation [website], <http://nikeinc.com/pages/the-nike-foundation/> [accessed 3 December 2012].

Oxfam (2004) 'Trading away our rights: women working in global supply chains', Oxfam International, Oxford.

Oxfam (2010) 'Better jobs in better supply chains', *Briefing for Business* 5 (international edition), Oxfam International, Oxford.

Rutherford, S. (2001) 'Any difference? An analysis of gender and divisional management styles in a large airline', *Gender, Work and Organization* 8: 326–45.

Scherer, A. G. and Palazzo, G. (2007) 'Toward a political conception of corporate responsibility: business and society seen from a Habermasian perspective', *Academy of Management Review* 32: 1096–120.

Scholte, J. A. (2005) *Globalization: A Critical Introduction*, Palgrave Macmillan, New York.

Sellers, P. (2012) 'Fortune 500 women CEOs hit a milestone' [blog] <http://postcards.blogs.fortune.cnn.com/2012/11/12/fortune-500-women-ceos-3/?iid=obnetwork> (posted 12 November) [accessed 3 December 2012].

The Adolescent Girls Initiative (2010) [webpage], World Bank <http://go.worldbank.org/I5PX4JETM0> [accessed 3 December 2012].

van der Gaag, N. (2011) *Because I am a Girl 2011: So what about boys?* Plan International <http://becauseiamagirl.ca/2011GirlReport> [accessed 3 December 2012].

About the authors

Dr **Kate Grosser** is a Visiting Fellow at the International Centre for Corporate Social Responsibility, Nottingham University Business School, and currently teaches corporate governance and corporate social responsibility at Monash University, Melbourne. Her academic work critically engages with corporate social responsibility research and practice from a feminist perspective. Kate has worked for numerous non-governmental organizations, and served on the Management Committee of the Women's Budget Group (UK). She has been a consultant to, among others: the Global Corporate Governance Forum; UNIFEM; Plan International; Oxfam International; the European Academy of Business in Society; and the Government Equalities Office (UK). She was a member of the Global Reporting Initiative's Gender Working Group (2010), and advisor on 'integrating a gender perspective' to the Special Representative of the United Nations Secretary-General on Human Rights and Transnational Corporations and Other Business Enterprises. Her work has appeared in numerous academic and practitioner publications.

Nikki van der Gaag is an independent writer and consultant specializing in gender and communications. She has held senior editorial and communications posts in the non-profit sector including Oxfam, The New Internationalist, and the Panos Institute. She is a member of the International Advisory Board of the Young Lives Project at Oxford University, a director of Just Change UK, a trustee of Asylum Welcome, and an advisory trustee to New Internationalist. She was the principal author for four of the 'Because I am a Girl' reports for Plan International. Other books include *Changing Lives in a Changing World* (Young Lives, 2012); *Speaking Out: Case Studies on How Poor People Influence Decision-Making* (Oxfam/Practical Action, 2009); *The No-Nonsense Guide to Women's Rights* (New Internationalist, 2008); *How the World Came to Oxford: Refugees Past and Present* (Oxford Literary Festival, March 2007); and *'Nothing is impossible for me' Stories from Young Lives Children* (Young Lives, 2009). She is writing a book about boys and men and gender equality.

CHAPTER 6

Lost in translation: gender mainstreaming in Afghanistan

Anastasiya Hozyainova

This chapter explores, from an institutional perspective, the factors behind the apparent minimal achievements in securing women's rights in Afghanistan. The contradictory approaches of international donors, the government of Afghanistan, and civil society have resulted in superficial reform that has fallen short of meeting some of the fundamental challenges that underlie the disadvantaged position of women in Afghanistan. This chapter argues that, 10 years after the West came to Afghanistan under the banner of protecting women's rights and liberalizing Afghanistan, there continues to be a mismatch between helpers and would-be benefi-ciaries. Neither side understands or speaks the institutional and cultural language of the other. The chapter concludes that unless this disconnect is mended, efforts to promote and protect women's rights in Afghanistan will continue to stall.

There has been significant progress for women in Afghanistan, and by 2011 more women have been able to work, have some access to medical and education services, and have greater access to justice than 10 years ago (Hozyainova et al., 2012). However, there remains a general scarcity of social services for much of the population, particularly for women, and women continue to have significantly less access to essential services than men. The achievements in improving the situation of women in Afghanistan, albeit mostly superficial, are increasingly under threat. This is particularly so as we approach the planned 2014 transition, which will transfer all respon-sibilities currently fulfilled by the international community to the Afghan government. Many advocates of women's basic rights fear rollbacks and the eventual obliteration of the gains made. This will be a disastrous outcome for Afghan women and a major failure of international reconstruction efforts, especially given the amount of funding, investment, and attention Afghanistan has received since the US-led invasion.

Two key observations can be made about the dynamics of change in Afghanistan since 2001. First, the pace of progress has been much slower than expected. Second, the progress achieved to date is unsustainable. Both of these are a function of fundamental misunderstandings of the Afghan context when promoting gender equality. Donor-led development programmes have

http://dx.doi.org/10.3362/9781780447780/006

rested on the rule and superiority of law above all else, including the need for a legal framework and a formal organizational approach to implementing programmes. This approach has failed to create spaces for community-first approaches, which are characteristic of Afghan institutions. The legalistic and formalized approach also goes against the experience and practice of Soviet-trained civil servants, who worked through community engagement in carefully organized forums facilitated by the state (regardless of the validity or relevance of some of the state-led interventions in social life).

In the 10 years since the fall of the Taliban and the (formal) introduction of a democratic system in Afghanistan, major differences remain in the predominant mental models that separate the international community, the Afghan population, and government officials. Neither side understands or speaks the institutional and cultural language of the other. Unless this disconnect is mended, future efforts at gender mainstreaming are likely to continue to stall and eventually be reversed after 2014.

In 2011, Afghanistan remained the most dangerous country for women, and the worst in terms of health, non-sexual violence, and access to economic resources (Thomson Reuters Foundation, 2011). The fertility rate was estimated at 6.48 children per woman in 2009 (World Bank, 2011), and it has the highest maternal mortality rate in the world, with an estimated 1,800 maternal deaths per 100,000 live births (UNICEF, 2011). Access to primary education for girls remains a major issue, with a 75 per cent dropout rate before the fifth grade (Jackson, 2011). Afghan women's contributions in the economy continue to be underestimated and unrecognized, despite the fact that they carry out a significant portion of value-adding activities in agricultural production as free or extremely cheap labour (Parto et al., 2011). The legal provisions for women to have inheritance rights over land, and control over income, remain ill-enforced at best, and socially and domestically unacceptable (Akbar and Pirzad, 2011). Women are incarcerated for *zená* (sex outside of marriage), even in cases of rape, and for the nonexistent crimes of running away from home and 'attempted *zená*' (HRW, 2009, 2012). The courts and society at large consistently rely on often arbitrary interpretations of Islamic *sharia* law to limit women's rights in economic and political spheres, mobility, marriage, divorce, and inheritance (individual interviews conducted by the Afghanistan Public Policy Research Organization (APPRO), June 2011–August 2012).

All key development and reconstruction objectives in Afghanistan include a gender component. Gender equity is enshrined in the Constitution. The government has signed a range of international, legal instruments aimed at creating gender equity, including the Convention on the Elimination of Discrimination Against Women (CEDAW). Since the 2001 Bonn Agreement, national policy mechanisms in Afghanistan have formally embraced and promoted gender equity (Kandiyoti, 2005). These mechanisms have included the Ministry of Women's Affairs (MoWA, established in 2002), the Afghanistan National Development Strategy (ANDS, finalized in 2008), the National Action Plan for the Women of Afghanistan (NAPWA, approved in 2008), and the

Elimination of Violence Against Women Law (EVAW, signed into law in 2009). Each of these mechanisms emphasizes gender mainstreaming in all matters of formal policy, and every Afghan ministry is mandated to have a separate gender policy.

While at formal, legalistic, and bureaucratic levels, the above developments are impressive, there is no convincing evidence to suggest these top-down measures have taken root, or started a process of institutionalized change in favour of women. The following sections provide a critical examination of some of these measures and their outcomes.

Ministry of Women's Affairs: key agency protecting women's rights?

The sole mandate of the Ministry of Women's Affairs is to be a leading agency in creating gender equality, including being a referral source with the capacity and authority to supervise all projects promoting gender equity. It has raised awareness about women and society, despite its weak position in the predominantly patriarchal system of government. For example, it is unclear what role MoWA may have played in the incorporation of gender equity requirements into ANDS, the finalization of NAPWA, the promotion of female leadership in governmental appointments, and the adoption of EVAW. It is now commonly acknowledged that MoWA can be instrumental in promoting women's rights in Afghanistan but faces a range of major challenges, including a lack of political authority.

The first challenge is that MoWA does not have a well-articulated vision to which it subscribes. It has not formulated its own mission, strategy, policies, and action plans; it is struggling to define its own priorities, and is faced with significant capacity shortages. A range of donors tasked with building capacity has reacted to this lack of resolve and strategic coherence by outsourcing the majority of MoWA's strategic thinking and programme design to international experts. As with numerous other ministries, international experts wrote MoWA's strategy in its entirety while giving the responsibility to present the strategy to the Cabinet (including NAPWA) to MoWA's senior personnel (SIGAR, 2010). As a consequence, there are numerous claims that MoWA knows the words of NAPWA and other progressive legal documents, but does not understand what they mean in practical terms.

The second challenge is that MoWA struggles to recruit capable and trained staff. It only has an administrative budget to cover civil servants' salaries. In comparison, other key ministries such as the Ministry of Rural Rehabilitation and Development (MRRD; hailed as the most successful ministry), the Ministry of Finance, and a number of others receive salary top-ups from donors for their experienced Afghan staff. The top-ups are provided in recognition of the fact that it is difficult, if not impossible, to retain experienced staff on measly salaries ranging from $150 to $250 per month. MRRD is notorious for operating mainly via national and international consultants, paid at rates comparable to those in the World Bank and USAID. MoWA only receives top-ups for some key senior personnel. Additionally, it does not have a development budget, beyond staff salaries and building maintenance, to sustain the ministry and its provincial departments.

Finally MoWA has not been able to gain legitimacy among civil society organizations and government institutions. As a response to the inability to live up to its mandate and recruit well-trained staff, donors encouraged MoWA to engage in short-term, high-profile projects. MoWA's staff saw this as an attempt to build their legitimacy, hoping that such projects would earn them credibility. These projects included gender awareness and vocational training for women in the communities. The Departments of Women's Affairs (DoWAs) and MoWA believed their problems would be solved once they had a project-implementing role.

However, taking on these projects pushed the ministry in the opposite direction. MoWA, being dependent on its donors, took on too many different tasks. It lost sight of its intended priorities. It then shifted focus to activities with immediate outcomes that were practical and achievable in the short term. As a result, it created a gap between its mandate and its current work, which ultimately differed little from that of any women's network or organization. As a result, the Ministry was incapable of developing a strategy that reflected its mandate, and started competing with civil society organizations for projects to promote women's rights.

Exasperated by MoWA's strategic inaction, and sensing a competitive relationship, women's rights organizations started to distance themselves, resulting in further competition and animosity between MoWA and the civil society it was set up to serve. The majority of women's rights organizations interviewed by APPRO reported strained relationships with MoWA. Nevertheless, women's rights organizations must register with the Ministry and report on their activities every six months. In some provinces, DoWAs hold monthly coordination meetings with women's rights organizations, although these rarely go beyond reports on the number of cases handled. These meetings are sometimes seen as a tool by which MoWA limits the work of civil society organizations, including controversial women's shelters. In 2010-11, MoWA yielded to pressure from conservative elements in the government, and attempted a takeover of all women's shelters. This was seen as supporting accusations that women's rights organizations are prostituting women who live in the shelters. This, and the general trend to take on various projects, resulted in women's rights organizations referring to the provincial DoWAs as an institutional barrier to women's liberation and the promotion of women's rights.

This situation has created losses for MoWA and, more importantly, for Afghan women. A key outcome of the short-term approaches has been their failure to advocate for longer term institutional change and regulatory reform in the government and legal service delivery. This has left the women of Afghanistan vulnerable and unprotected. MoWA has also become the institution donors love to hate. It is hailed as the least competent, least productive, and the most difficult to work with.

However, there is no recognition that MoWA is a creation of donors' ill-informed and poorly designed implementation strategies for mainstreaming gender in Afghanistan. As a nascent governmental body, with one of the most challenging mandates, MoWA was not provided with informed guidance, space to make mistakes and learn, and resources to have its voice heard in relevant national and international arenas. Left to fend for itself by the international donors, MoWA turned to other governmental bodies to gain support and resources; however, these bodies had become significantly more conservative (relative to 2005) since the presidential and parliamentary elections in 2009 and 2010.

Access to justice, education, health, and work: examples of failures

Policies and strategic plans, including gender policies, continue to be written by international experts, without extensive and meaningful contributions from local staff. This results in policies that are hard to implement and which have very little resonance with the national institutions. These policies underestimate the challenges on the ground and do not contain clear descriptions of the steps, resources, and timeframes required to implement them. For example, NAPWA states that it will work towards dismantling individual and institutional gender biases and patterns of inequality. However, it does not provide a detailed description of how to overcome these challenges. Changing laws or introducing affirmative actions in areas where discrimination against women is most serious does not sufficiently address the fundamental causes of discrimination.

These policies are also widely opposed by local staff, including some women, as they are seen to contradict some interpretations of Islam and traditions adopted by Afghan society. Even the introduction of direct services to women might backfire if women's realities are not closely examined. Examples of newly introduced services and approaches that have backfired include access to justice, secondary education, maternity services, and promotion of women's right to work in the public sphere. These are outlined below.

One of the objectives of Justice Sector Reform had been to facilitate a female-friendly justice mechanism, as the informal community justice system was seen as inherently biased against women. This push for greater use of the formal justice system (versus continuing engagement with the informal dispute resolution mechanisms currently in use) failed to take into account the fact that it is by no means kinder to women. It is also prone to systemic corruption, and often exposes women to additional hazards by removing them from community or family protection. Formal justice systems often punish women for bringing family law cases to court. Furthermore, had Afghanistan enforced all existing laws, including the 1976 Penal Code and the 1977 Civil Code, the situation of women's rights would have already been much improved. The exclusion of women from both informal and formal justice mechanisms stems more from underlying discriminatory social and cultural norms than from shortcomings in the system itself (Chopra and Isser, 2011).

One way to prevent this failure would have been to engage with communities to highlight positive experiences in the formal justice system, and reduce the gap in relation to informal dispute resolution mechanisms. This might have created an environment for women to 'forum shop' so they could identify the best opportunities for accessing formal or informal justice. Such a process would draw on international standards as a framework for addressing problematic social practices (Chopra and Isser, 2011). However, donors have largely ignored this recommendation.

A similar example is seen in efforts to institutionalize schooling for girls. A significant unforeseen outcome of these efforts has been a high dropout rate as girls reach the sixth grade (Jackson, 2011). The Education Strategy (regarded as one of the better sector strategies in Afghanistan) fails to address some seemingly tangential, but in fact crucial, issues related to education, such as extreme poverty, cultural and social norms, and security. The strategy also fails to see that in some areas, excessive focus on creating girls' schools meant that the demand for boys' education was met by informal *madrasas* that have allegedly been a radicalization tool. The Ministry of Education did not address these issues in collaboration with the Ministry of Interior and MoWA. Lack of attention to these issues partially stems from a short-term approach to development, which fails to see and utilize the wealth of knowledge in the education field, including ideas on how to address concerns such as creating home schools and providing chaperones for girls.

The provision of midwife services to ensure better care for women in childbirth has also faced resistance from many communities. There appears to be little understanding of women's needs within their cultural settings, so the services remain underutilized (Akbar, 2011). Labour and birth is an intimate period. Many women in rural areas are uncomfortable spending this period with strangers in impersonal hospitals. The cultural rift between educated and uneducated Afghans also means that rural women often face humiliation by educated hospital staff when they come in for delivery. It is not uncommon to hear stories of rough physical and psychological treatment of women by medical staff. Some staff seem to revel in being insensitive to the needs of women in labour. Midwife training has failed to bridge these cultural gaps, resulting in terrified women returning to their villages and telling stories to other women who, naturally, shun the idea of going to the maternity hospitals.

A lack of protection for women in the workplace is another worrying aspect of development policies driven by donors. Sex is a taboo subject in Afghanistan. A focus on high-level national development plans makes the whole country look asexual, where children are 'found' (a literal translation for a Dari word referring to birth), pregnant women are 'ill', and there is no sex before marriage. This asexual presentation of Afghanistan prohibits discussing sexual politics. Meanwhile, women in workplaces are subjected to continual sexual harassment and have no way to voice their concerns.

There have not been any studies on sexual harassment in the workplace, but anecdotal evidence is worrying. In a study on policewomen in Afghanistan conducted by APPRO, the majority of interviews showed unsolicited complaints of sexual harassment. Personally, I have heard a number of confessions from women who were raped at their workplace and had no place to go for help. When one rape victim requested her supervisor re-allocate her to a women-only room and suspend her travels into the provinces, the supervisor said this could not be done because they had to remain 'committed to promoting gender equity'. International experts are reluctant to deal with sexual harassment complaints, and have been known to refer these to their local counterparts for resolution without adequate supervision. Again, this is done in the name of empowering local investigative mechanisms and promoting gender equity.

International donors have focused on the numbers of girls studying, the numbers of women served by the formal courts or hospitals, and the numbers of women working. This approach fails to see the importance of the quality of services. It does not acknowledge or understand the barriers and threats felt by women in accessing these services or participating in public life. This has further embedded some of the traditional barriers that prevent women from accessing services, and armed those who oppose gender equality with arguments on why such policies should not be implemented in Afghanistan.

Philosophical differences

These failures are products of the interplay between Western social values, traditional Afghan norms, and institutional remnants that carry features from pre-Soviet, Soviet, civil war, and the Taliban times. Current interventions prioritized by Western donors rest on a tradition that sees the law as the key to social change. Introduction of the law is seen as the first necessary step to changing social reality. This is expected to lead to further social adjustments, as mandated by the law, to ensure equal protection guaranteed by the law. In the case of women, this means the state regulates such questions as daycare subsidies for working women or shelters for victims of violence. These adjustments, while important, are secondary to working with the traditional norms within the Afghan context.

The majority of the Afghan population lives with a social tradition in which change is brought about slowly, by consultation among community leaders, and any actions are agreed upon by consensus. This is partially due to the fact that Afghan tradition mainly relies on oral and customary legislation. Even judges in the official courts are not always familiar with the civil and criminal codes. Thus, any change to the legal structure in Afghanistan is likely to take years to take root. It is because of this resilient nature of the Afghan legal tradition that government structures and functions have survived various regimes and remain relatively unchanged since their last major reform in the early twentieth century (Leach, 2011).

There is another institutional inheritance. A significant number of Afghans were trained and lived in the Soviet Union until the late 1980s. Under the Soviets, there were massive women's equality programmes in the urban parts of the country. This approach saw the law as secondary to the adjustments that were needed in the society to protect vulnerable citizens from abuse and exploitation. It put day-to-day protection needs at the forefront of social development, understanding that it would take time for laws to be incorporated in practice. The Soviet approach tolerated the delayed development of legal mechanisms, prioritizing communities' efforts to protect their members. In the case of protecting women's rights, such initiatives included introducing quotas for women, the organization of women's associations, providing daycare facilities, putting limits on the types of occupations for women, and on the amount of time that women could work, and putting in place 'champions' to promote the cause of women's equality. Civil servants and other Soviet-era professionals who remained in Afghanistan still carry that perspective. This approach pushes policy initiatives away from larger legal frameworks and instead advocates for practical programmes.

The interaction between these three disparate perspectives creates the current stalemate. The international community's discourse is incomprehensible for those not previously exposed to Western legal systems. The apparent inability of Afghan recipients to adopt and appreciate the alleged benefits of the Western legal system is often misunderstood by the international community as inaction. The international community remains unfamiliar with the Afghan context and views the response to its efforts to address women's rights as unsophisticated and piecemeal. The civil servants and civil society organizations that implement gender mainstreaming interpret the need for change differently, depending on which side of the philosophical divide they find themselves. This creates further confusion among the donors and the targeted beneficiaries.

In this situation the donors control resource flows and determine which changes are brought to the official structure of the Afghan government. International donors do not understand, and cannot sufficiently influence or alter the traditional structures through which Afghans organize themselves. But these structures have been proven to be relatively permanent, and for better or for worse, are trusted by the majority of the population. This results in situations where efforts and resource allocations to promote change in one target area are misappropriated by Afghan counterparts to do something else, or the intervention creates new problems for both international donors and the Afghan counterparts.

These challenges are layered over the shifting political pressures and priorities of the donor governments, creating the perfect excuse to disengage from gender programmes. Since 2009, women's rights have started to slip from the agenda of international donors. Afghan and international women's rights organizations are worried that the international community will use women's rights as a bargaining chip to come to a political settlement with the insurgency groups in Afghanistan. The Western governments have a perfect excuse: if the Afghans do not want gender mainstreaming, why should the international donors? Both donors and conservative elements in the Afghan government can use years of failed interventions to support their claims that women's rights should not be a priority issue in peace negotiations and future development plans in Afghanistan.

Conclusions

The current stalemate in gender mainstreaming programmes in Afghanistan is a result of fundamental disagreement over how significant social and cultural changes could be brought about. The international donor community seems to think that adopting internationally acknowledged policies and legal frameworks are sufficient for ensuring sustainable institutional change in Afghanistan.

The dominant thinking appears to be ignorant of the fact that changes in women's lives, especially in the more liberal Western societies, took generations to come about. It took, among other things, struggle from within by the women of those countries to start the process of change. But so far, the sizeable critical mass of women and women's organizations that would be needed to act as a catalyst for such change in Afghanistan remains a distant possibility. This is not least due to the inability of international donors to tap into the historical momentum created for gender equality after the fall of the Taliban. Furthermore, the majority of development policies and gender mainstreaming models imported into Afghanistan after 2001 seem to fail the 'home test'. They present their home countries as the ideal that Afghanistan should strive to achieve, but the changes proposed by the donor community would not have been possible to implement in the donor countries at the same pace as envisioned for Afghanistan.

The donor community seems to prefer concentrating on short-term, measurable projects, instead of long-term engagement aimed at challenging the current situation. This preference is driven by the ever-increasing desire to see and show impacts of aid. The short-term postings of (often) young and inexperienced diplomatic and development staff further compounds the situation. Diplomatic staff spend an average nine months to a year in Afghanistan in total. The longest period spent is two to three years. The vast majority of posted staff do not speak the local languages and remain confined to their compounds, on security grounds. They are not able to move around and see Afghanistan as the context in which they wish to bring about change. This, along with ill-suited cookie-cutter interventions, creates resentment among Afghans. Expatriate staff hold the purse strings for the funds, while having little legitimacy. This environment has consistently inhibited any meaningful conversations about what needs to be done and which approaches need to be adopted.

Despite these examples of failure, there are areas where informed dialogue has grown with Afghan activists, civil servants, and leaders. This includes developments in providing legal aid and dialogue about reforming the Family Law. This was largely possible due to substantial mentoring for local staff, starting in 2002. It has resulted in the emergence and growth of local voices to advocate and develop conditions for sustained institutional change. Unfortunately, these examples are exceptions, and have not sufficiently taken root. Any one of these accomplishments could be rolled back as soon as funding and mentoring are withdrawn. The unique feature of these developments is their starting premise of understanding the local environment, listening through engaging with local counterparts, and learning how to intervene through pre-existing structures to minimize polarization and loss of legitimacy.

It is not too late to build on these developments. The key, however, is learning, which unfortunately has been rare in post-2001 intervention in Afghanistan. It is still possible for both sides to learn from one another. It must be done through genuine patient conversation between donors and their Afghan counterparts to exchange, rather than transfer, 'capacity' about how to address women's rights.

Acknowledgements

This chapter is based on research carried out by the Afghanistan Public Policy Research Organization (APPRO) since 2009. As part of this research, APPRO interviewed women's rights advocates and organizations, Ministry of Women's Affairs' officials, and other government representatives. This chapter would not have been possible without significant contributions from Ahmad Shaheer Anil, Nafasgul Karimi, and Zarghona Saify (APPRO's permanent research staff), Quinta Smit (intern for APPRO from June to August 2010), and Margaret O'Connor (Research Consultant for APPRO from October 2011 to April 2012).

References

Akbar, S. (2011) 'Maternal health and the midwife training programme in Afghanistan: perceptions, deceptions and the politics of birth', Oxford University Masters Thesis, Oxford.

Akbar, S. and Pirzad, T. (2011) *Women's Access to Property in Afghanistan: Law, Enforcement and Barriers*, Qara Consulting Inc., Kabul.

Chopra, T. and Isser, D. (2011) 'Women's access to justice, legal pluralism, and fragile states', in P. Albrecht, H. M. Kyed, D. Isser and E. Harper (eds), *Perspectives on Involving Non-State and Customary Actors in Justice and Security Reform*, International Development Law Organization and the Danish Institute for International Studies, Rome.

Hozyainova, A., O'Connor, M. and Karlidag, M. (2012) *Women and Reconstruction: Tracing Implementation of Afghanistan National Action Plan for Women of Afghanistan*, APPRO, Kabul.

Human Rights Watch (HRW) (2009) 'We have the promises of the world', HRW, New York. Available at: www.hrw.org/node/86805/section/1 [accessed 10 December 2012].

HRW (2012) *'I Had to Run Away': The Imprisonment of Women and Girls for 'Moral Crimes' in Afghanistan*, HRW, New York. Available at: <www.hrw.org/sites/default/files/reports/afghanistan0312webwcover_0.pdf> [accessed 10 December 2012].

Jackson, A. (2011) *High Stakes: Girls' Education in Afghanistan*, Oxfam, Kabul.

Kandiyoti, D. (2005) *The Politics of Gender and Reconstruction in Afghanistan*, UNRISD, Geneva.

Leach. M. (2011) *Whither the Sub-National Governance Policy?*, GIZ Afghanistan, Kabul.

Parto, S., Hozyainova, A., Mihran, R., Winters, J., Karimi, N., Saify, Z. and Gorter, J. (2011) *Gender and the Agricultural Innovation System in Rural Afghanistan: Barriers and Bridges*, APPRO, Kabul.

SIGAR (2010) 'Greater coordination needed in meeting congressional directives to address and report on the needs of Afghan women and girls', Office of the Special Inspector General for Afghanistan Reconstruction, Kabul.

Thomson Reuters Foundation (2011) 'The world's five most dangerous countries for women' [PDF] <www.trust.org/documents/womens-rights/resources/2011WomenPollResults.pdf> [accessed 7 February 2012].

UNICEF (2011) 'Midwife training programme aims to reduce maternal mortality in Afghanistan' [webpage] <www.unicef.org/infobycountry/afghanistan_47120.html> [accessed 7 February 2012].

World Bank (2011) 'World development indicators' [webpage] <http://data.worldbank.org/data-catalog/world-development-indicators?cid=GPD_WDI> [accessed 7 February 2012].

About the author

Anastasiya Hozyainova was Director of Research at the Afghanistan Public Policy Research Organization from March 2008 to September 2012. She managed the Human Rights and Aid Effectiveness research streams. She has a Master of Social Work from Columbia University, and specializes in policy analysis and rights-based development. Her recent work includes research on social and economic rights in Afghanistan, and mainstreaming gender-sensitive policies. Ms Hozyainova has also worked on protection, gender mainstreaming, and human rights issues in Central Asia, the UK, and the USA.

CHAPTER 7
Insulating the developing classes

Tom Scott-Smith

This chapter is divided into two main sections. The first part discusses the insulation of development workers, based on personal experiences in Malawi. The second part draws on the theories of Slavoj Žižek, and argues that development workers can be seen as a distinct class, embedded in ideology. The chapter concludes that the concept of development can be seen as a 'sublime object of ideology': something rarely defined but perpetually invoked, which gives meaning to the actions of development workers and explains their continuing reliance on rational management techniques.

It is remarkable how little has changed in development management since Robert Chambers (1983) called for us to 'put the last first', nearly 30 years ago. There may be more participatory techniques in regular use, and we may have seen the rise and partial fall of the logframe, but the voices of the poorest and most marginal are still largely excluded from decision-making. There are many management methods in use, but the result is too often the same: the nuances of life are mangled, local perspectives are excluded, and complex changes are simmered down into reductive summaries of achievement. As critics, we make a mistake in focusing our analysis on a single aspect of management. Adding a participatory method here, and subtracting a logical framework there cannot transform the development industry. We may succeed in pulling down one problematic management technique – like the logframe – but another will spring back in its place – for example, randomized control trials. Instead of directing our energies at criticizing particular management techniques in isolation, therefore, we need to analyse the very ideology of development itself. We have an underlying problem, a structural problem, which rewards crude declarations of success, and discourages subtle and critical reflection.

My task in this paper is to make a contribution to the more structural analysis of development, starting with the question: why do rational management techniques remain so pervasive? This is a particularly troubling issue because critiques of these approaches are now well established (Hulme and Edwards, 1997; Mawdsley et al., 2002; Mosse and Lewis, 2005; Wallace et al., 2006). Despite these criticisms, why have the majority of well-intentioned, well-educated development practitioners become so captured by rational management techniques such as the logframe, so pre-occupied with the funding cycle, with proving success, and with expanding their organizational

http://dx.doi.org/10.3362/9781780447780/007

size and remit? Why do they seem to accept that people's problems can be objectively known and set out in a linear framework? Why do they collude in the widespread lack of involvement from the poor, and a hierarchical system of funding whereby accountability always flows upwards to the donors rather than downwards to the beneficiaries?

In responding to these questions, I will move beyond the common explanation: that it is all about economic incentives. I believe it has become too easy to lay the entire blame on donors and the funding constraints of development agencies. The system of perverse incentives plays a part in explaining the persistence of rational management techniques, but does not explain why individual development practitioners fail to rebel against these methods. Instead, I argue that a central factor is the *insulation* of development workers, their *separation* from the lives of people at the receiving end of development. Practitioners have become ensconced in a divided world characterized by secure compounds, 4WD jeeps, and exclusive jargon. They tend to administer projects from an emotional and physical distance, and this makes them less able to conceive of creative alternatives to the logframe. As an example of this, I will draw on my own experience, focusing particularly on a period of work in Malawi as the manager of a teacher education project. I will describe how four 'layers' of insulation cut me off from local realities, and will use this description to build a critique of development more broadly.

In this chapter I aim to be self-critical, to turn the lens of analysis on myself; as a result, I can hardly complain if the reader blames me for my failures. The best development workers, after all, manage to overcome these layers of insulation, and find ways to live and work with local people, creating genuinely collaborative projects. But I hope my experience will shed light on the structure of development work, and, in particular, illustrate how it prevents many employees from learning about the lives of marginalized people. I want to demonstrate how easy it is for development practitioners to become preoccupied with management rather than engage in meaningful interaction with human beings, and how easy it is to convert the little interaction we *do* have into a depersonalized, jargon-laden vocabulary. I also want to show how, even though we often know the problems with our work, it is very easy to justify what we do with reference to the ultimate consequences: insisting that the final aim of development is just and good.

My aim in this chapter is also to use these experiences as a basis for some more general theoretical reflections. In the second part of this chapter I draw on Slavoj Žižek's (1989, 1991) concept of ideology to analyse the world of development and make two central arguments. First of all, I suggest that development workers can be seen as a distinct class: separated from other communities, controlling benefits and resources, and inhabiting a distinct, cultural world. Second, I argue that development workers have inculcated a strong conviction that what they do is both inevitable and justified. In this sense, they are embedded in an ideology, which circulates around the concept of 'development' as the final and noble end. Development *itself* has become an unquestionably good thing, an end that validates and vindicates our activities, and a 'sublime object of ideology' in Žižek's sense.

Four layers of insulation

Lifestyle

When I arrived in Malawi, one of the first things that struck me was the material standard of life amongst development workers – especially when compared with other sectors of the population. I was allocated a detached house in a wealthy neighbourhood, with a night guard paid for by my employer, and a local family living in a much smaller building, who did cleaning and gardening in return for free rent and a modest pay. I had access to cars and jeeps, which I could use for work trips, but also take home at the end of the day. I was invited to cocktail parties and receptions in upscale hotels or the private residences of senior managers. I had a generous salary, which could be used to swim in hotel pools, take trips to the beach, or eat in restaurants. None of this was specific to me as an expatriate: the previous occupant of my post had been a national member of staff, and the pay and conditions were similar to everyone I met who worked in development in Malawi.

Pointing out these elements of the development worker's lifestyle is by no means new, yet it opens up an interesting debate. Practitioners often get angry when their way of life is criticized: don't they deserve some basic comfort? Isn't the way they live a completely separate issue from the work they do? Practitioners argue that they deserve comfort, rest, and relaxation; or they argue that the way they live has no relevance at all, as long as they fulfil their job description and help their organization to function well. Often, they suggest that such comfort actually helps them do their job better, as they go to work rested and ready to confront the issues required of them.[1]

I have three main problems with this line of argument. First, it presents development as just another wage-earning job: a role we fulfil, with targets to meet, which is completely separate from our private decisions and our personal wealth. This ignores how development, at its best, is a political position, a commitment to working with others, something you struggle with, make sacrifices for, and achieve through solidarity. Second, it ignores the inequality fostered through such lifestyles. Development is meant to solve problems, but the influx of large quantities of aid frequently causes problems: pushing up prices and rents, creating greater resentment between people, and leading to a more divisive society. The third problem is that this lifestyle *insulates development practitioners*; it separates them off from the society and communities they are living in. This is the problem I wish to focus on, since I believe it makes us worse at our jobs, dividing us from the very people with whom we are meant to be working.

The problem with the 4WD jeeps, the smart restaurants, large houses, and high walls is that development practitioners end up with less opportunity to understand the lives of local people, less chance to sit with them, eat with them, and experience their challenges directly. Even if we assiduously implement our participatory workshops, and go on our regular field visits, retreating to a more comfortable world at the end of the day sets us apart from the lives of people we should be trying to experience and understand. But there are also some difficult moral questions that arise from this isolation, questions that were at the forefront of my mind throughout my first months in Malawi. How could I possibly justify having two spare bedrooms in my house, when a family with three kids were living in a single room next door – employed by me, and on my property? How could I eat foods costing more than the average monthly wage, in tranquil surroundings that actively blocked out the lives of most Malawians? How could I travel in large white jeeps and not use the many buses or shared taxis? All these queries may be dismissed as middle-class guilt, but they sprang from a deep-seated political conviction: I strongly believe that the massive difference between the development worker's lifestyle and those of the people living in such close proximity is indefensible – with negative consequences, but also *intrinsically* problematic. As philosophers of egalitarian justice like Gerald Cohen (2011) have argued, no difference in skill, ability, effort, choice, intelligence, or worth can justify this level of inequality, and the circumstances of life that lead one person to sit at a smart table inside the restaurant, and the other to beg outside it, are largely the result of luck and inheritance, rather than desert and aptitude. Inequality should be something we fight against, not contribute towards.

Despite all these misgivings, I did not actively change the way I was living as I settled into Malawi. I should have made a greater effort to get out of my personal vehicle, take public transport, scale down my housing arrangements, and live more modestly, but overcoming this first layer of insulation met with several difficulties. First of all, everything was laid out before my arrival: the house was waiting for me, as were the night guard and the 'garden boy'.[2] The cars and jeeps were there, as were the hotel bookings for workshops and visits. The meals in smart restaurants were part of my induction, justified as team-building and put on the organization's expense account. Taking a job in development often involves accepting this constellation of practices, and questioning seems like fighting the wrong battle, at the wrong time – after all, it offers a direct challenge to one's colleagues, who already live like this.

But I also failed to change my lifestyle because of a perennial obsession with security. I was rapidly inculcated in the development practitioner's fear – a fear maintained through constant cautions from my colleagues. 'Don't walk alone in your neighbourhood', 'don't visit the park', 'don't go down to the bottle store', 'don't go to the restaurants near the bus station'. These entreaties were always accompanied by horror stories of muggings, break-ins, attacks, and a completely absent police force. I was told that the cars, night watchmen, and the carefully vetted accommodation were all there to ensure that our good work could continue, leaving the task of development uninterrupted by crime and inconvenience. I accepted all this readily, but it is unclear why.

After all, I had been to Malawi previously: I had drunk beer in those very same bottle shops, eaten at the very same restaurants, paced unmolested along the very same streets; but back then, it was always as an idealistic traveller. Now, as a professional development worker, I had a different set of calculations. Given the risks that were constantly spelled out to me, I felt there were more important things than eating and drinking with a diverse selection of people – I had work to do, a project to manage, and making use of the comforts and luxuries helped me do my job.

Formalism

My role in Malawi was to manage an in-service training programme for primary school teachers. This was a project funded by DfID and managed in partnership with the Ministry of Education. One of my biggest successes in the first few months was to expand the programme to 15 new districts, doubling the number of trainers, and getting a donor to contribute a fleet of new vehicles to expand our reach. I was very pleased with these accomplishments while in post, but, looking back on it, recognition for my achievements reveals a second layer of insulation: the problem of formalism, and the restrictive and usually quantitative measurement of development success. The focus of my work was on increasing impact – but increasing impact always meant growth, and growth had to be numerically provable. Increasing impact meant enlarging the programme, it meant more numbers, more jeeps, more areas of the country being covered. Increasing impact meant more dollars coming into the project, and more trained teachers spat out of the project. The whole process was like a sausage machine: if you add more inputs, you can get more outputs, producing a grand, developmental banger.

The problem was we weren't actually running the project very well at its existing size, so the best way of increasing impact would have been to focus on the detail, not the scale. We had problems being inclusive – something that was repellently called 'buy-in'. District-level education officers complained of being excluded from decision-making. Head teachers were reluctant to release staff for training programmes they had little role in devising. Class teachers had little incentive to attend – lured only by the debilitating structure of per diems and perks. One of the most central issues was the class teachers' pay and conditions, which affected their morale and status, and which never seemed to change. But we also had problems with the content of the training: the curriculum had been poorly thought out, the material was delivered didactically, and the teachers had problems applying what they learned, because of their limited resources.

Then there were problems with the logistical arrangements. Project workers never spent long enough in any one place, and moved rapidly around the country in their 4WD jeeps. The use of project vehicles was already causing problems, without adding a fleet of new ones. The jeeps were a prized and scarce resource in the districts, and consequently were squabbled over, commandeered for status trips, and used for self-interest, while all the time isolating their inhabitants (the education officers, teacher trainers, and NGO staff) from the parents and children in the local area, the very people whose lives the project was designed to improve. As for gender issues, they were never raised, and I was never challenged to include them. We rarely talked to women, because women were rarely in positions of power. If I had any anecdotes of female voices being excluded and suppressed, I would recount these gladly, but this exclusion was so total that the perspectives of women barely entered my experience as a manager.[3]

But the project looked great on paper. We covered hundreds of schools, ran thousands of workshops, produced detailed training manuals, and could point to surveys and in-depth interviews that illustrated the value of our work. This was important, because for my employer it was the *paper* project, the *image* of the project, which mattered most of all, since it was the image of success that was used to leverage more funds. And since the paper project mattered so much, I spent a great deal of my time in the company of paper: writing reports, shuffling numbers in budget sheets, recruiting staff, negotiating partnership agreements, and submitting quantitative 'results' of our work to headquarters. It was easy to become preoccupied with the tasks that sat in my in-tray every day and to lose sight of the bigger picture. It was easy to be thankful for small successes – getting a minister's signature on a key document, securing some additional funding, gathering some quarterly statistics, recruiting some new staff – but all the time I was losing sight of the process itself, and ignoring the constituency I was there to support: the rural villages who had little education.

Language

After several months, I finally realized I was missing the point. I was rushing from an evaluation meeting in one district to a supervision meeting in another when the strap holding the load in my pickup truck came undone and the contents scattered onto the road. I stopped and collected the paraphernalia I had been carrying – a mixture of teaching materials, refreshments, mattresses, and baggage – and a group of people who were walking alongside the road stopped and helped me, forcing a break in my schedule. The clear-up and the thanks I owed them made me pause. I gave them a lift, and we discussed education in their area. I realized I had barely had an informal, detailed conversation with a non-development professional for some time. This is not to say I had been skimping on my commitment to participatory techniques. My organization valued them, and had written them into detailed policy documents. I had been trained in how to use them, and had studied them at length. But as the academic literature has now established, these methods had become so formalized that they ended up as just another piece of paper, another policy, another best-practice box to be ticked (Cooke and Kothari, 2001). I had become so preoccupied with formal tasks that 'participation' had become just another aspect of management. Even by using these techniques,

I was only interacting with people through the circumscribed framework of policy.

We have a real problem when formalized participatory techniques are our only way to talk to people, when we live such an isolated, privileged, home life that all our interactions with local men and women happen at work, in a highly structured way. But we have an even bigger problem when these participatory workshops become outcome-oriented activities written into project plans, converting local perspectives into 'development speak' by using terminology, phrases, and structures that mean little to the people whose opinions were ostensibly being sought. 'Development speak' operates as an exclusive language of development practitioners, excluding many people from its often opaque reference points (Cornwall and Eade, 2010). But it also tends to paper over disagreements *within* the development community, making liberal use of banalities, generalities, and poorly defined terms.

Allow me to take one example, an outline phrase specifying the aims of a project, in very common development language: 'this is a youth-led programme run by a local community-based organization to tackle social exclusion and generate greater participation in local politics'. The usual approach of 'participation' critique is to question whether this phrase reflects what was actually said in the meeting, and to examine the power dynamics that led to its acceptance. But perhaps a more interesting line of analysis is to ask what a phrase like this really means. The language of development, after all, deals in generalities that are hard to dispute, even amongst development practitioners. No one is likely to challenge this formulation, partly because it would take too long, and partly because everyone knows that being youth-led, promoting participation, and combating social exclusion are all good, uncontroversial things. But what constitutes the 'community'? In what way are the partners 'community-based'? How is the project youth-led? What does it mean to be youth-led? What counts as participation? Is greater participation in politics always good? How might this affect the 'community'? What is social exclusion anyway? Who is being excluded, and from what? What, for that matter, is 'development' – this capacious term which is the end of all our interventions and the final arbiter of our success?

We could sit around working through each of these questions, and use up a day of our time, getting embroiled in definitions of each individual word in each individual policy. Or, we could trust that everyone knows what they are talking about, assume that everyone means the same thing, and get on with funding the project. The latter path is more regularly taken, but these assumptions – that everyone agrees on basic concepts, that everyone supports the aims of the project, that our overall objectives are good – tend to disguise the contested nature of our work, and obscure how often we become separated from the way people speak, think, talk, and desire at the local level.

Economic relationships

The insulation of development workers does not just take place at the level of lifestyle, through excessive formalism, and at the level of language. There is also a fundamental separation based on the economic relationship. After all, development always involves one party granting access to resources and opportunities, and another party receiving these benefits. However hard we try to eliminate this distinction through participatory techniques, it remains an ever-present dynamic.

I was particularly aware of this dynamic when forming new partnerships with smaller community-based organizations. What I wielded in these circumstances was the ability to grant access to a whole world of opportunities: not just funds, but also advice, contacts, kudos, and alliances – the very things that would determine whether an organization would thrive or fail. In some circumstances, the inequality of this relationship was made painfully obvious by the attention lavished on me as a guest from a more powerful organization. During visits to Cameroon, for example, gifts were given, however small, to take back to my office, and elaborate welcoming events were carefully staged to give the best impression. This unequal dynamic operates right down the aid chain. Smaller NGOs have a patron–client relationship with *their* beneficiaries, granting or withdrawing advantages on the basis of strategizing in their offices, and driving into rural areas to receive obsequious thanks.

Of course, what applies to the smaller organizations also applies to the larger ones – so as we rise up the aid chain, my organization, in turn, was also chasing contacts, grants, alliances, and funding. We were always willing to bend our aims and objectives to the demands of donors, because the mantra was growth: more income, more impact, more results. All of this created the tendency to gloss over mistakes and write reports of unqualified success, but, more crucially, this illustrates how the relationships at every level of development are infused with inequality – a division between those who hold the funds and those who do not. In the large INGOs we flattered our donors just as our beneficiary organizations flattered us. We took corporate trust managers out to lunch and laid on platters of projects that would tickle their fancy, just as the local NGOs *we* funded took care of us overseas: feeding us, taking us out, and hosting events to welcome and honour our presence.

Theoretical reflections

Class

The personal experiences I recount cannot be said to apply to all development workers, but they can be the basis for some theoretical analysis. After all, I did not lead an isolated lifestyle, but one that was being shared by a whole group of people, a group that can perhaps best be described as a particular class. This is by no means an original suggestion – Robert Chambers (1983: 2), for one, suggested such 30 years ago – but the implications of understanding development workers as a class has not always been spelled out – especially insofar as it relates to ideology.

'Class' is a deeply unfashionable term, and for good reason. It is a crude label, which obscures as much as it elucidates, and like all analytical categories it has disadvantages as well as benefits. As post-structuralist thinkers have pointed out, the very idea of 'class' is an historical and cultural construction, emerging from language, not from an external reality that pre-existed it, and when we apply 'class' to a group of people, we subsume all sorts of other identities – race, gender, ethnicity, nationality, sexuality – to its totalizing and all-inclusive logic. In addition, many scholars have concluded that class is an outdated concept: in today's post-industrial, post-Fordist, postmodern world, economic relations have far greater complexity than they used to, and people can be simultaneously labourers, landowners, and shareholders. It is very hard to work out what class people are in today, and it is certainly more complex than the simplistic divisions in Marx's time, when classes could be defined as those who had capital, and those who only had their labour power to sell.

Nevertheless, there appears to be a number of key, shared characteristics that unite development workers as a group, and which point to the relevance of class as an analytical category. Just as we might speak of the 'working classes' for those that work, and the 'ruling classes' for those that rule, I think it makes sense to speak of the 'developing classes' for those who develop – for those who 'do' development. In the orthodox Marxist sense, class is usually defined as a *patterned set of economic relations between groups*, each having different rights and powers over productive resources. Surely, development workers and their beneficiaries fit this description, because each has a different relationship to development funds: the developing classes are united by the possession of money and resources that are needed to 'produce' development, and the beneficiaries are united by their *receipt* of those resources, and their obligations to report to those further up the aid chain.[4]

This objective side to class – which is defined by economic relations – can be supplemented by a more subjective account of class – which encompasses the cultural world in which a group of people live. Class in this more recent ('cultural Marxist') sense involves sharing a set of subjective ideas and worldviews, participating in similar rituals and talking a similar language. Again, it is easy to see how this conception of class applies to development practitioners since shared experiences and worldviews are at the heart of my narrative above. Development workers tend to live a similar kind of lifestyle, eat in similar restaurants, stay in similar places, drive similar cars, and have similar aesthetic sensibilities. They share a common idea of what is good, what is bad, what we are working for, and what we are working against; they also use a similar kind of language, adopting the same acronyms, terms, and discourse.[5]

Ideology

Class is a useful concept in describing the separation of development workers from the rest of society. But ideology is perhaps more useful, since it can help answer the question I set myself in this paper: why do so many people still use reductive, rationalist management techniques, despite knowing their manifold limitations? The answer, as I indicated in the Introduction, lies not just in economic incentives, but also in the realm of ideology. In a classical Marxist sense, ideology is a purely negative force: a false belief, a false consciousness, which papers over the contradictions of class conflict. Marx argued that ideology involved the concealment of people's true interests, both from themselves (in the case of false consciousness) and from other people (in the case of ruling ideologies). Ideology therefore involves an illusion, which obscures the class-based antagonisms that only Marxism – as an objective science – can reveal. Can we say that development workers are ideologically blinkered in this classical Marxist sense? I think not. The traditional notion of ideology is problematic because it places the scholar in a privileged position. With typical arrogance, it assumes that only enlightened Marxists are able to reveal the true situation, the real circumstances of the world. It presents ordinary people as dupes, who are unable to see behind the ideological smoke and mirrors, and who possess a level of faith in political leaders and ideologues they certainly do not have. As applied to development, it seems particularly misguided, because development workers are perfectly capable of understanding what they do, and many of them are highly critical of their lifestyles and working practices.

So, no, I am not suggesting, in a crude classical Marxist sense, that development workers are brainwashed, dupes of capitalism, and that they do not know how their actions and lifestyle create social stratifications. But I *am* suggesting that they are affected by ideology. This is where Žižek's work comes in. Slavoj Žižek's great contribution to the notion of ideology is to reject the absurd idea of ideologically imprisoned, credulous persons living under false consciousness, but maintain that the concept of ideology still has salience. Ideology, Žižek argues, cannot be identified in the realm of what people know, or in what they say they know; rather, we can identify ideology by studying what people *do*. According to Žižek, ideology functions today not through false consciousness, which can be summarized as the idea that 'they do not know it, but they are doing it', but rather through a kind of partly acknowledged, self-limiting action, which can be summarized in the phrase 'they know it, but they are doing it anyway'.[6]

Žižek provides countless examples of this tendency. People may know that their political leaders manipulate them and the parliamentary system does not represent them; nevertheless they still vote. People may know that the media misrepresents the world in the pursuit of a good story or according to editorial policy, but they still consume this media and base their conversations around it. People may know that life chances are deeply determined by circumstances, that wealth buys advantage, and that private education creates social inequality; they send their children to private schools never-theless. People may know that companies use corporate social responsibility (CSR) to change their image and increase consumption and profits, but they will buy one coffee rather than another (and feel good about it) because of CSR publicity.

The division here is between what people know and how they act, and Žižek's key observation is that the way people talk and think often does not translate into any change in their actions. People may *think* critically, independently, and sceptically, but they still act in a way mediated by ideology.

Hopefully the relevance of this to my discussion of development is now clear: we can identify ideology operating not in what is said or even believed by development workers, but in how they *act*. Even though they may know the problem with their lifestyles, housing arrangements, 4WD jeeps, and imported foods, they still consume these things. Even though they know that logframes are crude devices for capturing reality, that their reports overemphasize success, and their targets prioritize numerical growth over subtlety and understanding, they do not change the way they act. Why? Because the whole arrangement can be justified in the name of development. 'Development' becomes the crucial and laudable end point, the ideological hook onto which all actions are hung. We consider our actions to be right because they correspond with the notion of development success, and we justify our large houses, jeeps, and logframes because they make us more effective at doing development work and meeting development targets.

Development is an excellent example of what Žižek calls a 'sublime object of ideology' (1989): it is an end point of ideology, which gives meaning to our actions and structure to our lives. 'Sublime objects' are grand ideas – like the nation, or God, or the economy, or development – which are perpetually invoked, but rarely defined or analysed. They are sublime because they are part of a fantasy that gives meaning to our life; they arrange our pleasure, our enjoyment, and are the end point of our aims and desires.[7] When we do things in the name of development, we are invoking something impossible to pin down, but something that structures what we see as valuable. Striving to achieve development gives our action meaning, and structures our world in deep and troubling ways.

Conclusion

In the context of this book, my argument moves beyond the identification of 'perverse incentives' in development, calling for greater attention to the way development workers interact with others. I believe we need to analyse the structured relationship between development workers and their 'beneficiaries' as well as the incentive structure of the aid chain. The task of this chapter has been to examine why rational management techniques persist, despite widespread acknowledgement of their limitations. To put the argument succinctly, these techniques persist because of the insulation of the developing classes. To put it more subtly, *ideology* plays the crucial role. But the argument is similar, in that development workers remain somehow blinkered in their activities, and captured by a structure that revolves around the transcendent position of development as a 'sublime object' in Žižek's sense.

As I stated in the introduction, one of the central problems for development critique is the lack of *systemic* analysis, the lack of attention to the structure as a whole. I believe that Žižek's approach is important here, because it applies not just to small issues – like examining the persistence of rational management techniques amongst development workers – but also on a more fundamental scale, providing the tools to bring Marxist ideas back into development studies more broadly. Since the decline of dependency theory in the 1980s, Marxist ideas have more or less been consigned to a wilderness in development, replaced by more deconstructionist 'post-development' paradigms that offer very few concrete alternatives for the activist. But Žižek's thought – and particularly his revival of ideology critique – helps us look afresh at the world of development. Žižek reminds us that we need to pay attention to the disconnection between what we say and what we do, between what we think and how we act. He reminds us to be wary when we justify concrete actions in the name of abstract concepts like 'development'. He warns us to beware if our actions aim at indistinct but seemingly laudable aims. And he reminds us to think critically about our private choices and lifestyles, demonstrating that the way we seek pleasure and enjoyment often supports the very social stratification and marginalization we oppose.

Notes

1. A very interesting articulation of these perspectives can be seen in a recent debate around Oxfam's swimming pool in Nairobi (http://oxfamblogs.org/fp2p/?p=8258).
2. This phrase is widely accepted in Lilongwe for a man of any age who lives on your property and helps with gardening and other domestic chores.
3. This, of course, was as much a fault of mine as anyone else's, given that it was an issue I never raised during my time in post.
4. Of course, the same individual can move from one position to the other: beneficiaries can become developers, and developers can become beneficiaries, but there is always a distinct relationship to the resources of development and the power dynamics associated with this.
5. For a vivid and amusing portrayal of the shared culture of aid workers, see the blog, 'Stuff Ex-Pat Aid Workers Like' – <http://stuffexpataidworkerslike.com>.
6. Žižek's notion of ideology is spelled out in his first, and most influential, translated book (1989), then expanded in his second (1991). Of more accessible introductions to his thought, perhaps the most useful as regards ideology, are Dean (2006), and Sharpe and Boucher (2010).
7. For Žižek the notion of *jouissance*, or enjoyment, is central to politics. The main influences on his thought are Marx, Hegel, and Lacan, and here, in the notion of unconscious drives and *jouissance*, the influence of Lacanian psychoanalysis appears particularly vividly.

References

Chambers, R. (1983) *Rural Development: Putting the Last First*, Wiley, New York.
Cohen, G. A. (2011) *On the Currency of Egalitarian Justice, and Other Essays in Political Philosophy*, Princeton University Press, Princeton.
Cooke, B. and Kothari, U. (eds) (2001) *Participation: The New Tyranny?* Zed Books, London.
Cornwall, A. and Eade, D. (2010) *Deconstructing Development Discourse: Buzzwords and Fuzzwords*, Practical Action, Rugby.
Dean, J. (2006) *Žižek's Politics*, Routledge, London.
Hulme, D. and Edwards, M. (eds) (1997) *NGOs, States and Donors: Too Close for Comfort?* Macmillan, London.
Mawdsley, E., Townsend, J., Porter, G. and Oakley, P. (2002) *Knowledge, Power and Development Agendas: NGOs North and South*, INTRAC, Oxford.
Mosse, D. and Lewis, D. (eds) (2005) *The Aid Effect: Giving and Governing in International Development*. Pluto, London.
Sharpe, M. and Boucher, G. (2010) *Žižek and Politics: A Critical Introduction*, Edinburgh University Press, Edinburgh.
Wallace, T., Bornstein, L. and Chapman, J. (2006) *The Aid Chain: Coercion and Commitment in Development NGOs*, ITDG, Warwick.
Žižek, S. (1989) *The Sublime Object of Ideology*, Verso, London.
Žižek, S. (1991) *For They Know Not What They Do: Enjoyment as a Political Factor*, Verso, London.

About the author

Tom Scott-Smith is a former development practitioner now completing a DPhil at the University of Oxford. His research examines the history of humanitarianism and applies critical theory to development institutions. He has worked across sub-Saharan Africa and the Middle East, and is currently writing a history of humanitarian technologies in nutrition, sanitation, and emergency shelter.

CHAPTER 8

Reconnecting development policy, people, and history

David Lewis

This chapter considers two important and interrelated problems within current development policy and practice. The first is the way policymakers focus predominantly on the 'perpetual present' of policy, in which terms and ideas are constantly reinvented and fashions followed, in ways that diminish the possibility of reviewing and learning from past experience. The second is the turn towards a highly technocratic and managerial version of development policy and practice. This has gradually shifted the focus of the work of development 'upstream', further than ever from people's everyday realities. Two examples are discussed from the context of Bangladesh – the story of the 1989–93 Flood Action Plan, a largely forgotten, failed, megaproject, and the ongoing Swedish International Development Cooperation Agency (Sida) Health and Education Reality Check project, which aims to try to better understand how large-scale health and education reforms are being experienced by ordinary people around the country who live in poverty.

The modern aid industry first took shape in the years after the end of the Second World War. Yet the opportunity to learn from more than six decades of experience appears to have become ever more elusive. The lessons (both positive and negative) that have emerged from the history of countless projects, operating concepts, and policy initiatives seem only rarely to have received attention from development professionals. Furthermore, as Western development policy has recently become more and more concerned with the management of aid resources, relationships, and impacts, so the lives of ordinary people in developing countries have, perhaps paradoxically, become even more remote from policymakers and development professionals. The 2000s saw the rise of new aid instruments such as direct budget support, sector wide approaches (SWAPs), and aid coordination and harmonization efforts that, while often well-intentioned, nevertheless contributed to a new concentration of administrative effort that took place far away from the everyday realities of peoples' lives at the grass roots.

Within this context this chapter attempts to explore two important (and related) problems within current development policy and practice. The first is the turn towards a heavily managerialist, technocratic activity within

http://dx.doi.org/10.3362/9781780447780/008

the organization of development agencies that has shifted the work of development 'upstream', with the result that people's grass-roots realities have become further and further away from the locus of activity and power. The second is the way that policymakers within the aid industry are conditioned to operate in an ahistorical way. They tend to ignore history, and the lessons that it might provide, in favour of what might be termed the 'perpetual present' of policy (Lewis, 2009). These problems are directly relevant to the challenges of improving the way development work is undertaken. However, such issues have received comparatively little attention in recent discussions about the relevance and effectiveness of development intervention. They illustrate the need to find ways to reconnect people, policy, and history in order to establish that the needs and priorities of the poorest should be at the centre of efforts to address development problems.

Decontextualization, history, and learning

The past decade has seen the emergence of what has come to be termed 'the new architecture of aid' in which projects have been moved away from the centre of aid priorities in favour of good governance and policy reform. The emphasis has been on privatization, economic liberalization, and the increased use of market mechanisms to bring about growth and greater efficiency (Mosse, 2005). Although 'poverty reduction' has been stated to be at the centre of these approaches, it has generally come to be framed more in terms of the impersonal language of indicators – such as the United Nations Millennium Development Goals – than in terms of human experience and perception. The idea of making an effort to engage more fully with social experience from the participants' point of view – embodied, for example, in the 'humanistic' tradition of social science described and advocated by Plummer (1983) – surfaced briefly in the World Bank's *Voices of the Poor* study (Narayan et al., 1999), but has rarely been brought centre stage within mainstream development donor priorities or activities.

Neoliberal policy orthodoxy has increasingly come to dominate thinking about development, but it is also, of course, increasingly at the centre of many other aspects of social and economic life. Trends in the world of development are part of wider changes in the ways Western societies are organized. At the organizational level, the ideology of managerialism is rife. The logical framework approach to planning has long been the orthodoxy and it has more recently been joined by the idea of results-based management. While I was visiting Bangladesh during early 2012, I learned from DfID staff that they must now prepare their proposals for development interventions as 'business plans'. This ideology of managerialism pushes a relentless emphasis on novelty and change. Power (1997) has drawn attention to the 'rituals of verification' associated with the rise of a measurement and audit culture. Such effects form part of the wider dominance of ideologies of manageri-alism within the worlds of development agencies (Roberts et al., 2005). The organizational characteristics of development agencies, and the human resource management strategies that they adopt, both contribute to an exacerbation of the problem. For example, short-term expatriate staff tend to be appointed by agencies for postings of two or three years only, making it hard for them to gain in-depth knowledge of context and distil lessons from their experiences, or for agencies to preserve their institutional memories and learn from them.[1] The bureaucratic logic within many agencies also tends to create incentives for a new appointee to a particular position to show their effectiveness by deliberately downplaying the ideas and work of their immediate predecessor, and beginning new work as a way to demonstrate their own particular 'added value'.[2] The result may be the unnecessary development of new initiatives, terms, and approaches in a process that further contributes to the suppression of past experiences and restricted learning.

In the world of development policy, all this has reinforced a set of ahistorical tendencies. Development terms and intervention ideas are constantly being reinvented, leading to new development fashions that may be slavishly followed for a few years until new ones take their place. The language of projects has turned into that of programmes, donors have become partners, and these days country 'ownership' is increasingly emphasized. All this diminishes the possibility of reviewing and learning from past experience, wider history, and local knowledge. In discouraging engagement with the past through an emphasis on novelty and change, a decontextualization of practice takes place. Ideas or practices that originally might have had radical meaning and implications become assimilated into the mainstream and drained of their original power. For example, Cornwall and Brock (2005: 243) analyse how 'development buzzwords' such as 'empowerment', 'participation', and 'poverty reduction' help maintain 'the imagined, decontextualized world of the consensus narrative'. The result is that the history of previous policy is only poorly remembered, if at all. At the same time, the career trajectories of short-term international aid agency staff, in which they are moved between countries in two- or three-year cycles, work against preserving 'institutional memory' within agencies. This contributes to the unhelpful phenomenon that Sogge (1996: 16) terms 'the continuity of discontinuity'. He argues that development agencies are often rewarded simply for 'being active', and points out that that they can 'just keep moving'. For example, Northern NGOs may simply make sustainability someone else's problem by ending a project or partnership process and leaving matters in the hands of local 'partners' like the children of 'unwed mothers'.

This ideology insists on what is at best a limited sense of historical perspective, and at its worst an active suppression of historical depth and distance. It resonates with James Scott's (1998: 95) analysis of 'high modernism' in which, he argues, 'the past is an impediment, a history that must be transcended' and that 'the present is the platform for launching plans for a better future'. The future-centred stance of high modernism is therefore an important part of its ideological purpose and operation. The consequences are also felt at the level of larger scale donor projects and interventions. For example, Rachel Wrangham's ethnography (2004) of a project in Mozambique illustrated well how project staff became strongly focused on imagined views of the future, obscuring discussion of important political and institutional continuities with the past. She argued that the project design paid insufficient attention to three important sets of historical factors: a comparatively recent civil war, local perceptions of outsiders, and livelihood diversity. She concludes that 'ignoring history' (ibid. 124) led project staff to develop an apolitical analysis of the reasons for rural poverty and, as a result, a set of inappropriate objectives for the agricultural component of the project.

These problems are related to broader changes that go beyond the development industry. In examining wider trends of modernity, the historian Eric Hobsbawm (1994) has also commented on the way that the past is not simply ignored but also actively suppressed or dismantled:

> The destruction of the past, or rather of the social mechanisms that link one's contemporary experience to that of earlier generations, is one of the most characteristic and eerie phenomena of the late twentieth century.

The expansion of communications technology and new media, such as the rolling news phenomenon, for example, can be seen as part of this process. Every hour, each new item of news immediately 'overwrites' the previous one, making historical perspective narrow, collapsing into what feels like permanent present time. The result is what postmodern theorist Frederick Jameson (1998) has termed an ahistorical 'perpetual present':

> The disappearance of a sense of history, the way in which our entire contemporary social system has little by little begun to lose its capacity to retain its own past, has begun to live in a perpetual present and in a perpetual change that obliterates traditions of the kind which all earlier social formations have had in one way or another to preserve.

In the following sections, two cases are briefly discussed from Bangladesh. The first is the Bangladesh Flood Action Plan (FAP), a largely forgotten, failed, flood control project from the 1980s that spent US$5–10 billion on hundreds of technical studies and river embankment infrastructure construction. This example is used to illustrate the problem of lack of learning from the past in the context of today's debates on climate change, where there is a pressing need to learn from and ultimately avoid repeating previous, largely top-down, attempts to control Bangladesh's river systems. The second is the Sida Health and Education Reality Check project in Bangladesh. This experimental initiative is a 'listening study' in which specially trained field workers stay with households each year to record their views and experiences. The aim of the project is to learn in more direct ways exactly how ongoing large-scale health and education reforms are being understood and experienced by ordinary people living in poverty. By trying to bridge these voices with upstream policymakers, the project aims to reconnect people's voices to the policy process, and to 'humanize' policy processes by putting faces and voices to facts and figures.

Repeating the past? The FAP case

In Bangladesh there have long been concerns about flood control, and these have regularly attracted attention from government in the form of proposals for large-scale flood prevention schemes. For example, the British colonial authorities commissioned many large-scale public works in the struggle to manage rivers and embankments (Iqbal, 2007). When Bangladesh was known as East Pakistan, another major initiative was undertaken in the form of the 1964 'Master Plan' funded by USAID and the World Bank, drawn up after serious flooding had occurred during 1954–6 (Adnan, 2000). During the late 1980s, after two decades of relative neglect, international donors once again became interested in flood control. There were disastrous and well-publicized floods during 1987 and 1988. Environmentalists at that time linked increased flooding to growing Himalayan soil erosion brought about by deforestation upstream in the mountains of Nepal. The country's long-standing 'flood problem' suddenly became a donor priority and high-profile international cause. This renewal of attention to Bangladesh's flood problem was widely credited to reports that Madame Mitterrand, the wife of the French President who had been visiting Dhaka during the floods, had noticed water coming under her hotel door (Boyce, 1990).

During what was to be the final year of the authoritarian government of Gen. H. M. Ershad in 1989, a large, multi-donor project that became known as the Flood Action Plan (FAP) was designed. A communiqué was issued from the July G-7 summit stating:

> Bangladesh ... is periodically devastated by catastrophic floods ... [There is] ... need for effective, coordinated action by the international community, in support of the Government of Bangladesh, in order to find solutions to this major problem which are technically, financially, economically, and technically sound. (World Bank 1989: 23, quoted in Adnan, 1991: 8)

FAP was formally approved in May 1990. It included a total of 26 studies and pilot schemes, 11 'main' components, and 15 'supportive' components. The aim was to construct embankments along Bangladesh's three main rivers. The French government joined with Japan, UNDP, and USAID to engage a wide range of foreign experts, including engineers and later social scientists, to devise flood prevention and control schemes. FAP was a mega-project designed to be one of the largest development projects ever undertaken.

However, FAP became controversial for four main sets of reasons. First, the top-down manner in which the plan took shape at a London meeting under World Bank leadership led to questions about accountability and consultation. The donors had not considered earlier flood control measures when finalizing FAP, nor had they held public consultations (Adnan, 1991). When the Ershad government fell in late 1990, a new interim government led by Justice Shahabuddin took power. A new government FAP Task Force set up in February 1991 reported on these concerns and now set about fostering public debate.

Second, FAP's primarily technical emphasis on engineering solutions to problems of floods, based mainly on the construction of embankments and sluice gates, paid little attention to the potential of 'softer' people-centred solutions, drawing on past traditions of community management of floods, to build upon the generations of local experience of dealing with the problem. FAP also seemed unaware of the likely political and administrative complexity of managing such infrastructure equitably. Conflicts of interest quickly appeared within government and donor bureaucracies, and within foreign consultancy teams. As a result, international opposition began to mobilize: for example, the US International Rivers Network argued that intervening in a powerful regional river system would actually worsen the incidence of floods (Custers, 1993). Others contributed to the discussion older experiences from the colonial period. Building river embankments was known to seriously threaten local agricultural productivity and to hasten the deterioration of rivers (Iqbal, 2007). Kolkata-based Professor Prasanta C. Mahalanobis's study of the 1922 North Bengal floods had reported that embankments tended to worsen floods because they raised the levels of the riverbeds (Adnan, 2000).

Third, the project relied predominantly on donor expertise gained from 'exotic' contexts such as the Netherlands and Mississippi, both out of step with Bangladesh's own distinctive ecology. At a technical level, problems also quickly became apparent, with experts failing to understand the complexity of Bangladesh's environment and natural resource systems. For example, the view of Bangladesh in the 1970s as a 'basket case' unable to feed its people was challenged during the 1990s when the rapid intensification of smallholder agricultural production brought the country close to food self-sufficiency (Bradnock and Saunders, 2002).

Fourth, FAP soon began to dominate development activities in Bangladesh. Hundreds of preliminary studies were commissioned to consider a wide range of water-related issues around the country, engaging large numbers of local and expatriate researchers, consultants, and administrators, and drawing them away from work on other equally important issues. Development in Bangladesh, it seemed, had now become subordinated to the central problem of flood control.

By 1993 FAP had fizzled out. An embankment system in Dhaka and another one built in Tangail were the only tangible results of what was to have been a government and donor showcase project. There were by now hundreds of consultants' studies that cluttered the shelves of government and donor offices. Contestation from within local communities, such as the well-documented protests in Beel Dakatia, contributed to the growing international anti-FAP mobilization by a range of groups (Adnan, 2000). Expert knowledge was by now under challenge by local voices and local community memories, ultimately forcing those in power to reconsider and perhaps finally to engage with history. As Wood (1999) points out, the FAP had been a contestation over water resources in which little or no space had been given to ordinary people in relation either to problem diagnosis or to the design of policy solutions. A key lesson was therefore that privileging the 'expert knowledge' of engineers, bureaucrats, and development specialists was a poor substitute for an engagement with local communities, institutions, and indigenous knowledge. Yet today's elevation of the climate change agenda by donors into a central position within development policy in Bangladesh seems set to begin this process all over again. Already there is talk of ill-conceived large-scale infrastructural responses to flooding, and a new rising tide of community-level protests in response to top-down policy planning (Lewis, 2011).

Listening to people? The Sida Reality Check

The Reality Check is an initiative established by Sida in 2007 as a way of using ethnographic participant observation to learn more about how local people experience sector policy reforms. In Bangladesh, billions of dollars of international donor money have been invested in attempts to improve basic services through major health and education sector-wide reforms. The US$3.5 billion Health, Nutrition and Population Sector Programme (2004–10) and the US$1.8 billion Second Primary Education Development Programme (2003–10) were flagship sector-wide approach (SWAP) initiatives. This initiative has been trying to address the challenge of monitoring outcomes on the ground through connecting directly with people's perceptions and experiences. Field teams visit and spend quality time with ordinary households who live in poverty in different parts of the country, and try to understand – through listening – whether these health and education sector reform programmes are actually working. The teams spend five days and four nights living with some of the poorest families, listening to their stories and helping to document their experiences. A distinctive aspect of the approach is that it is household-centred. The approach makes it a priority to engage each of the members in conversation to ensure that voices not usually heard – such as those of children, older people, and women – are listened to properly. Each year these conversations and observations are written up in an annual report for policymakers and the reports are widely circulated. The following year, the teams return to the same households and update the stories.[3]

Some of the findings that emerge each year are already known and contribute further to the knowledge base. But many are new, providing potentially useful information to policymakers to take action on, or opening up new issues for further monitoring or research within the programmes. Some are good news stories. For example, parents continue to believe in the value of gaining an education for their children, and in working hard to try to make it happen.

People tell us that traditional birth attendants and untrained pharmacists often do a good job meeting basic health needs, even when local conditions are harsh and few resources are available. When effective leadership exists at a local school or health centre, people say, and our observations confirm, that this makes an enormous difference in the performance of such facilities. But with only a rudimentary public health and education system in place that struggles to meet people's basic needs, the reality check approach (RCA) reminds programme officials that there is much that still needs to be done. For example, while Bangladesh now boasts near universal primary education levels, quality remains low. The government has begun emphasizing a new culture of 'joyful learning' to try to improve quality, but the atmosphere in many classrooms remains uninspiring.

In view of the household-centred methodology used, there is a wide range of useful gender insights from the RCA. For example, boys in particular say they get little from classes in terms of relevance and engagement. Despite many parents' determination to send boys to school, many become tempted to truant or to drop out altogether. When it comes to health care, despite recent large-scale investments, public hospitals and clinics seem to perform very poorly. People report that they are unpopular because they have very few useful services to offer and they impose informal charges on people who try to gain access. Many women report that they prefer home births with a traditional birth attendant whom they know, and are frightened by the prospect of hospital deliveries. Doctors point out the lack of cleanliness that exists in many public hospitals, and they confirm that home births are often safer. Public health facilities are in some cases only places for people to go to collect supplies of free, often unneeded, drugs such as high strength antibiotics.

One important way that the RCA challenges current policy norms is that it offers a stark reminder of the high level of agency demonstrated by people living in poverty and the need to try to harness more of this energy. The reports each year speak of households constantly strategizing on how to improve their position as best they can, and trying to make things work for them, however imperfect the options they face. For example, many people struggle to piece together a viable system of services to meet their needs – using whatever public, private, non-governmental, and informal providers they can access. This patchwork approach makes it possible for many to survive, but it is far from adequate. The RCA aims to convey this grass-roots information 'up' to programme officials and policymakers quickly, so that they can either take action and make course corrections, or, if they wish, investigate the issue in more depth using conventional monitoring, evaluation, or research. For example, informants regularly report their dislike of the ineffective and bureaucratic school stipends system, and support is now gathering for extending preferred school feeding programmes.

The RCA work has potentially important implications for wider development policy. For example, in the face of weakly performing public service systems, how do we reform them more effectively, and how do we better regulate private and non-governmental providers to help strengthen provision? It also reminds us of the potential dangers of development policy becoming too 'technocratic', inflexible, and distant from the everyday worlds of ordinary people. Although the 2005 Paris Declaration on Aid Effectiveness may have helped to bring better coordination among international donors and greater efforts to foster local ownership of reform processes, it has also moved policy-making further 'upstream', and away from people. Simply asking people how they see things, and taking time to engage with each member of a household in detail and depth, is one way to begin closing some of this distance.

As a new form of 'listening study', the RCA therefore aims to offer a way to reconnect people and policies. Yet in practice the RCA has also shown how difficult it is to get the attention of policymakers. The work highlights, in stark terms, the 'disjuncture' between the upstream discourses and assumptions of development agencies, and the everyday lives and experiences of people who are poor. Many donor and government staff report to us that the reports are not like the statistical studies or evaluations that they are used to, and therefore that they are not 'usable'. The material in the reports also challenges some of the assumptions held dear by donors. For example, while rights-based development is at the heart of Sida's stated principles, each year the voices in the RCA describe the sense of powerlessness experienced by people who are quite unable to register their dissatisfaction with the quality of health services through the totally unusable 'citizen charter' placed on the hospital wall, or unwilling to risk fragile status and livelihoods by participating in a fledgling parent–teacher association to question the quality of local education provision. Reading programme literature, one could easily get a rosier picture of the rights of the poor than actually exists. The RCA also highlights the worrying gap between the type of impersonal information being collected within sector programme monitoring systems and the subjective experiences of those people who try to use services. One programme staff member confidentially observed:

> The monitoring system concentrates mainly on gathering information on financial monitoring and budgetary information and other performance indicators. The type of information contained in the Reality Check reports is not currently available to us. (sector programme staff member, personal communication)

Despite the complex management information systems put in place to provide information to guide the large sector reform programmes, the RCA seems to show up existing information systems as unwieldy, difficult to access, or out of touch with ground realities.

Conclusion

Robert Chambers has recently set out some challenging thoughts and ideas. In a section in which he wryly offers some 'assertions to tempt you or turn you off', he sets out a list of assertions among which the following seem particularly apposite:

- The realities of poor people around the globe are changing ever faster ...
- Powerful professionals are increasingly out of touch with the realities of poor people ...
- Development practice is in perpetual tension between a dominant paradigm of things and a subordinate paradigm of people. (Chambers, 2012)

Each of these assertions needs, of course, to be further debated across different contexts where they may or may not be found to apply. But these problems of professional distance – both from ordinary people and from the lessons of the past – are highly relevant to the context of contemporary Bangladesh, where development policy and practice seems to be moving further and further away from the realities of ordinary people and towards an increasingly silent world of development policy history. Perhaps now is a particularly good time to engage with what anthropologist Paul Connerton calls 'types of structural forgetting which are specific to the culture of modernity' (2009: 2). We need to decide now whether we wish to continue unlearning the past or whether we wish to learn from it. There is no simple way to learn from the past, as historians are fond of reminding us, but nor does it make sense to close off the potential benefits that might come from engaging more fully with historical knowledge in relation to development policy and practice.

Notes

1. As Tom Scott-Smith (2013) argues in Chapter 7 of this volume, development professionals also increasingly live in heavily 'closed off' worlds, isolated from others.
2. See Ashish Shah in Chapter 15 of this volume on the issue of 'making a mark' in an organization.
3. See http://reality-check-approach.com for more details, and to access the full text of each of the five Sida Bangladesh Reality Check reports produced to date. The author is an adviser to the project, but writes here in a personal capacity.

References

Adnan, S. (1991) *Floods, People and the Environment: Institutional Aspects of Flood Protection Programmes in Bangladesh, 1990*, Research and Advisory Services, Dhaka.

Adnan, S. (2000) 'Explaining the retreat from flood control in the Ganges-Brahmaputra-Meghna Delta of Bangladesh', unpublished paper, South Asian Studies Programme, National University of Singapore.

Boyce, J. K. (1990) 'Birth of a mega-project: political economy of flood control in Bangladesh', *Environmental Management* 14: 419–28.

Bradnock, R. W. and Saunders, P. (2002) 'Rising waters, sinking land? Environmental change and development in Bangladesh', in R. W. Bradnock and G. Williams (eds), *South Asia in a Globalizing World: A Reconstructed Regional Geography*, pp. 51–77, Pearson Education, Harlow, UK.

Chambers, R. (2012) *Provocations for Development*. Practical Action Publishing, Rugby.

Connerton, P (2009) *How Modernity Forgets*, Cambridge University Press, Cambridge.

Cornwall, A and Brock, K. (2005) 'What do buzzwords do for development policy? A critical look at "participation", "empowerment" and "poverty reduction"', *Third World Quarterly* 26: 1043–60.

Custers, P. (1993) 'Bangladesh's flood action plan: a critique', *Economic and Political Weekly*, 28, 29/30 (July 17–24): 1501–03.

Hobsbawm, E. (1994) *The Age of Extremes: The Short Twentieth Century, 1914–1991*, Allen Lane, London.

Iqbal, I. (2007) 'The railways and the water regime of the Eastern Bengal Delta, c1845–1943', *Internationales Asienforum*, 38: 329–52.

Jameson, F. (1998) *The Cultural Turn: Selected Writings on the Postmodern, 1983–1998*, Verso, London.

Lewis, D. (2009) 'International development and the "perpetual present": anthropological approaches to the rehistoricisation of policy', *European Journal of Development Research*, 21: 32–46.

Lewis, D. (2011) *Bangladesh: Politics, Economy and Civil Society*, Cambridge University Press, Cambridge.

Mosse, D (2005) 'Global governance and the ethnography of international aid', in D. Mosse and D. Lewis (eds), *The Aid Effect*, pp. 1–36, Pluto, London.

Narayan, D. with Patel, R., Schafft, K., Rademacher, A. and Koch-Schulte, S. (1999) *Can Anyone Hear Us? Voices from 47 Countries*, Vol. 1 of World Bank *Voices of the Poor* study, World Bank, Washington, DC.

Plummer, K. (1983) *Documents of Life*, Unwin, London.

Power, M. (1997) *The Audit Society*, Oxford University Press, Oxford.

Roberts, S. M., Jones, J. P. and Frohling, O. (2005) 'NGOs and the globalization of managerialism', *World Development* 33: 1845–64.

Scott, J. C. (1998) *Seeing Like A State: How Certain Schemes to Improve the Human Condition Have Failed*, Yale University Press, New Haven, CT.

Scott-Smith, T. (2013) 'Insulating the developing classes', in T. Wallace and F. Porter (eds), *Aid, NGOs and the Realities of Women's Lives*, pp. 101–113, Practical Action Publishing, Rugby.

Shah, A. (2013) 'I don't know ... and related thoughts', in T. Wallace and F. Porter (eds), *Aid, NGOs and the Realities of Women's Lives*, pp. 199–211, Practical Action Publishing, Rugby.

Sogge, D. (1996) 'Settings and choices', in D. Sogge, with K. Biekart and J. Saxby (eds), *Compassion and Calculation: The Business of Private Foreign Aid*, pp. 1–23, Pluto Press, London.

Wood, G. D. (1999) 'Contesting water in Bangladesh: knowledge, rights and governance', *Journal of International Development*, 11: 731–54.

World Bank (1989) *Bangladesh Action Plan for Food Control*, World Bank, Washington, DC.

Wrangham, R. (2004) *Negotiating Meaning and Practice in the Zambezia Agricultural Development Project, Mozambique*, unpublished PhD thesis, London School of Economics.

About the author

David Lewis is professor of social policy and development at the London School of Economics and Political Science. An anthropologist by training, he has worked mainly in South Asia and specialized in international development policy and the role of non-governmental organizations. He has published *Bangladesh: Politics, Economy and Civil Society* (Cambridge University Press, 2011).

PART II
Changing conversations

CHAPTER 9

Taking our lead from reality – an open practice for social development

David Harding

This chapter suggests that the way of engagement with the world that has increasingly come to dominate in social development work – with its hard technical and instrumental ground – is a wrong and inappropriate model for the social field. But it is one deeply rooted in Western ways of seeing and engaging with reality, and one that we find it difficult to see beyond. The chapter explores a radically different way of being for social development work based on an open, responsive practice, presenting both key ideas and illustrations from the author's own practice. Rather than seeking to engineer the world into our own simplistic formulations, an open practice allows divergent realities to speak with their own voice, in their own language. It provides a basis for a respectful, adaptive engagement in our work through coming to an understanding with others.

Over the past 15 years I have both run and taken part in hundreds of small group, open conversations around questions facing people in their work in the social development field – with teams in organizations, with cross-organizational groups, and with groups in learning and academic programmes. I have worked in this way in regions and cultures as divergent and different as Central and Eastern Europe, West Africa, Southern and Eastern Africa, Latin America and the UK. This has become an important way of working for me.

Why is this so? What can this 'small-scale' work give to participants? And what helps make these open conversations effective?

'*Small* group' does mean small. Between 4 and 8 participants seems optimal. Everyone can be fully and actively engaged in the conversation.

The ground for the conversation needs to be the *concrete living experience* of someone or some people in the group. Invariably this experience will be a rich situation presenting many questions, where the presenters are struggling with their understanding, and how best to act. Work on the ground, management, strategy, working relationships – the content can be varied but is always this active, present, challenging work experience.

This is enough to generate an intense and engaging conversation. No further structuring of the path of the conversation is required. Once going, it is

http://dx.doi.org/10.3362/9781780447780/009

allowed to develop and run, going where it goes. No prior guiding framework, or pre-set range of questions is needed or helpful.

But what is meant by *open* conversation here? It is a conversation that stays open to all possibilities, does not rush to judgement or closure. It works with a mutual exchange of questions and views – listening to, responding to, and building on what others say – to describe and explore deeply the concrete situation. Just that allows us to get to know the situation in all its complexity and subtlety and from different perspectives.

We work with an approach to time that is provocatively, radically, different from the usual tight management and highly structured use of time. We allow more than enough time to naturally exhaust a conversation (although this is often different to concluding around the situation). And we do not pre-structure our way into the time allowed. Time here is an inviting empty opportunity – time *pressures* do not weigh down. The focus is more on the quality of the *journey*, than on some final thing we are 'getting to'.

And, yet, in this work, the participants do indeed 'get somewhere', usually a much richer shared understanding of the situation – a deeper, more global and subtle sense of what is going on overall. Often there is a very significant shift in understanding – a 're-framing' of the situation. This richer understanding often unlocks a different sense of the potential in the situation. There *will* then emerge some immediate sense of how to respond to, or engage differently with, this situation – though this will often be expressed more as 'we might *try* this' rather than a hard action plan.

There is an interesting energy in many of these conversations – they really engage participants. People stay alert. There can be a quiet but intense feel to the work as the story builds and dips off into side stories and new strands to explore. There are often moments of heightened attention when people sense a significant shift in understanding here, or when a particularly difficult aspect is being talked about at another point.

As well as the immediate, alive feel to the process and the immediate 'results' coming out of these conversations, many people notice, over time, something else. Many note – very sharply and positively – how different it feels to how they normally work. How surprising it is to get such depth on a situation in such a short engagement. How much they learn from others' experiences, and how much they get from others' open questions in this empathic but quietly challenging process. And, most powerfully, how these simple processes somehow *do* take them to the real practice heart of their work and its challenges. These differences from their normal work-fare can also, however, often feel disconcerting (destabilizing) and uncomfortable.

I have noticed and felt the same in this work, and come to realize a change in how I now see it. When first working in this way I saw this approach as another (but effective) means of 'getting somewhere' – reading a situation better, getting good agreement, effecting learning. But reflecting on the practice over time I realized that this way of working also offered, in a microcosmic way, something as radical as a different 'way of being' in our engagement with the world, and our particular current concerns in that world. A way of being that rubbed up very uncomfortably with the dominant way of being that many of my small group colleagues, across many different situations in the social development field, were increasingly having to work with.

While we were, for many years, absorbed in our intense but energized conversations around our tables, there was a growing, rumbling noise from outside of a very different approach to engagement.

The prominence of a particular technical-rational model

Over recent years (as many other chapters in this book bear witness) work in the field of social development has increasingly come under the close influence of a particular technical-rational and bureaucratic approach to development management and practice.

Both inside our organizations and in our engagement out with others, our daily work has been ever more tightly shaped and comprehensively covered by this approach. Every step taken, from senior management to field level, is supposed to be guided by and filtered through prescriptive systems, frameworks, and procedures. Work paths into the future are pre-set into frameworks and plans, tagged with objectives, indicators, and performance targets. We are guided by comprehensive manuals and toolkits. We report into pre-established frameworks and categories, against the targets and objectives agreed. Our own work and our very working relations are targeted, measured, and reviewed within similar frameworks.

If there are underlying premises to this now dominant approach they are the need to aspire to *control* the external world, and events in it, through our work, and the need to have a strong degree of future certainty around our path forward in that world. These needs can be achieved through tight, measured planning into the future – modelling the future we want to achieve – and detailed micro-management of subsequent activities to get to our pre-set goal. This is the 'path to an effective result'. And although this trend originated in Western institutions we now find it extended globally as a conditional element in the provision of social development resources.

This approach presents a tough, confident face to the world, very sure of its ground and language, confident in its objective 'grounding', and tough in holding people to the rules and procedures. It is an approach that seems certain of itself and is looking for certainty in its work.

And yet so much of our daily, lived, working experience, and some cursory critical reading around the human sciences, brings a firm message that this 'model' – despite its self-confidence – is simply neither effective nor appropriate for working in the complex, ever shifting, highly relational field of social development.

In his survey of the history of high modernist social projects, James Scott notes that these 'thin simplistic formulations' (Scott, 1998: 309) of the rational-technical model are always inadequate as a basis for *effective practice*.

The formal structures they produce are 'always and to some considerable degree parasitic on *informal processes*, which the formal scheme does not recognise, without which it could not exist, and which it alone cannot create or maintain' (ibid. 310).

Donald Schon, writing in the 1990s on 'reflective practice', similarly questioned the fundamental appropriateness of a rational-technical approach to social questions:

> Technical rationality holds that practitioners are instrumental problem solvers who select technical means best suited to particular purposes. Rigorous professional practitioners solve well formed problems by applying theory and technique derived from systematic, preferably scientific knowledge ... But, as we have come to see with increasing clarity ... the problems of real world practice do not present themselves to practitioners as well formed structures. Indeed they tend not to present themselves as problems at all but as messy, indeterminate situations. (Schon, 1991: 93)

And critics from a variety of perspectives have driven a convincing stake through the heart of the rational-technical position that it is somehow viable or effective to base your model for action on the possibility of accurate, tight, causal projection into the future. Scott again: 'if the only certainty about the future is that the future is uncertain, if the only sure thing is that we are in for surprises, then no amount of planning, no amount of prescription, can deal with the contingencies that the future will reveal' (Scott, 1998: 344).[1]

The reality we face in our day-to-day *practice* in social development work is always more white water rafting than building a railway track across known and placid terrain. We need therefore to have our eye on what is moving and changing – the surprises, shifts, and unforeseen consequences of our and others' actions and responses. We must be prepared to adapt, to work constantly with relations with others – across gulfs of power and culture, and in politically and socially contested contexts. We must work with our own local relations and teams in our organizations – and the challenge of managing bright, highly committed staff in social sector organizations often draws the well-known phrase 'herding cats'.

To navigate these difficult and surprising waters with insight, equanimity, and compassion, we need fully rounded, fully human qualities, skills, and responsive, skilful ways of engaging – difficult to define at times but easy to recognize in action. Here Scott's 'informal processes' at work and Schon's 'artistry' in reflective practice become central to an *effective practice* in this social field.

For the rational-technical proponent these informal, skilful processes are a foreign land. We are in 'soft' territory outside the technical domain. When it comes to reading and making meaning of dynamic social situations, the rational-technical approach falls far short. It has its 'phrase books' – its list of pre-set questions for organizational assessments, surveys, etc. – but these standardized frameworks cut across our being able to listen properly to the real, ever-changing news from the ground. Our own noise – our heavy load of assumptions and pre-determined positions – jams the more subtle and difficult-to-entice voices that speak of emerging newness, of what is not working, and of the relational challenges brewing in the work situation.

On relational working itself, the rational-technical has little to say. Having worked so hard to get the volatile 'subjective' human elements out of its game, it has no language or way of engaging with this central concern.

And this approach, despite being all about *effecting change* towards our goals, has no praxis for engaging with change as it happens, of recognizing and working with the new *as it emerges*. It can only advise – as we look in dismay at the now irrelevant and wrecked structure of the initial tight, certain plan for the future – that we cook up another speculative framework, with another idealized mix of hard measurable goals, tight track of implementation, and key performance indicators.

Why, though, do we persist in working with these 'thin, simplistic' frameworks, which then come to dominate our work-space and time? Why do we indeed often voluntarily embrace them as good practice? Could we not more productively employ our time paying more attention to developing and practising our 'informal processes', and our reading of, and skilful adaptation to, newness and change in our work situations?

The short answer for many organizations working in social development is you do not survive if you do not comply. Many of these frameworks and models and their assumptions have been brought in as conditional requirements by the major institutional players in this field, who in the past decade have increasingly aligned in both ideology and practice around development management. For them these methods respond to important bureaucratic and political needs (as James Scott so clearly demonstrates); in the modern bureaucratic institution, control over work and control out into the world are primary drivers. And mistrust of both its own people and the outside world is seemingly a strong characteristic of the modernist institution. Over the past 20 years many social development organizations have become more and more dependent on large institution funding and are in a weak place to challenge or resist what they may still inwardly see as an unhelpful path.

There is, however, a possible longer and deeper answer. In the Western world we seem to have got caught in a deeply embedded, narrow perspective on how to engage with the world. We seem to want a definitive language that will provide a universal, objective knowledge base for work. For the social field, we seem to think we have found this language by importing the certainties of a nineteenth-century natural sciences language (ironically at the same time as the natural sciences begin to talk of 'uncertainty principles', 'chaos', and 'complexity'). Even older Western thinking leaves us attached to the idea that we must model some ideal path into the future (to know where we are going), and act forcefully to get there, if we are to be effective players in the world.[2]

In an article that explores these questions, the Canadian philosopher Charles Taylor suggests that it is precisely here that the 'whole model of (Western social) science is wrong and inappropriate' (Taylor, 2002: 126).

For the social sciences (as opposed to the natural sciences) human meaning is at the heart of the game. Claims to have developed a 'universal', 'final', and 'objective' language in a world of very different human cultures and languages, and thus a world of often deeply contested positions and understandings, are hard to sustain intellectually, and much harder to gain agreement around in practice. Taylor suggests we pick up on the work of the phenomenologist Hans-Georg Gadamer, who suggests that an appropriate ground for knowledge for the social sciences can be found rather in 'coming to an understanding' (ibid.) with others.

Coming to an understanding with others, though, involves a type of relationship with people, situations, and texts that 'can never have this finality' (ibid. 127) of the Western pretension. It is an exercise of *mutual* active engagement and representation of views. Different people, faced with the same situation, will present different understandings to us. Different situations will challenge *our* understandings derived from *our* own experience. Any under-standing we or others hold may change over time as the situation, anyone's own understanding, or the context changes. Surprise and 'talking back' are just part of the game in play. This field of engagement, full of rich differences, gives us the beauty and the challenge of engagement in the human world, and provides a source of constant renewal of understanding and action. There is never a 'universal', 'final', 'objective' ground, or language, or, indeed, any persisting certainty.

The modernist technical-rational, managerial approach, and its underlying understanding of how we engage with the world, has left us in the development field in a dangerous mess. It provides a working model not fit for purpose; a model that does not give us an appropriate ground to work with complex social situations and processes, or change, or encompass the relational threads so deeply woven through work in the social field – a detached, cold model, wary of a fully human language and practice. This model asks us to spend most of our daily energy in managing for an unrealizable tight control of reality, on a basis of an ungrounded mistrust. Yet it seems to be a way of engaging with the world that we in the West find it difficult to see beyond, and one we have aggressively exported across the world.

A different way of being?

If we were looking for a different way of being in our work in development, where might we look for guidance and inspiration? We do not need to start from scratch.

Over the past hundred years, broad currents of critical *praxis* have developed in response to the dominant trend in Western thinking and way of being in the world. Critical developments in philosophy and in particular phenomenological thinking, radical and humanist developments in psychology and psychotherapy (for example, in the work of Eric Fromm and Gestalt therapy), insights from the 'new sciences', and inspiration provided by many global social movements and grass-roots practitioners offer the possibility of a different ground for understanding and practice. Older expositions of praxis have found a renewed recognition and reception – the Buddhist practice of 'skilful means'; J W Goethe's 'delicate empiricism', for example. Amidst all the subtle differences of language and practice some common threads light up a different way of being, and illustrate just how different it is.

If the dominant path in Western thinking has sought to grasp the world into its own categories and render the world into its own language, common to many of these different approaches is a sense of the importance of coming to an understanding with reality *on its own terms, in its own varied languages.* As a core statement from the phenomenological tradition has noted, the intention is:

> To let the situation (itself, actors in it) 'which shows itself be seen from itself in the very way in which it shows itself from itself.' (Moran and Mooney, 2002: 284)

This asks that we work with 'a certain disposition of patient attention towards the world ... not annexing it, exploiting it or ransacking it for congenial meanings' (McGilchrist, 2009: 151). It asks that we come to a situation with an ability and willingness to be radically open to what presents. This is a process of patient, gentle exploration to uncover and know the situation, and others' understanding of it, in its own terms.

To be truly open here, however, means that we must not only be able to hear and see the other, the situation, as it presents to us, in its own voice, but that we can allow ourselves to be moved (in all senses), to be jostled, to be surprised into a new understanding. As Charles Taylor suggests, 'the slogan might be – no understanding the other without a changed understanding of self' (2002: 141).

In coming to an understanding in this way we must engage with lived experience first-hand – with that immediate thick, local experience in each situation. To allow us best to engage with what is, as it is, we enter the field with a minimum of pre-prepared method and framing. We dispense with our usual baggage of familiar filters, lenses, and expectations.

We are active, reflexive agents; we interpret and make meaning of what we hear. We may offer that meaning back into the conversation. We hope the other may also be open to being surprised, open to changing understanding. But this is a delicate and sensitive presentation of our own provisional position, not an adversarial argument, or an imposition from superior knowledge. We recognize that we never have a 'final knowledge', that the process of 'coming to an understanding' with the other is important *in itself,* and that in that open dialogue we may all come to a different and higher understanding.

We are also asked to acknowledge the primacy of relationship. Underlying these different critical positions is an understanding that the world we live in is best understood fundamentally in terms of relationship and process. Our world is a dynamically complex and interdependent reality where no thing (including particularly us as humans) stands apart as some sort of 'object in itself', or has a self-standing identity. We are all in the swim, formed and forming in relationship, and there is no detached, objective 'view from nowhere'. Our conversations with others are relational events. Their effectiveness (in coming to an understanding with others) will depend on the quality of the relations developed in the process – which will depend on the relational skill and disposition we bring to the table.

We inhabit a constantly renewing world of radical impermanence. Seeking certainty, fixity, predictability is somehow beside the point. Looking for *control* over how our actions run in the world is not just a lost cause but a potentially harmful and distorting practice.

Of course we act, with intention, into this world, on the basis of the understanding we come to with others. In that sense we *are*, always, co-creating and co-creators in this constantly renewing world, but never exactly as we intended, as our actions enter, and are turned by, the swirl of others' intentions and actions (these in part of course in response to our action) and the resultant overall emergent patterns of change. Appropriate action within this understanding of change will work most effectively if local, incremental, and at a cautious scale.

Ian McGilchrist reminds us that 'the kind of attention we bring to bear on the world changes the nature of the world we attend to' (2009: 28).

We are looking at establishing a patient, receptive, and respectful attention which allows the other to come forward and speak in their voice, and (with human interaction) to have some trust that there can be an authentic 'fusing of horizons' (Taylor, 2002: 133). We are looking at a way of being rooted in holding an open conversation with the world we engage with.

In this different way of being, energy and focus is in the situation and, with those working on that situation, to develop a deep reading and a co-creation of responses to a moving, changing reality – an active, practical 'coming to an understanding'.

Working with FDC – an example of practice

In mid-2008 I was asked to work with FDC (Community Development Foundation), a small but growing national level organization in a European country. In many ways the organization was a success story. Between its inception in 2002-3 and 2008 it had grown from a small core of 4 staff to 16, seen a sevenfold increase in its grant budget, and a similar increase in its overall turnover to around £1 million annually.

It had a very strong reputation for effectiveness and integrity in a context not generally marked by those attributes. Donors were coming to

FDC – including some of the major bilateral players in the region. Central government was interested in working with this young organization around local and community initiatives.

Yet there was a feeling in the mind of the director and his board that things were also 'out of order'.

The brief for the review was deliberately short and open: to explore with them whether the work was working, whether FDC was grounded in the right work, and to surface strategic questions.

The review process itself ran over three working weeks. At its heart was an intensive set of conversations – some 35 in all – with FDC's staff and board, partners and grantees, and other local actors. Some conversations were held on a one-to-one basis, others in small-group sessions. Some conversations took place in the field with both grantees and staff. Generally these conversations ran for about 1.5 hours but with groups often longer.

Each conversation started with participants being asked to talk about their own work and about their relationship with FDC, and to share their perception of FDC and its work. In initial conversations there were no other pre-set questions. I worked with what arose, exploring further, different lines of interest, with open but focused questions.

In parallel to these conversations were two other streams of discussion. Every few days I met with the six FDC programme team staff – young, committed, but struggling with some of the roles and the challenge of reading complex situations in the work. I also met regularly with a 'contact group' – mainly senior managers. With these two groups I talked about what was emerging through the conversations and began to offer my own emerging understanding of key themes, questions, and strategic concerns, encouraging them to talk through these, providing me perhaps with confirmation, or a check, or ground for further exploration.

The process was an iterative one. The parallel conversations would often prompt me to follow up more deeply with some previous interviewees, and then subsequently bring back the revised interpretation or understanding. New depth in any area, changing emerging questions, were brought back to both teams in an evolving, building, picture.

Over three weeks a living picture of the organization and its work was developed. In a series of one-day meetings my reading of this picture was offered to staff and the board, and explored further.

The picture emerging did confirm the positive and special reputation of this organization – their commitment and their integrity. But it also confirmed that sense that things *were* somehow out of order. What came through strongly was that significant degrees of transformation in many different areas in the organization, and the world it sat in, had not been noticed or attended to throughout the period of rapid growth in resources and workload. Coming together, these transformations had created a set of tensions and dangers for the organization which had been felt, but not really seen or understood.

Out of this very rich picture let me pick a few 'transformations' as examples.

FDC had passed through several 'glass ceilings' in its rapid growth. It was now a medium size organization with a need for different ways of working. But leadership had not brought its organizational processes and structures into line with the changed reality.

It was still run like the 'family firm', with a very high concentration of responsibilities (and almost all strategic thinking) held by a now deeply exhausted director. He was several ways caught. He felt he *was* the one who took all the pressure and made it all work, but did not feel able to let go enough of his power to allow a supported devolution of responsibility to develop. He expressed frustration at other senior managers not 'stepping up', but also doubted their capacity and commitment to do so. For other senior staff there was a mix of respect for the director's capacity, frustration, and some resentment about their lack of role in high-level management. But some were also comfortable in their dependence and reluctant to take on higher responsibilities. There was an exhausted, tense, relational gridlock.

The organization had built its reputation around one particular programme that worked openly and supportively with small grassroots organizations – many too small and young to be on most funders' radar screens. Even in 2008 this programme was seen as the 'spirit' of FDC, especially by programme staff. This open flexible programme was supported by an equally flexible general purpose grant from an international foundation.

But, by 2008, the weight of this programme in the overall programme portfolio had shrunk from around 60 to under 20 per cent. The original flexible grant was still there. But two major new programmes now occupied 70 per cent of the grant budget, both programmes strongly shaped by the major donors who supported them. FDC had drifted into a situation where its programme work was not where most staff wanted it to be, and its funding had become strongly dependent on several major donors, with their own strong strategic interests. FDC wanted to grow, to have a more significant impact. It did not lack funding suitors, in fact it was under pressure from some donors to 'come on board'. But it somehow seemed to have lost its own strategic orientation.

Perhaps at the heart of all this was a sense that the organization was caught in a style of working which seriously prevented it from maintaining a good strategic awareness of where it was. Chronic busyness that accompanied rapid growth and the overdependence on the director had all shut off space for the ongoing conversations which *would* have allowed the organization to see these transformations as they developed. There *had* been a three-day strategic planning process some six months before the review which had not uncovered this picture. The ensuing document could have fitted any local (or indeed regional) organization. FDC had severely dropped off that necessary continual awareness of where it was.

The response to the review 'picture' was a mix of deep recognition, surprise, some questioning on emphasis, and some consternation that they had not seen all of this. And yet it was they themselves, and those other actors they engage with daily, who, offered an open chance to voice their understanding, built this picture. It was a picture built by a 'coming to an understanding' across many voices.

In the end it was a picture that identified some very important strategic questions, gave a clear sense of strong current dangers, but also pointed to some important opportunities. Not a picture you would respond to with an 'action plan', or to be 'resolved' in a few months, but one which gave a strong, nuanced basis for ongoing conversations allowing the development of responses to those strategic questions.

Preparing for a different praxis

This praxis of open engagement with lived experience, of coming to an understanding with others, of acting into uncertainty, is one where the *quality of our own practice*, and the *nature of our own disposition*, rather than any surrounding shell of ideas, methods, frameworks, and toolkits, is of primary importance.

This way of being in the work, set around open conversation with others, asks us to 'go naked into the conference chamber'. When Nye Bevan used that phrase he was seeking the reassurance of a nuclear weapon. For us, in our usual work modes, the reassurance is usually the support of some technical framework. First we may look to have a definitive language and framework for 'capturing' the world, a structure, a toolkit, a range of questions in the back pocket. Further down the line is the comfort of finding a definitive 'solution', and devising a plan to guide us there. But this different way of being asks us to go in radically, openly, ourselves, and give attention to what comes up in its own language. It is a method-less method, suggesting minimal pre-structuring and framing. It asks us not to rush to conclusions, or stay with pre-judgements. And it suggests that wherever we then arrive together will always be provisional.

This request to ourselves, and our immediate practice, can be enormously energizing. At the same time it can be fundamentally disconcerting, can seem to take the ground away from under our feet. Where the conventional Western approach is settled on a 'ground of certainty', in language and in how we pre-organize our way into work and the world, this broad 'different way' wants to constructively start from a radical openness – to the world and others, and to the uncertainty of the future.

If we wanted to bring this understanding into our work how might we do so? How do we prepare ourselves for working in this way? What qualities and dispositions does it ask of us?

This is clearly not a way of working you impose on others, or structure in unilaterally. It is a practice you can offer, a practice you can live in your work.

So if, as a practitioner in the social development field, sitting wherever you sit, you feel that this language, this way of being in and engaging with the world, makes sense, draws you in, then the questions are 'How do *I* best prepare to be able to work in this broad and open way? How do I best ensure that I will be able to offer this way of being in my work, effectively, appropriately and sensitively, when the opportunity arises?'

At the core of this different way of being is the practice of openness. And I stress *practice*. We may come to the conference chamber 'naked', but not empty. We are all the children of our own social past and socially formed development. We always bring with us our pre-judgements and our dispositions. Our pre-judgements are the existing understandings we bring. Some of these we may have developed quite explicitly, through a careful critical sieving of our experience. Others are more beneath the explicit surface, part of our daily way of understanding our world, of which we may not be so immediately aware. Our dispositions, however, inform how we engage with the world, the nature of our attitude towards the world and others. An open disposition will breathe patience, respect, and compassion into any encounter; it will have an easy settledness in self, with no need to assert power or control over others or impose understandings.

What we bring, and *how* we bring these pre-judgements and dispositions to bear in any encounter with others will shape how open our practice is, how willing we are to be surprised and accept change in our own understanding. Developing a greater awareness of our pre-judgements, and of how we are in the world, an awareness of how our dispositions and attitudes appear to others, feels to be an important first element in preparedness for engaging openly with others. Moving from greater *awareness* to slowly developing an open *practice* is a next step.

But another key challenge may be the ability to do less. In the modern Western way of being we are asked to be over-prepared and over-determined and tasked to 'stay in charge' in engagements with others – hyperactive players in the game. This different way of practice asks us to come in more patient, receptive, and less driven for control over process and ends. This can be difficult; it touches often quite deep drives and anxieties in us.

Aside from these more self-directed challenges, we also need to be able to improve our ability to read and make meaning of situations. As well as developing an openness to what the situation or those within it say, we need to be able to work in an imaginative and synthesizing way with what is then before us.

Preparedness to work with this way of being means engaging differently and more skillfully with the living realities we encounter in practice, not just at the level of ideas – which is where we come full circle to small group conversations. Small group open conversations embody this other way of being. They also provide an excellent forum for practice around 'coming to an understanding' with others. Forming such a group, with willing colleagues, across or within organizations, enables you to practice open engagement, explore working with open questioning, build capacity for reading and making meaning of situations, reflect together on the process, and over time come to a deeper understanding of the quality of your own practice in this work. From the confidence you build here, you will be better placed to offer this way of working out in your wider work world.[3]

Notes

1. The most thorough and convincing work draws on insights from the 'complexity sciences'. For a good recent exposition see Chris Mowles (2011) on the implications for management.
2. For a fascinating account of just how 'Western' these ideas are, how deeply embedded, and in many ways unhelpful, see Francois Jullien (2004), who contrasts Western thinking with a radically different Chinese tradition.
3. A fuller version of this chapter can be found at <http://proteusmasters. wordpress.com/interim-readings>.

References

Jullien, F. (2004) *A Treatise on Efficacy: Between Western and Chinese Thinking*, University of Hawai'I Press, Honolulu.

McGilchrist, I. (2009) *The Master and his Emissary: The Divided Brain and the Making of the Western World*, Yale University Press, New Haven, CT, and London.

Moran, D. and Mooney, T. (2002) *The Phenomenology Reader*, Routledge, London and New York.

Mowles, C. (2011) *Rethinking Management: Radical Insights from the Complexity Sciences*, Gower, Farnham.

Schon, D. (1991) *The Reflective Practitioner*, Ashgate, London.

Scott, J. (1998) *Seeing like a State*, Yale University Press, New Haven, CT, and London.

Taylor, C. (2002) 'Gadamer on the Human Sciences', in D. Dostal (ed), *The Cambridge Companion to Gadamer*, pp. 126-143, Cambridge University Press, Cambridge

About the author

David Harding has worked for 30 years in the social development field – in Latin America, Africa, and Central and Eastern Europe – after starting his work life in community development in the UK and Spain. He works mainly with the non-profit sector around questions of organizational effectiveness, strategy, and working with change. In recent years he has been particularly interested in what he sees as the central question of practice in social development – what makes for an effective and appropriate practice in this difficult but engaging work, and what sort of qualities and faculties do we need to offer and develop in ourselves for this? He works with organizational teams, and individuals, facilitating and supporting their engagement with their own work situations, and their learning around practice arising from this. He is part of a small international team offering a master's programme on reflective social practice.

CHAPTER 10
Women on wheels

Meenu Vadera

*One major influence on current development aid spending is the focus on cost effec-
tiveness, low transaction costs, and low unit costs. INGOs seek 'a bigger bang for
your buck': only £2 a month for vaccinations, £20 a year to train a para-vet, etc. The
more privileged invest thousands of pounds to get 'employable'; the poor must 'gain
employability' from the investment of a couple of hundred pounds. The pressure to
change the lives of the many 'at cost' often leads to a focus on one-step solutions: e.g.
bed nets for malaria, market prices by phone for agriculture, micro-credit loans for
women's groups. The complex causes and effects of poverty often lead into unexpected
results and failure or problems in the longer term. There are no short cuts to transforming the lives of the poor! Women on Wheels in India enables such women to get
out of the vicious intergenerational cycles of poverty and disadvantage and change
the lives of their families and wider networks.*

The beginnings

The year is 2007. I have been thinking of doing something different, feeling
tired of doing the same workshops, trainings, meetings, and so on. Personally,
my life demands I am more based in Delhi, with a young six-year-old daughter
and an aging mother. For the first time in my life I start considering work
possibilities in Delhi itself. Various strands start coming together in my mind.

The census had been out recently. And I remember being shocked. We all
knew about discrimination against the girl child, also about the fact that some
people terminate their pregnancy rather than give birth to a girl child, but the
size of the challenge of female foeticide indicated by the declining sex ratio in
the age group 0–5 years was brought home officially in the 2001 census. Delhi,
with Punjab and Haryana, was amongst the 'red states' (regions with the
worst figures on female foeticide). The census underlined the debate between
economic growth and development. I would have loved to start something in
Punjab, where the CSO activity is still limited. But I was living in Delhi and
I thought 'Why not do something here?'

Growing up in the development sector landscape in India, I had learnt
in my younger years that one had to go work in far-flung areas and remote
villages to understand poverty in India. This was true to a very large extent,
but it did not mean there was no poverty in the cities and urban spaces of

http://dx.doi.org/10.3362/9781780447780/010

India with plenty of scope to work here. My work then, with elected women representatives in the local government structures, inspired me also to think of myself as a citizen, rather than just a 'development worker'. I started thinking more about how I could contribute in the society around me. I decided to get more active in our residents' welfare association and started looking at Delhi as a city where I could perhaps find a meaningful role for myself.

During my five years in Uganda, Delhi seemed to have metamorphosed into a very different creature. I was struck with the Baristas, CCDs, the multiplexes, flyovers, business processing organizations (BPOs), and the internet everywhere. There were many more young people on the road, many more young *women* on the road and in public spaces. BPOs had provided employment, and with that came a higher disposable income, a propensity to spend in the new upcoming malls and multiplexes – and crime against women. Delhi has had the dubious distinction of the highest incidence of rape in the country. The media had also become a 24/7 presence, so crimes against women were more visible and talked about.

Somewhere then, all these strands were coming together in my subconscious, and it struck me that Delhi did not have a 'transport service for women'. I had known of similar services in London when I was studying there in 1994. The idea grew from there.

Rationale

Urban poverty has increasingly become a challenge to address in India; the numbers of urban poor have steadily increased and in some states are becoming the majority of the poor (Government of India, 2009). Women, of course, continue to be the most marginalized and oppressed within the population of urban poor, gendered power relations ensuring they remain by-and-large confined within the narrow walls of their shanty dwellings. The majority of the livelihood options available to resource-poor women remain within the traditional realm in the informal sector. They work on unequal terms, for discriminatory wages, and in mostly unsafe workspaces for long hours with low returns. The multiple domestic and livelihood burdens on a woman make her more vulnerable to exploitation at the workplace. Though these glass ceilings have been broken by some, the stories are too few and scattered to alter the overall picture. Large-scale livelihood programmes are mostly skewed in favour of poor men. At best, they offer to women shorter livelihood training in domains aligned to, and reinforcing, stereotypical occupations (tailoring, beauty and grooming, tiffin services, etc). Since women have restricted mobility, they are trained in occupations that do not require them to move beyond their neighbourhoods. This severely constrains their earning potential.

There is a strong need, thus, to demonstrate engendered and high-return livelihood options for women to be able to:

- imagine new roles for themselves;
- get opportunities to work in safe and respectful environments and enhance not just their economic status but also their self-respect and dignity;
- build social capital for women as they transform their own lives and those of others around them.

Women on Wheels

Thus was born the idea of Women on Wheels to enable resource-poor women to become qualified and competent chauffeurs. Commercial driving has been and continues to be a very male domain. In a country with more than a billion people, one could easily count the total number of commercial women chauffeurs. A hybrid institutional structure combining not-for-profit and for-profit was conceived to handle the two ends of the spectrum – training/capacity building – creating a pool of trained and competent women chauffeurs on one hand and employment through nurturing markets for women chauffeurs on the other. The not-for-profit Azad Foundation was set up to identify, motivate, and register young, resource-poor women to enrol themselves for the training. Sakha, the for-profit partner, was set up to provide employment for the qualified women chauffeurs. Over the past three years more than 100 women have registered with Azad, of whom nearly 80 completed their training and acquired a permanent license; 35 of these have been employed through the efforts of Sakha.

Who are these women?

It is important to understand the profile of women who come to Azad Foundation to be trained as women chauffeurs. Nearly all reside in one of the slums or 'resettlement colonies' of Delhi. They come from households living on the edges of survival. Even by the highly questioned and contested definitions of poverty proposed by the Planning Commission, they come from families living below poverty lines with monthly family earnings of 3000–5000 INR (US$60–100). The average education level is class VIII, and many have never travelled alone outside of their colony (residential area) in a public bus. Apart from the big challenge of poverty, the most pervasive and perhaps more difficult challenge they face is that of violence, or the threat of violence, largely at the hands of male relatives. Listening to the everyday stories of violence ranging from abuse, eviction from home in the middle of the night, shadowing, slapping, and more severe blows, I wonder sometimes whether we live in a peaceful, democratic country or a war zone. Looked at from the eyes of many women trainees, freedom is a dream – freedom to choose a livelihood, to wear what they want, to travel where they want, to study as much as they want, to choose the subjects they wish to study, to marry or not, to choose a partner – the list is endless. It does make one question whether in 1947 India did become a free country for ALL its citizens. And if in 2012, large numbers of its population still do not enjoy basic rights and freedoms, have we at all been serious and committed to the principle and practice of freedom for *all* citizens?

The fact that women have been able to overcome all these odds, and aspire to a programme that requires them to spend long hours in training, is evidence of the determination and resolve many of them have. Several of the women who come have professed that, secretly, they always nurtured a desire to learn to drive. For these, then, it is a dream come true, and reflects later in their resolve to continue to resist all pressures from homes as they hold on to jobs offered to them. A few women, though, do get support from their families. However, it soon turns into questioning when they see them keep long working hours. For most, it continues to be hard negotiation on boundaries imposed by their families, neighbours, and the society they live in.

The learning journey

Being on Delhi roads, working with a very different socio-economic clientele, and moving out of their homes for extended hours has not been easy for the women who enrolled. It was not sufficient just to equip them with driving skills and put them on the road. Azad thus had to invest resources – human, financial, and physical – in ensuring the women had opportunities to gain confidence, self-esteem, learn how to defend themselves, speak a bit of English, acquire grooming and personal hygiene skills, and, most importantly, learn to be 'professional'. Without these vital, non-driving-related skills, they would not be able to cope with the pressures and challenges the new employment would pose.

A tie-up with Maruti IDTR (Institute of Driving and Training Research) ensured the women received cutting-edge training in driving-related skills. This was further supported in-house, and Azad ensures that every woman trainee is able to acquire the relevant licenses and get a minimum of 100 hours of practice on the road.

To enable women to become more confident, Azad has linked with the Delhi Police Crime Against Women Cell, which provides training in self-defence. Links with other resource institutions/persons ensure women get exposed to spoken English, learn more effective communication that helps them be assertive in dealing with clients, and acquire skills to be well groomed and smart.

The reality of violence that most women face almost on a daily basis necessitated their learning about the legal and policy infrastructure that provides them with choices when faced with violence – at home or on the roads. Interestingly, women have faced little violence on the road. Where they have, they have mostly been able to handle it, sometimes singlehandedly, sometimes in groups. But the violence women face at home is an entirely different story. Almost 90 per cent of the women who register for training have stories of dealing with the challenge of violence at home. Mostly the perpetrators are male relatives, fathers, husbands, brothers – even younger brothers and brothers-in-law. The forms are many – verbal abuse, occasional physical abuse which in more extreme forms leads to bruises or broken bones, denying mobility and enforcing restrictions against moving out of home, being evicted from homes in the middle of the night, and, in a few cases, being forcibly married or sent to in-laws' homes. Devastating in its impact, and ever present, the violence stops them from doing anything to transform their living conditions. Apart from learning about their entitlements, women trainees have also learnt to exercise their options of filing police complaints, bringing cases for separation or protection, and, sometimes, deciding to live on their own. In each situation they are also supported by counselling services, with counselling support at times extended to families.

Despite the web of support services and comprehensive training, women trainees have dropped out. Azad has seen nearly a 40 per cent dropout rate, though this is very positive as compared to most other such organizations. The majority drop out for domestic reasons. Brothers suddenly get protective, husbands get suspicious, women are required to undertake domestic tasks that do not allow them to go out, or families are unwilling to redistribute the domestic responsibilities to create space for women to work. The need to have women at home defies logic; families are willing to forego potential incomes that are more than their existing family incomes in order not to lose the control they exercise over their women!

It is hard work, then, to almost literally hold and nurture those who are able to escape these constraints and build a future for the 35 women working, a further 30 almost at the end of their learning journeys waiting to get employed, and more than 70 in other stages of training; this is where we are after almost three years of intense effort. And we celebrate and salute the efforts of each of these women.

Interfacing with donors

We thought our logic was clear and compelling: a unique initiative that helps break boundaries for women, that helps them transform their living conditions in perhaps irreversible ways. For once they are there on the roads having completed their learning journeys, driving powerful cars they had not even dreamt of, engaging with a class they had only seen from a distance, earning salaries that no one in their families had ever earned, building lives for themselves and their families, unleashing their dreams, they became different persons. They just have to be met to demonstrate this transformation. Many of them have been interviewed, and covered in the media.[1] They have become attractive stories for anyone wanting to write about 'change'. We thought donors would love to support an initiative demonstrating change in a group living on the periphery. Having previously worked with an international aid agency, I know there are few examples of interventions able to achieve an impact of such depth.

But we had surprises in store. The near universal refrain thrown at us over and again was concern about 'scale'. It is near impossible to imagine that so many fund providers – whether they are donors or investors – are so completely obsessed with scale. For investors, one could argue the bottom line is commercial returns and perhaps achieving a certain scale is critical to that. Investors are not there to change the world; they are there to make profits and strengthen their financial bottom lines. But donors? Time and again we have had to engage with some very difficult mindsets, all of which are but different ways of saying 'scale' – cost per trainee, returns on investment, and so on.

Tyranny of concepts, frameworks, and practices promoted

Cost per trainee

At Women on Wheels it takes a woman with the profile mentioned above (very low skill base and even lower levels of self-confidence) between eight to ten months to become a skilled, employable chauffeur. The cost of sustaining a capacity-enhancing programme over this time is approximately 5,000 INR ($110) per month which includes costs of mobilization, outreach, various training components, modules, helping to acquire all the relevant licenses and qualifications, providing at least 100 hours of driving practice and making available basic social security in the form of interest-free loans returnable once in employment. In themselves, these costs appear very reasonable for helping transform a resource-poor woman into an empowered professional who often becomes the principal breadwinner of her family.

This amount is, however, very much more than the average costs that donors or government have budgeted for 'livelihood training programmes for women'. The maximum perhaps that these budgets offer is 10,000 INR ($220) per person – far too little; but of course the expectation of a successful outcome remains the same. Little wonder, then, that a majority of these livelihood programmes offer little to women. In fact they often do a disservice to them by continuing to perpetuate the practice of offering them low-paid jobs within the traditional gender stereotypes and restricting themselves to only offering 'technical' skills. Many do not address those basic constraints that exist within the women themselves nor those in the external, social context that will continue to deny them the ability to exercise their choice in various spheres of their life.

A small initiative such as ours has to deal with the huge monolith of institutions that work within budgets which have been decided on the basis of who knows what. Who decided, how, and why that only 10,000 INR ($220) was the cost of empowering a resource-poor woman to change her life circumstances for the better, especially if it meant a quantum change in her life, and in the life of her children, particularly her daughters? The fact becomes even more difficult to understand when one compares it to the investments the more privileged classes make in ensuring their daughters and sons become employable.

One could argue that in a country where perhaps the majority of the world's poor live, one must look at 'low-cost' models of change. While low costs are generally good practice to avoid wastage of resources, when low cost becomes a defining principle only in provisions for the poor in the society there seems something almost unethical about it. It is okay for billions of rupees and dollars to be pumped into wars, into technologies that promote war, into the entertainment industry, into technologies that the majority of the world's poor would perhaps never use – but not okay to break the tyranny of low costs when it comes to making quantum changes in the lives of resource-poor women. It seems almost a moral obligation to question this tyranny when working with completely unskilled women, with little or often no education and over a period of nine months, transforming them into confident young professionals able to earn decent wages for now and ever. The shining, glittering India would spend this amount on a single air ticket for its holiday abroad, or annually on pizzas or cinema tickets. Do donors think this is too much to be invested in ensuring a family is food-secure for all its life? A hard question but the development world must reconsider its own practice against its larger ideological perspective.

Returns on investment

At Women on Wheels we are not just looking at an exceptionally high-end livelihood activity, we are also looking at an intervention that breaks through deep-rooted gender barriers. In fact, as our experience tells us, it is not just deep-rooted gender barriers; it is also barriers of class, caste, and culture that are getting broken. There are few other livelihood interventions that are as disruptive and as high end.

From our perspective the returns on investment are exceptionally high especially if we impute value to all economic as well as non-economic gains. Consider this. Using a purely economic framework, the total cost per trainee (50,000 INR/US$1,000) is recovered by the trainees within ten months of their working. So in effect the costs are recoverable in a period of less than a year. Added to this, however, is the social capital of bringing into the mainstream empowered women professionals, the networks of support that the women build amongst themselves, and the impact of this transformation onto the families and communities where the women come from (see Box 10.1).

We have often been told that the donors will be happy if we can demonstrate that women who are now employed are contributing back to the institution to enable other resource-poor women to benefit as well. On the face of it, this sounds, well, logical, until one asks how many of us from the more privileged classes were forced to contribute to our respective *alma maters* so that others who came after us could benefit. There have been some voluntary initiatives

---

Box 10.1 The story of Savita

Savita joined Azad Foundation when she had just turned 18. Having studied up to class V, she was forced to drop out due to economic constraints. Savita lives in a small temporary structure with her family of four siblings and parents. Her father used to sell bread and, to make ends meet, her mother worked from home making small packets of chillies for the shops nearby. A crisis happened when her father stopped working, as they believed he had been cursed by the spirit of her grandmother for not having properly performed her last rites when she had died.

Savita was determined to change her family circumstances. She successfully completed her course and got a job in a period of ten months. However, the curse of the spirit seemed to come over her as well. Azad team supported Savita with a lot of professional counselling and treatment. That, along with her own determination, helped Savita to break out of this curse and continue with her employment. Gradually, she was able to convince her father and older brother as well that they could also break out of this curse.

Today Savita is one of the best chauffeurs working commercially in Sakha Cabs for women. Her father and brother have once again taken to selling bread and doing odd jobs.

As I write this, Savita is now busy building a permanent one room structure for the entire family! She has wings in her feet and has aspirations and dreams of driving a BMW one day!

---

where very successful professionals and entrepreneurs have contributed back to their universities and institutions to expand their facilities and upgrade their technologies, etc. But I do not know even a single learning university that would impose this caveat upon its students. When we consider the opportunities available to the poor, why should we have such expectations? At the risk of repeating myself, I find it unethical that we continue to perpetuate unequal benchmarks, unequal expectations that privilege those who have while demanding further sacrifices from the have-nots. It is as if our society is doing a favour to the poor by helping them break out of the vicious traps of poverty and totally disclaiming any sense of responsibility at having in the first place failed to provide and ensure basic rights to all citizens.

The social cost–benefit analysis is a much disputed and debated concept even in pure economic theory. Applied in real life it can become a very questionable basis on which we either legitimize a given initiative – or not.

Scale

Ah! The issue of scale is perhaps the deadliest one to deal with. Negotiating with donors/investors on this is like 'scaling' Mt. Everest! And pardon me if my fatigue filters through my words. But this issue I have argued over endlessly, sometimes getting pushed so hard on the need to work with tens of thousands of women that I begin to question whether there is any point in working with a few hundred – even though it means a world of change for them.

Their logic is irrefutable. In a country with 1.2 billion population, of which 200 to 600 million would be in the category of poor depending upon which estimate one considers, changing the lives of a few hundred women seems almost irrelevant in the larger landscape of change. And if it means taking almost a year, then the initiative becomes even more questionable. We need models that can bring thousands of women out of poverty in a period of three months. In a meeting with representatives of Delhi State Government we were told our initiative is great and very innovative. But why are we talking such small numbers? We should be able to prepare a thousand women and in three months! After all, how long does it take for someone to learn driving? Yes, the argument goes, it is a new area; yes, it breaks gender stereotypes; yes, these women are path-breakers; but what is the problem in working with thousands of these path-breakers? Surely the slums and resettlement colonies have enough women who fulfil our eligibility criterion of minimum age 18, minimum education qualification standard VIII, an aptitude to learn driving, and commitment to working as a chauffeur for a period of at least three years.

Yes to all of the logic. We have over the years made increasing investments in financial and human resources for our Outreach and Mobilization programme. The reality is that in our three years of work we have reached out to thousands of women; we have 3,000 names of potentially eligible women; we have had conversations with almost a 1,000 of them but only a 100 of them were converted into successful registrations for the programme through which we offer employment as part of the training package. The challenges we face are reflective of the social reality we work within. To share a few:

Driving as a career for women. Most families balk at the idea. It is unheard of. They would much rather send their sons to learn driving. It is not just unheard of for daughters to become drivers; they do not really believe their daughters – whom they have really never considered worth any significant investments – could actually learn driving.

The women themselves. Though many get excited at the thought of being behind the steering wheel, many do not really believe that they can do it. Once they get some counselling and get excited at the idea, however, addressing the scepticism of the family and neighbours is another task. We learnt that several women who participated in our training programme did not tell their families and neighbours that they were training to become chauffeurs until much later, not wanting to face the sneers and looks of disbelief.

Concerns around security. Professional driving has built an image for itself of male drivers often drinking, smoking, living life on the edge, rough and hardened by the life on the roads – definitely not a place for women to be! There are concerns about how women will handle themselves amongst the large community of male drivers and how they will protect themselves from advances from male passengers. Azad Foundation, therefore, works with the police on developing the women's self-defence and how to conduct themselves in challenging situations. During their training the women also develop broader assertiveness and self-confidence so many have taken recourse to saying 'no' to domestic violence by resisting abuse, calling the police, registering cases at legal aid clinics or women's organizations, or even choosing to walk out of homes. As a result of Azad's broad-based approaches the women are learning to navigate the hazards facing a female chauffeur as well as those of the male-orientated world.

The investment of time in training. Most other training programmes for women offer two-hour daily modules. That is convenient. Women can finish all their domestic chores and then 'indulge' themselves in doing some training or other. Since most of these trainings are free, women often register themselves in several such courses, learning tailoring, art and craft work, cooking, beautician work, and so on. Every such training also enhances their eligibility for marriage. In the vast spectrum of these very convenient training programmes, this driving training programme stands alone. Women must give almost six to eight hours a day for between eight and ten months. They must travel far from home. They learn things that start bringing a visible change in their personality and behaviour. All of this requires tough negotiation at family level and a lot of counselling support for the women and often for their families. The confidence they gain also helps them acquire boyfriends and girlfriends. The women make new relationships, as they begin to question the existing ones that they have experienced as violent or less than satisfactory. It becomes a delicate balance to support them in meeting their very natural needs for acceptance, affinity, and affection, while also assuring the families that their *izzat* (honour) will not be stained.

The list of reasons and concerns that will not allow an average Indian woman to pursue a career and growth that will make her economically independent and empowered to make her own decisions in life is endless. In a livelihood intervention that is as socially disruptive as ours, each individual woman who chooses to complete her training and build a career as a professional chauffeur must be held within a carefully managed web of institutional systems that supports, advises, guides, counsels, and nurtures, that helps build on her strengths and launches her as 'a professional chauffeur'.

In this context, 'scale' must have a new meaning. The depth of change must be considered as a critical factor, and an understanding that quantity is not always a preferred yardstick to quality. It is difficult for most fund providers, as they prefer dealing with big institutions who talk about training tens of thousands. It is much easier (and cheaper) to provide large funds to a handful of institutions than having to deal with several smaller ones. The logic of convenience in management overlooks the fact that large institutions often spend more money in sustaining themselves. There is no one true solution to this debate on 'scale'. There is a need for large-scale programmes, for large institutions that can cover several districts and states or even countries. There is also a strong need for smaller institutions working on new, innovative, initiatives that demonstrate new alternatives and new worlds. The danger is when we begin to believe in only one 'narrative of change'; a 'single story that talks about scale and numbers' as the only real way of bringing social change. In following this belief we close ourselves to new possibilities, to new ways of thinking, doing, and being, to new horizons and fresh dreams. We prevent chances of those few hundred women becoming lighthouses in their small communities and we close the doors on 'possible seeds of revolution'.

Afterword

It is important to mention here that despite the often-experienced hegemony of the donor/investor concepts mentioned above, Azad Foundation and Sakha have continued in their work. And for this we must acknowledge those several individuals and our key donors – Shell Oil, iPartner (a charity based in the UK), and Human Dignity Foundation (based in Ireland) – who have believed in alternative narratives, trusted in processes and the experience of those on the ground, and supported us in flexible and thinking ways. If not for them, we would not be here to even tell our story!

Notes

1. See www.azadfoundation.com/weblinks.php [accessed 15 June 2012].

References

Government of India (2009) *India Urban Poverty Report,* Ministry of Housing and Urban Poverty Alleviation, New Delhi. Available at: <www.undp.org/content/dam/india/docs/india_urban_poverty_report_2009_related.pdf>

About the author

Meenu Vadera is a feminist development practitioner who has worked for 25 years both nationally and internationally on issues of women's rights, such as reproductive rights, land rights, women in governance, violence against women, women with HIV/AIDs, and women living in conflict situations. During this time Meenu has worked with both local and international NGOs. Her experience on the ground is supported by her Masters in Social Development and Public Policy from the London School of Economics, where she focused on gender studies in health and education. She is currently working on an innovative intervention, 'Women on Wheels', which she co-founded a few years ago. Women on Wheels has received a lot of praise and won awards for its innovative approach. Meenu was also awarded first prize in the Business and Enterprise category of the 100 Unseen Powerful Women, listed by One World Action from across 40 countries in October 2011.

CHAPTER 11

Too young to be women, too old to be girls: the (un)changing aid landscape and the reality of girls at risk

Seri Wendoh

About 16 million adolescent girls give birth every year. Pregnancy-related complications are a leading cause of death among girls aged 15–19 years. Adolescent births are more likely to occur among poor, less educated, and rural populations. Gender inequality, undervaluing of girls, gender-based violence, sexual exploitation, and deepening poverty are key drivers. The realities of adolescents at risk of pregnancy are not part of discussions on aid and in relation to sexuality education. Anxious to deliver on their own and donor requirements, aid agencies adopt strategies that exacerbate the challenges rather than leading to empowerment and transformation. Drawing on research conducted by IPPF and FORWARD, this chapter examines poor girls' realities in Freetown and Sierra Leone and shows that girls who are out of school want access to information and sexual and reproductive health services, and empowerment to be self-determining for themselves, their children, and communities; both are imperatives and human rights.

Today's generation of young people is the largest in history. Nearly half of the world's population (almost three billion people) is under the age of 25 with a significant number of adolescents and young people in the countries of the South (UNFPA, 2005). UNICEF's (2010) report showed half of the world's out-of-school population live in conflict countries. However, the discussions and approaches currently promoted around universal access to health and education often ignore this and do not relate clearly to the analysis of and thinking around poverty and how to reach the poorest. Currently sex education and sexual and reproductive health programmes are most accessible for young people in schools, showing a weak grasp of how many young people, girls especially, are out of school. Approaches, useful for young people within the school environment, fall short for those who do not fit neatly in a school curriculum. Young girls out of the school safety net, forced out due to pregnancy or early marriage, are significantly impacted by poverty, gendered inequality, and limited access to information and education, thus narrowing both their agency and opportunities.

http://dx.doi.org/10.3362/9781780447780/011

The numbers of out-of-school girls, especially by secondary level and particularly in parts of Asia and Africa are significant, with only 67 and 76 girls per 100 boys, respectively, enrolled in tertiary education (UN, 2010). In many countries less than 50 per cent of girls are in school post primary. Girls are out-of-school for a range of reasons: poverty and the preference for supporting boys in education; early and forced marriage; teenage pregnancy; and negative attitudes towards girls' education rooted in attitudes and beliefs that endorse gender inequality at national and local levels. This situation continues despite many excellent constitutions and policies introduced to promote women's and girls' rights in many countries of the global South. Shadow CEDAW (Convention of the Elimination of Violence Against Women) reports show how slowly things are changing in many African countries for women and girls, who largely remain marginalized and subordinate in the household, community and wider society (CEDAW, 2007; Zimbabwe Women Lawyers Association, 2012).

Young girls, already in poverty and often living in slums or poor rural communities, do not hear the health messages and lack access to key services that are designed without taking their specific contexts into account. They often lack access to contraceptives, condoms, sexual and reproductive health services, information, and gender-based violence services. Many are married and bearing children very young, others are unmarried mothers at an early age, and many suffer from sexually transmitted infections (STIs) including HIV and AIDS. The problems of non-consensual sex in marriage or outside can lead to many health problems and reinforce a cycle of poverty and deprivation. Countries where the gross domestic product is above a certain level are now cut off from health aid, yet they have swathes of children in poverty to cope with, leading to the assertion that the new context of global poverty means that the focus of aid should target 'poor people not poor countries' (Kanbur and Sumner, 2011).

Quick-fix, target-based approaches undermine agency for girls at risk

This world's not going to change unless we're willing to change ourselves. – Rigoberta Menchú Tum

In contexts with prevailing gender inequality and entrenched gender norms that devalue women and girls, 'one-size-fits-all', quick-fix strategies merely serve to stunt girls' growth. In particular, gender frameworks designed without a clear analysis of the complex realities on the ground and local concepts of family inadvertently cause damage to those for whom they are intended. These strategies focus more on donor priorities and less on articulating and investing in broad, rights-based approaches that have the potential to contribute to social justice and lead to transformation. The challenge is aptly captured in an analysis by one NGO:

[D]onors continue to insist on large technical assistance components in most projects and programmes they fund. They continue to use technical assistance as a 'soft' lever to police and direct the policy agendas of developing country governments, or to create ownership of the kinds of reforms donors deem suitable. Donor funded advisers have even been brought in to draft supposedly 'country owned' poverty reduction strategies. (Action Aid, 2006: 5–6)

Even though there is clear evidence that maternal mortality and morbidity for adolescents is highest for poor girls, it is ironic that these girls are not put at the centre of interventions. Even though there is growing support for the introduction of policies and laws intended to protect and promote the rights of poor girls, these are still sketchy and few of these girls benefit from sexuality education and the related health benefits. Projects designed to support these girls fall within short timeframes with quick results. As one frustrated girl noted, 'it is a case of jumping from the frying pan into the fire ... they (NGO) took me and just hang me like that' (Freetown).[1]

The push for 'harmonization', 'alignment', 'targets', and time-bound quick results has far-reaching effects on poor girls. Frameworks developed without the meaningful involvement of young people mean, for example, that comprehensive sexuality education is packaged for school-going girls, while overlooking girls who are not grown-up enough to be women (and so receive targeted aid) or fall outside the school safety net. For example, one young pregnant woman living with HIV was given nutritious food at a health clinic, yet the agency despaired because her health did not seem to change. Only after a long time did they learn that the food she was given was shared with her husband and children once she got home. The concept of extended family and kinship is often not taken into account when strategies are designed.

Realities facing girls at risk

It is well known that forced and early marriage affects girls from poorer households (UNFPA, 2005). Gender norms and power imbalances leading to relationships that expose girls to risk of violence and infection further exacerbate girls' vulnerability. Evidence shows that pregnancy-related complications are a leading cause of death among girls aged 15–19 years in developing countries and unsafe abortion is a key contributor to these deaths (WHO, 2009). Most of these girls are those who have dropped out of school and, in many cases, face sexual exploitation in their efforts to make a living or are forced into marriage as a compromise to alleviate parental and family poverty. These girls remain on the fringes not only of the development agenda but more specifically of health interventions targeting young people.

This chapter explores the vulnerabilities affecting young girl mothers and girls at risk of unintended pregnancy. It traces some of the underlying risk factors confronting these girls and suggests that the one-size-fits-all approach, which is often presented as the panacea to sexual and reproductive health challenges faced by girls at risk, is lacking in differentiation and nuance. Drawing on findings from the International Planned Parenthood Federation's (IPPF) and FORWARD's work with girls at risk in Freetown and Liberia, the chapter examines the reality of girls within the wider umbrella of gender inequality and women's empowerment, positing that when girls at risk are meaningfully included in interventions designed to empower them and enable access to resources, they can excel and enhance the quality of their own, their children's, and their families' lives.

The Girls at Risk Project

Sierra Leone and Liberia have some of the highest maternal mortality rates in the world, with 15–24 year olds accounting for 40 per cent of such deaths. Recognizing the gap in sexual and reproductive health service provision for adolescents and young mothers, IPPF and FORWARD collaboratively undertook participatory research using the Participatory Ethnographic Evaluation and Research (PEER) methodology,[2] with member associations in Sierra Leone and Liberia. The aim was to examine why teenage girls from poor backgrounds are so at risk of teenage pregnancy, the impact of teenage pregnancy and early motherhood on these girls' lives, and girls' own views and recommendations on the availability of appropriate services and information. The findings underscored the fact that unequal gendered power relations are bulwarked by tradition, while cultural and religious beliefs collude to marginalize girls – especially those out of the school system. Dichotomies of 'good' and 'bad' mean that poor girls who become pregnant are either disowned by their parents or forced to go out and work and/or face unsafe abortions often with tragic consequences. The stigmas attached to teenage pregnancy and the fear of being branded 'bad' means that girls do not seek access to health services or information and so are at real risk, including an increased risk of violence.

From the horse's mouth: girls' research findings

The PEER in Liberia and Sierra Leone provided space for girls, between the ages of 15 and 24 years, to become researchers and listen to the realities of their peers in the communities about their experience of life, sexual matters, and access to services. The findings show that many girls do not have access to information and education and where services exist, they are a source of stigma: 'we know where the clinic is, we know we can get condoms, but there is fear to be called "bad" and sometimes you can meet your aunt there' (Monrovia) and 'some people are ashamed to buy condoms because when they go to where it is been sold, they are been judged wrongly.'

Limited access to services heightens risk: 'most girls will try an abortion anyway as the first stop anyway and some are successful ... they will pay someone to help them with this or they will just take some remedy for it at home – sometimes it ruining their stomach and womb, sometimes they even die from this' (Monrovia). With almost no access to information, strategies adopted by girls expose them to further risk:

> They use herbs, special potions, all types of things. They also use special chalk, they put it inside themselves, sometimes they put it in by themselves, sometimes the boyfriend will put it on his penis to insert it, other times it will be the traditional healer that will put on his penis for you. Other people use a mixture of ground cassava leaves, ground up glass bottles and mix with blue (bleach for clothes) and they drink it. It damages you so much it even kills you. But they will have to do it anyway. (Monrovia)

Risks of unsafe abortion are exacerbated by gender-based violence and sexual exploitation. Girls at risk aspire to a better life and want the same things as their peers in school; however, their opportunities are impacted by their circumstances.

> There is a girl who went to live with her aunty because her parents were killed in the war. Her aunty had a 27-year-old son that used to sleep there on weekends. One day when no one was home he called the girl in his room and he raped her. When she told her aunty the lady said that she was lying for her son so she beat the girl mercilessly. (Monrovia)

In the case of Mariana, a 14 year old from Monrovia with two children from two different fathers, she first got pregnant when she was 12 and used to help her mother to sell rocks. A man came to the mother and said that he wanted to help the girl by taking her from the rock hole, but instead he went and got the girl pregnant and threw her out. It happened the second time when another guy came and said that he will help her with the baby but then gave her another baby. All this happened to this girl because her parents were poor and not able to properly care for her.

Often girls are forced to support their families:

> It is common for girls to have sex with people they don't want to have sex with. They say, 'close your eyes and bite the centipede' – it is for a greater goal than the actual act. An unpleasant thing you just have to get on with it. These sugar daddies, they come along as the cotton tree, big and strong and able to assist your family. So you have sex with them. (Freetown)

Many of the girls' experiences are shaped by the post-conflict effects in both countries and those in Freetown are mirrored in Liberia:

> There is a 15-year-old girl in my community whose father was killed during the conflict. Her mother can send her out every night to go and bring $25. She says she doesn't want to know where the child will get the money, but the money must be there in the morning. So every night the girl goes and sleeps with men. In the morning she comes home with $20 and that is very okay with the mother. (Monrovia)

> In my community there is a girl who started doing girl business at the age of nine. It all started because her aunty wanted to make some money out of her. She is now 20 with a 10-year-old child.

As these experiences of girls in Freetown and Monrovia show, risk factors for girls are deeply entrenched in the social fabric and require more investment of time and resources to provide long-term and transformative change. Yet the push for targets and quick results means that work comprehensively addressing the root causes of inequality, violence, and lack of access to services is not happening. These girls need multiple approaches including support to return to school, alternative livelihoods, basic parenting skills, dialogue with parents and community leaders, and ways to promote the enforcement of policies and laws that ensure protection for girls and respect for girls' voices.

Why investing in girls matters: enabling girls' voice and agency

The PEER found that out-of-school girls want the same things as other girls their age – access to services, opportunities to improve their own lives and those of their children and families. They do not want labels of 'victimhood' and sympathy; they want a chance to speak and act on their experiences. The following cases highlight their needs and how they are able to change and grow given appropriate support.

Regarding access to services:

> We want somewhere only for young people. We don't want to meet up with our mothers there. There is no privacy there and we don't feel free to say what we want. We want to speak to someone who we have confidence in, not some old person asking us a lot of questions and embarrassing us.

Seventeen-year-old Adama (Sierra Leone), whose baby is 13 months, had initial difficulty fitting in with her peers: 'I thought I was the only one who had been forced to leave school because I was pregnant, but now I see I am not alone.' After three months' research among peers in her community, Adama was the spokesperson for the research team and fielded questions at a panel organized to share the research findings with the national media, representatives from civil society, and Ministries of Health and Gender. No longer feeling stigmatized, Adama spoke for her friends:

> They want a place for girls and girls only, confidential and secret. They want the information to come from peer educators, people their own age. A library, books and videos, most of them see their future as downcast they don't see their future as bright. Show them videos of girls like themselves who have got pregnant but have made their future bright. Not just peer educators there but also older people there who can mentor them; also classes in how to be healthy when you are pregnant, antenatal classes and talking about it, how to eat well for you and your

baby. Also after birth how to take care of yourself and your baby well, parenting skills, how to feed the baby well. There can be stigma between those who are at school and those who are not, we need to encourage those not in school to still believe they have a future.

In Monrovia, on qualifying as a peer researcher and listening to the stories of her peers, Marcontee Okai was inspired to set up a girls' club, a space of their own for learning vocational skills and for continuing education: 'Twenty five girls attend the club which is located in the YWCA. I help them improve their reading skills and develop good manners. My plan is to ensure that every young girl in Liberia has a quality education and information about sexual and reproductive health – but I will need more support to make that happen.' Using this girls' only space, Macontee wants to empower her peers by enabling them to share and exchange information, to provide health education and promotion programmes to counter myths, stigma, and misinformation as well as confidence and self-esteem-building initiatives and vocational training to foster economic independence.

Mariama was 11 when she was abducted and witnessed her father being killed. She missed her mother but did not know where to find her. One day, somebody gave her directions.

> When they saw me coming they said, 'don't reach here, you are now a rebel wife, stay where you are' – even though I am my mother's only daughter. I started to plait hair and help older people and when they cooked they would give me some food. In 2005, I went to an aid agency and explained that I needed my mother and they helped to reconcile us. Now I live with my mother, my brother has agreed to pay school fees and my family is doing well.

Zainab was driven out because:

> I am a rebel with the habits of a rebel, even my baby is a rebel … yet I went with the rebels to save the lives of my aunt and uncle. One agency talked to my aunt and she took me back – I live with her, do the domestic work, bring my baby to the centre and then go to school. (Makeni, Sierra Leone)

Conclusion

> Involving young people in designing and running programmes aimed at helping them often leads to unique approaches, improving the projects' success rate, while teaching the young people communication, negotiation and civic participation skills. (UNFPA, 2011)

To achieve 'a world where women, men and young people everywhere have control over their own bodies, and therefore their destinies' requires tackling entrenched gender inequality in many countries and communities which

---

Box 11.1 Barrie's Story

'The sinking ship has got into a slamming ocean without sinking.'

My father had many wives. When my mother died, my stepmother mistreated me and did not treat me like one of the children in the home. She used me and made me work for her children like their servant. One day my father kept 250,000 Leones in their bedroom and my stepmother came in and took the money. She accused me of taking the money. They flogged me and I ran for my life. I went to live on the street. I lived there for one year. One night, there was a lot of movement and we were frightened because we thought there was some ritual and they were going to come and take us, then we thought it was the police. We were afraid of being captured. It turned out that it was HANCI people with some former street children who persuaded us it was alright to go with them. They took us to the centre, gave us food to eat and water to wash. On the street we were not living like human beings and access to water only came when it rained on us.

Every morning HANCI prepared food for us. One week later, they started verification and after that they asked us if we had been to school. I'd gone up to SS2 but I was not happy to go back to school because the friends I had before had gone ahead and even on to college and they used to see me on the street and mock me. Instead I asked for a trade in tailoring and HANCI gave me finance, trained me for a year and six months. When I was training they visited me every two weeks to be sure I was ok and if I was still attending the college. When I got my certificate, HANCI gave me a sewing machine and asked me if I want to be reconciled with my parents. I refused because my parents had humiliated and cursed me. After more counselling, I agreed and I was reconciled with my parents

Two months after completing training, the co-ordinator invited me to help train girl mothers and to counsel them.

After work, I go home and continue working and practising my sewing. I have saved money and bought myself a second sewing machine.

Now I help my parents and support my younger brothers with their school fees. My parents now respect me and I have become a role model in my community. In my family, no decision can be made without my consent. They all listen to me. I can also train and counsel others to leave the street: *'The sinking ship has got into a slamming ocean without sinking'*.

Source: adapted from HANCi, 2008, evaluation report

---

teaches young people in many contexts that 'differences between their bodies mean differences in how they are treated, in how they are expected to behave, in what they are praised and criticised for and in what they are allowed to do' (UNICEF, 2011). These differences relate especially to young people's sexuality and sexual expression. For example, misleading messages, based on notions of femininity and masculinity that focus on 'chastity', 'fidelity', and 'purity' for girls, mean that they have only limited information that contrasts with their evolving understanding of their own bodies. The 'abstinence only' approach of faith organizations colludes with some 'cultural/traditional' messages but fails to recognize the real world in which young people live and relate. Many young people are sexually active and have a right to information and education that will enable them to make informed choices. Culture and/or religion should not be used as a reason to deny them such rights, so exposing young people to unnecessary risks.

Eliminating inequity will include provision of free services for the poor, and commodities and anti-retroviral drugs. Eliminating gender stereotypes, which prevent girls from making the decisions that profoundly affect their own health and well-being, can be encouraged through comprehensive sexuality education not only in the school curriculum and teacher training, but also in communities. Along with education, specific laws to enforce zero tolerance for gender-based violence, including child marriage and female genital mutilation, should be enforced ensuring the full involvement of the community in its achievement for which the support of public health campaigns is also needed.

Investing in poor girls' empowerment is critical – it is an imperative and a human right. Investing in sexual and reproductive health knowledge and services for early adolescents is critical because some children are engaging in sexual relations in early adolescence. Empowering adolescent girls in particular with knowledge of their sexual and reproductive health and the gender-related protection risks they face in many countries and communities enables them to start taking some control. Research suggests that, at present, adolescent pregnancy is related to factors beyond girls' control (McIntyre, 2006).

Efforts to ensure universal access to education, reduce poverty, and achieve gender equality are best served when girls at risk are at the centre of development interventions. Quick-fix solutions cause further damage, negate gains, and entrench poverty. One- to three-year project cycles intended to empower girls often fail because donors are unwilling to undertake a critical analysis of the complex realities on the ground, including entrenched gender social norms, the effect of conflict on girls' lives and family fabrics, deepening poverty and how it impacts on girls' ability to access sexual and reproductive health services. At the same time the tendency for many NGOs to focus on those issues that may be 'in vogue' for donor governments and agencies undermines their efforts to reduce poverty in its broad manifestations and the attainment of social justice.

Reaching girls at risk may be difficult and even costly, but shunning this effort only entrenches marginalization and impacts on their contribution to development. Ignoring their voices is not only a violation of human rights but also a curtailment of their empowerment.

Notes

1. The findings presented here are all based on personal interviews in Liberia and Sierra Leone by and with the author.
2. See the PEER website: <www.options.co.uk/peer/>.

References

ActionAid (2006) *Real Aid, Making Technical Assistance Work*, ActionAid, London.

CEDAW (2007) 'Sierra Leone Shadow reports 2007: initial, second, third and fourth reports on the implementation of CEDAW', United Nations, New York.

Help a Needy Child in Sierra Leone (HANCi-SL) (2008) 'Evaluation of HANCi-SL and ChildHope (UK) project: to promote peace and reconciliation in post conflict Sierra Leone', <www.street-child.co.uk/sl.php>.

Kanbur, A. and Sumner, R. (2011) *Poor Countries or Poor People? Development Assistance and the New Geography of* Poverty, Cornell University, New York, cited in Glennie, J. (2012), 'What if three quarters of the world's poor live (and have always lived) in Low Aid Countries?', ODI, London [PDF], <http//www.odi.org.uk/resources/docs/7681.pdf>.

McIntyre, P. (2006) *Pregnant Adolescents: Delivering on Global Promises of Hope*, World Health Organization (WHO), Geneva [PDF], <www.who.int/child_adolescent_health/documents/9241593784/en/index.html>.

UNFPA (2005) 'Adolescents fact sheet: state of world population 2005' [webpage], <http://www.unfpa.org/swp/2005/presskit/factsheets/facts_adolescents.htm>.

UNFPA (2011) 'The world at 7 billion: top issues–fact sheets' [PDF], <www.unfpa.org/webdav/site/global/shared/documents/7%20Billion/7B_fact_sheets_en.pdf>.

UNICEF (2010) 'The children left behind: a league table of inequality in child well-being in the worlds richest countries', Innocenti Research Centre, Florence [PDF], <www.unicef-irc.org/publications/pdf/rc9_eng.pdf>.

UNICEF (2011) 'Sexual and reproductive health matters', in *The State of the World's Children: Adolescence – an age of opportunity*, UNICEF, New York [PDF], <www.scribd.com/UNICEF/d/49542133/11-Sexual-and-reproductive-health-matters>.

United Nations (UN) (2010) 'Millennium Development Goals fact sheet 3' [webpage], <http://www.un.org/millenniumgoals/pdf/MDG_FS_3_EN.pdf>.

World Health Organization (WHO) (2009) 'Women's health, fact sheet no 334' [webpage], <www.who.int/mediacentre/factsheets/fs334/en/index.html>.

Zimbabwe Women Lawyers Association (2012) Zimbabwe's civil society shadow report to the CEDAW Committee, Zimbabwe, Harare.

About the author

Seri Wendoh is the Senior Technical Officer, Rights and Gender at the IPPF. She has researched extensively into how relationships of power are manifested in sexual and gender-based violence. She has over 20 years' experience as researcher and trainer with grass-roots and national women's organizations in Africa. She has a degree in Education from the University of Nairobi, a doctorate on the intersection between race, class, and gender from Leeds University, taught literature and gender studies at the University of Nairobi, served as an advocate for gender and rights at Transform Africa, and works as a social development consultant. At IPPF, Seri works with programmes on the implementation of gender, rights, and sexuality based on the framework of the IPPF Declaration on Sexual Rights which seeks to ensure access to sexual and reproductive health services and advocate for the rights of all, especially the poor, marginalized, and stigmatized.

CHAPTER 12
Looking beyond the numbers: reducing violence against women in Ghana

Kanwal Ahluwalia

The Nkyinkyim Anti-Violence programme stands out as a beacon of good development practice and has resulted in significant improvements in the lives of women and girls in Ghana. The programme focused on achieving changes within the lives of predominately poor, rural women and girls experiencing violence and the changes in attitudes and behaviours of those around them. The programme took a bottom-up, responsive approach and enabled women themselves to determine what needed to change. Women themselves shaped, altered, and benefited from the programme. However, this approach became increasingly 'at odds' with donors in the UK who were under pressure to demonstrate success through quick results for large numbers of women. The challenge for the NGOs involved was how to remain true to the principle of enabling women to lead the changes in their own lives while trying to comply with ever-changing and increasing donor demands.

As a practitioner working on women's rights and gender equality, I am constantly asked for examples of good practice. What works? What can we replicate and scale up? Can we really change power relations between men and women and can we do this in short time frames? How can we measure these changes? In trying to respond, one programme still stands out as a beacon of good practice. The Nkyinkyim Anti-Violence programme[1] in Ghana, coordinated by the Gender Studies and Human Rights Documentation Centre (Gender Centre), made a significant difference to the lives of poor, rural women and girls experiencing violence[2] in their homes and communities. So what makes this programme stand out? Perhaps the key is in the name, 'Nkyinkyim', an ancient *Akan* symbol, which translates as 'twisting' and symbolizes innovation and versatility. This was the bedrock of its success.

The origins of the project

Following a spate of murders of women in Accra, the Gender Centre undertook nationwide research on the prevalence of violence against women and girls (VAWG). This research provided insights, which were used to design a pilot to tackle the issue and then a scaled-up programme to reduce domestic violence.

http://dx.doi.org/10.3362/9781780447780/012

This was development work at its best – trial and error – building a culturally responsive model, which was adapted as time went on, building on what was and was not working. At each stage women and those around them were involved in the development of the response; vitally, the work done to bring men on board and the lobbying for a law to criminalize domestic violence helped spearhead and sustain change.

Based on women's own perceptions of what needed to change, the programme focused on achieving changes within the lives of individual women experiencing violence, and changes in the attitudes and behaviours of those around them. In order to understand and track change, primarily qualitative data were gathered. This approach was a far cry from the world of logframes and SMART objectives and the pressures of demonstrating success. The approach became increasingly 'at odds' with donors in the UK who, in response to pressure from the Treasury, were pushing NGOs to prove impact mainly through quantitative data collection to illustrate quick results for large numbers of women. Is it possible to marry these two very different approaches?

Action-based research and consultation

The Nkyinkyim Anti-Violence programme developed following nationwide research[3] on the prevalence of violence against women and girls, the ways in which women and society responded to this, and what the barriers were to effectively reducing violence. Findings indicated that one in three women and girls had been subject to physical abuse (e.g., being slapped or beaten), three out of four had been subject to psychological abuse (being shouted at, humiliated, ignored, prevented from seeing family or friends), and one in three had been subject to sexual harassment or rape (Coker-Appiah and Cusack, 1999). Interestingly the main cause of violence was when women and girls were seen to be stepping out of their defined traditional roles by, for example, not living up to expected household responsibilities or refusing to take 'instruction' from their husbands or fathers. The pressure to not report violence to family members or friends was strong, even moreso to outsiders such as the police or social workers, which would bring dishonour to their communities. Women feared the consequences of reporting, which, potentially, included divorce from their husbands, removal from their homes, and ostracism by their communities; in many cases women and girls were blamed for the violence. Many women interviewed held the view that domestic violence was a private matter and one that the state should not interfere in. As we often see, many women and girls themselves articulated the same views on violence as its perpetrators, illustrating how deeply they had internalized patriarchal social attitudes and norms. The research also highlighted the lack of government or customary law to tackle violence – particularly within rural areas.

Following the research, extensive consultation was undertaken with community members and staff from state agencies including the police service, the Ghana Commission on Human Rights and Administrative Justice, local health centres, the social welfare department, and local government officials in order to develop a pilot project, initially in three rural areas and later in a further 15. The communities had very different contexts. Some were in the southern regions of Ghana – predominantly Christian with matrilineal kinship systems. Others were in the north in primarily Islamic, more patrilineal, communities, which experienced far higher poverty levels, political marginalization, and a long-standing conflict.

The programme had three core elements:

(1) a community response for women experiencing or at risk of domestic violence in rural communities which had little access to government services, a model which became known as the Rural Response System;
(2) sensitization work with community members and staff from state agencies to ensure a deeper understanding of the types, causes, and consequences of violence in order to reduce the acceptability of violence; and
(3) alliance-building with other NGOs to undertake advocacy work to push for the passage of a Domestic Violence Act to protect women and girls in law.

The Rural Response System was developed by women themselves and their communities. They selected volunteers to form anti-violence teams known as community-based action teams or COMBATs. The teams had equal numbers of women and men based on their view that men needed to be involved right from the start. They agreed on the support needed for women and potential sanctions for perpetrators. Consultations also took place with state agencies about effective referrals and with other NGOs working on violence to agree an advocacy plan.

An interesting element of the Gender Centre's approach was that they were not directly operational but worked in collaboration with other civil society actors. They identified six partner organizations[4] working in the target areas, known to and trusted by the communities. Most of the partners were mainstream development organizations (not women's rights organizations) and the Gender Centre built their capacity on gender by working alongside them, supporting staff to identify and challenge any unconscious negative attitudes they had towards violence against women and girls.

Implementation

The power and influence of traditional chiefs and community elders remains strong in rural Ghana so getting them to understand that violence was a form of abuse and had negative consequences, not only for the women themselves but the wider community, was vital because they were the ones who usually presided over cases of violence in the community. Ghana continues to be a deeply religious society and so priests and imams were also targeted as key stakeholders to ensure they actively discouraged violence using verses from the Bible and Koran to highlight the importance of love and respect to all.

Initially COMBATs were trained to work as peer educators to sensitize community members. Using focus group discussions, *durbars*,[5] plays, and songs they began to get communities talking about violence. They discussed what constituted violence and that it was not just physical or sexual but also included emotional (refusing to talk to a wife or eat the food she had prepared) as well as economic violence (such as refusing to pay for a daughter's school fees on the basis that she was not worth investing in). They also talked about how violence prevented harmonious relationships and further subjugated women. A deliberate attempt was made, however, not to use the language of gender and rights, because these are often seen as a Western imposition; local concepts and ways of thinking were used instead. This was complemented by work with the media to ensure journalists did not report violence in sensationalist ways and radio programmes were promoted to allow communities to further debate the issues.

As COMBAT members were selected for their good standing and trustworthiness in the community (including some religious or traditional leaders) they soon became the first point of contact for women and girls experiencing violence as well as a deterrent to violence happening in the first place. COMBAT members, working in pairs, would offer a range of support based on a woman's specific needs. This could include first aid or accompaniment to a health centre; counselling; mediation with her partner if this was what she wanted; and support with taking her case to the chief or the police and social workers. Women were also referred to existing microfinance, revolving loans, or seed grants where they could access finance and skills to increase their economic security because many women felt they could not leave abusive partners due to their economic dependency. Each case was meticulously written up by a literate COMBAT member to document the woman's particular situation and the course of action she decided to follow; the final outcome was also recorded.

In some areas, chiefs and community members developed a sanctions system for the perpetrator – for minor offences it might be public apology by the perpetrator or the 'gifting of eggs', which is seen as a sign of a new beginning. In the Upper East Region, some chiefs instigated by-laws to institutionalize the prevention of violence in their communities. This mechanism of using traditional and community-based safety nets and responses complemented the formal justice system that women could still access when appropriate.

Education work with state agency staff helped to ensure that when women reported cases they would not be faced with what is termed 'secondary victimization' by being blamed for the violence. The Gender Centre also developed a module on gender and VAWG, which was incorporated by the national police force for use in training all new recruits.

The community work was complemented by policy work. The Gender Centre, together with other mainstream and women's organizations, formed the Domestic Violence Bill Coalition. Then began the arduous task of drafting and promoting the passage of a Domestic Violence Bill. For many years the Bill's reading within Parliament was stalled over the repeal of a section of the Criminal Code that related to marital rape, which many MPs wanted removed. The Bill was finally passed in 2007 without the clause on marital rape. However, the government invited the Coalition to help develop a National Plan of Action on the Domestic Violence Act and to be a member of the Domestic Violence Management Board.

The impact of this work

During regular visits to the communities involved in the programme I spoke to many women who talked about how violence had reduced substantially in their homes, whether by their partners or from other family members, e.g., mothers-in-law. Their stories, as well as those from men about how their lives had been transformed, struck home; one story of Joyce and Mensah from the village of Akawani stays with me still.

Joyce, a nursery teacher, had volunteered to be a COMBAT member. Mensah, her husband, regularly beat her and objected to her attending meetings; he would hide her slippers to try and prevent her going but a determined Joyce would borrow her friend's slippers and attend anyway. When I first met the couple I asked Mensah what had given rise to his behaviour towards his wife. He told me how he felt: he was 'suffering to pay for everything' so felt that he should be making all the decisions at home and he would not share his money with Joyce even though she needed it. Joyce would resort to stealing it and this would result in fights. Mensah explained that he started to change when Joyce brought back materials from the meetings, which he would read on the quiet. Eventually he agreed to attend community meetings with her and they realized that violence was common in many households. Mensah said he realized that violence was affecting his relationship with his wife and their five children badly. He started listening to Joyce's views and they began to make shared decisions; he also spent more time looking after his children and helping out with housework.

Time and again I visited communities across Ghana listening to women and men talk about the project – in packed churches, in school halls, or on village benches in the dappled shade of trees. Women and men talked openly and with confidence about violence, its effects, and what had changed in the community. I remember a particularly wizened chief telling me that 'his food no longer went cold' because of dealing with cases of violence; the presence of COMBAT members in his chiefdom had reduced them.

These testimonies were common across the life of the programme and went beyond supporting women experiencing violence to a change in rigid gender roles. Community members demonstrated a deeper understanding of violence that included physical violence, neglect, withdrawal of support, and emotional abuse. Through the sensitization work, the role of women and girls within rural, traditional society was examined and community members began increasingly to value their contributions. Women's role in decision-making increased, for example, from the pooling of household income and joint decisions on how it was used to agreeing together when to have sex. Men who previously had prevented their wives from working on the basis that they should not be economic providers or that they should have limited exposure to other men agreed that their wives could usefully contribute to household income. Daughters were more likely to be cared for and attendance at schools increased. Men began supporting their wives in domestic work (Ampofo, 2008).

Involving male power brokers was crucial. Support from chiefs in particular as well as religious leaders, staff from state agencies, and male COMBAT members was important in changing behaviours, creating positive role models, and sustaining change (Ampofo, 2008). However, the pace of change varied across the different project areas and communities in the northern regions of Ghana that were more patriarchal were more resistant to change, so it was even more important to bring those men who were influential on side.

Levels of violence reduced. Community members and state agencies' staff reported significant declines in levels of violence, including emotional and economic violence, all of which was ascribed to the work of the COMBATs. In focus group discussions towards the end of the programme between 65 and 90 per cent reported a reduction of violence against women in their communities and between 60 and 90 per cent reported greater levels of decision-making by women.[6] Another stark indicator of success was the fact that women and men from adjacent villages to those where the COMBATs worked came to learn about the programme, because they had heard about and seen for themselves the decline in conflict within the COMBAT village and wondered whether the programme could be expanded to include their own villages.

The passage of the Domestic Violence Act provided police and judiciary members with a stronger mandate to deal with cases of violence. Awareness-raising work through the print and broadcast media helped to substantially increase visibility of the issue, sparking much public debate and aiding the passage of the Bill.

The process of piloting the work to enable continuous learning and capacity building of partners was crucial. Initiating a process of sensitization and dialogue and then institutionalizing an ongoing process of education and critical reflection at the community level was very successful (Waibel, 2004). The Gender Centre and their UK NGO partner, Womankind Worldwide,[7] were commended in successive evaluations for their partnership approach to increasing the capacity of partners on gender, programme implementation, and organizational development, which enabled the work to increase its reach and effectiveness.

Beyond the programme

Since the end of the programme the Rural Response System was adopted by the Domestic Violence Secretariat, within the Ministry of Women and Children's Affairs, which is tasked to implement the National Plan of Action on Domestic Violence. The Rural Response System is being developed and implemented in 12 communities in one region with a view to further scale-up. The Gender Centre is working with the Secretariat to undertake a new study on violence against women and girls. Implementing partners continue to use the RRS model but are seeking funds to continue the work in adjacent areas. The Gender Centre has since undertaken action-based research on the links between gender inequality, violence, and HIV and is currently working with partners to address the susceptibility of women to HIV infection as a result of negative gender norms.

The challenges of demonstrating change

Throughout the duration of the programme, Womankind supported the Gender Centre to focus on learning from the work. The donor's reporting format was adapted to allow for documenting change but by the end of the project real challenges around reporting emerged. The donor context in the UK had substantially shifted; the need to assuage a donor-fatigued general public and justify spending on aid had started to take centre stage. Donors were increasingly asking for more 'robust' monitoring and evaluation systems primarily concerned with numbers, and less interested in changes in attitudes, behaviour, and women's own perceptions of change – a key element of any work to achieve gender equality. The Gender Centre felt the sharp end of this shift. They felt that these donor demands 'to demonstrate success in numerical terms' were hindering real learning, leaving less time for qualitative analysis with partners and communities, and jeopardizing their ability to find funding for this sort of work.

The purpose of data collection was not always clear in terms of what the donor needed, partly because this changed quite dramatically over the course of the programme. Initially qualitative data sufficed but towards the end the demands were increasingly for quantitative information. Each COMBAT meticulously wrote out case studies of women experiencing violence, believing these were necessary for the donor, only to discover they were not in fact the kind of numerical data required. Case studies were not longitudinal studies so they were seen as anecdotal by the donor and not sufficient to demonstrate impact. Mountains of data that took hours to compile lay unused.

The Gender Centre and Womankind knew, however, that positive changes *had* taken place from conversations with numerous different stakeholders, and most importantly the women themselves. A very participative mid-term review, which brought together stakeholders from all the different project areas, many of whom had left their villages for the first time and were able to meet and share experiences and strategies, generated real learning about women's lives and what enabled positive change. It was an unmitigated success for stakeholders but did not produce the sort of statistical data that donors now demanded. By the time of the final evaluation there was strong pressure to try and make the qualitative data more quantitative retrospectively. So, in focus group discussions stakeholders were asked about 'before and after' and to quantify their perceptions of change in an effort to 'improve' the qualitative data.

The Nkyinkyim Anti-Violence project was on the threshold of two quite different approaches. On the one hand there was a bottom-up, responsive approach that enabled participative monitoring and evaluation processes, where stakeholders themselves shaped, altered, and benefited from the programme; they defined the change that mattered to them. On the other there was a much more top-down approach driven by the demands of those far away from the coal face of development requiring data that fitted their definitions of measuring change for women, and demonstrated accountable and effective expenditure. The challenges of bridging these two apparently clashing approaches were brought into sharp relief in the Nkyinkyim programme. The challenge was how to merge these two elements when one is championed by those who hold the power and purse strings. How far are these two approaches mutually exclusive?

Certainly there is a need for upward accountability to ensure that money has been used ethically and for the benefit of those that it was intended for and all NGOs have stringent, audited accounting procedures. There is space for the collection of *both* qualitative and quantitative data in order to gauge to what extent impact is taking place. NGOs want to know – perhaps more than donors – that the work they are doing is making a difference for those with whom they are working. NGOs such as the Gender Centre equally want to ensure downward accountability to the very people the project is aimed at. In practice meeting both agendas requires different methodologies, and different ways of collecting data and working with communities. All in all, it requires a great deal of staff time and diverse skills, which are not paid for within project funding.

Staying true to our practice in this context is increasingly the challenge. Ensuring that the women and men at the heart of our development work lead the changes in their own lives, and that we serve to merely facilitate that process, is so often what seems to be missing from our work now. The de-politicization of international development is well underway. The rhetoric of rights, social transformation, and power has faded while the mantras of replication, scale-up, and value for money ring in our ears. Funding for development work – and particularly for work on gender equality – is proving harder to obtain, partly due to the pressure to demonstrate numerical impact in short time frames. Competition is increasing amongst NGOs and our communications messages get simpler. Gone is the nuance of development messaging and old 'instrumentalist' arguments have reared their heads again: poverty can be fixed overnight; those at the very margins of society can transform the world with a few pence or a few days of training. These messages serve only to exacerbate the problem. The general public understand less and less about the complexities of reducing poverty and tackling unequal power relations because we feed them simplified messages. This puts pressure on our governments and in turn NGOs to demonstrate quick results. Even NGOs like Womankind, which has always striven to redress power imbalances in its relationships with Southern partner organizations, feel the pressure to adhere to increasing donor demands. This in turn impacts on how NGOs in Ghana spend their time and use their resources for learning.

In this difficult context, we have a great responsibility to keep downward accountability at the core of our work and to renew our vigour, to challenge ourselves and others about who is actually leading the agenda and how to shift the power back to the people. It is essential to continually remind ourselves of the need for trial and error in development work; to enable interventions to be moulded by the people that they are intended for; and to remember it is their own perceptions of success that matter. Change can and does take place but often it is not well explained by simple numbers; more relevant is who is looking, learning, and benefiting.

Notes

1. The Nkyinkyim Anti-Violence programme took place between 2002 and 2007 and was coordinated by the Gender Studies and Human Rights Documentation Centre, together with six implementing NGOs. It was funded in the UK by Comic Relief and managed by Womankind Worldwide, a London-based international women's rights organization.
2. The UN definition of violence against women and girls refers to 'any act of gender-based violence that results in, or is likely to result in, physical, sexual or psychological harm or suffering to women' (UN Commission on Human Rights resolution 2003/45).
3. The research was conducted in 1998 in all 10 regions of Ghana with over 2,000 women and girls.
4. Partner organizations included General Agricultural Workers Union (GAWU) in the Eastern Region, Centre for the Development of People (CEDEP) in the Ashanti Region, Amasachina Self-Help Association in the Upper West Region and in the Upper East Region, Centre for Sustainable Development Initiatives (CENSUDI), Associates in Development (ASSID), and Bawku East Women's Development Association (BEWDA).
5. Community events usually presided over by traditional authorities.
6. Focus group discussions by partners did not include Centre for Sustainable Development Initiatives (CENSUDI) communities.
7. Womankind Worldwide is a non-operational NGO working with women's rights organizations in the global South to improve the lives of women. It has a long history of identifying strategic women's rights organizations and providing targeted support to strengthen the women's movement in a particular country.

References

Ampofo, A. A. (2008) 'Final external evaluation of the Nkyinkyim Anti-Violence Programme, Ghana – January 2005–December 2007'.
Coker-Appiah, D., and Cusack, K. (eds) (1999) *Breaking the Silence and Challenging the Myths of Violence Against Women and Children in Ghana: Report of a National Study on Violence,* Yamens Printing and Packaging, Accra.
Waibel, G. (2004) 'External evaluation of the Nkyinkyim Anti-Violence Programme, Ghana – March 2002–May 2004'.

About the author

Kanwal Ahluwalia has an MA in development studies and has worked in the field of international development for 17 years with specific expertise in women's rights and gender equality. She has worked for a range of agencies including WomenAid International, the Humanitarian Policy Group of the Overseas Development Institute, ChildHope, and Womankind Worldwide. At Womankind her work focused on gender transformative programming in the areas of reducing violence against women and HIV as well as increasing women's role in political processes. Currently Kanwal is Gender Equality Advisor for Plan UK, tasked with mainstreaming gender equality and girls' rights into all of Plan's work. Kanwal has been or is involved in either a trustee or advisory capacity to Collective Artistes, Gender and Development Network, International Centre for Health and Human Rights, a multi-donor initiative to tackle female genital mutilation, and the Darbar Arts and Culture Heritage Trust.

CHAPTER 13

From local to global and back again – learning from Stepping Stones

Alice Welbourn

This chapter charts the history, development, and spread of a programme called 'Stepping Stones' over the past 20 years, since the author, Alice Welbourn, first learnt that she had HIV. The programme, built on the participatory learning and action movement, takes a holistic, life-enhancing, and rights-based approach to the challenge and opportunities of a crisis like HIV, enabling 'ordinary' community members, without any formal education, to develop powers of critical literacy around their own experiences in their own contexts. Through explicit acknowledgement of issues of difference along gender and generational lines, and through implicit trust and belief in the inherent wisdom of people most affected by an issue to work out their own mutually supportive solutions, the programme has spread, often by word of mouth, across cultures, countries, and continents – and is still spreading. This has been achieved despite, rather than because of, the externally imposed formal 'evidence base' required increasingly by public health experts, academics, and donors.

Background

This is a story of a long-term development initiative that grew from a small seed and became a global approach; a story of perseverance at times, of cooperation, of multiple players. It is a story about learning, change, and adaptation and the way understanding of the complex issues around HIV and AIDS has deepened over time.

Stepping Stones (Welbourn, 1995), a training package on gender, HIV communication, and relationship skills, started with an idea, from an HIV and AIDS communication project, Strategies for Hope (Williams, 1989). In 1993 Glen Williams identified the need for a booklet on HIV and women. This was a few months after I had been diagnosed with HIV and, in what I thought were to be the last few remaining months of my life, I desperately wanted to do something useful, to make some sense of this diagnosis. I asked Glen, who was one of the very few colleagues who knew my status, if he might be prepared for me to write this booklet. He agreed, and also agreed to a different kind of publication. Thus the idea of a short booklet grew over time to be not just about women, but about women and men and relationships, and instead

http://dx.doi.org/10.3362/9781780447780/013

of a short booklet it was a manual for an 18-session participatory training activity to be held over nine weeks, with scope for younger and older age groups to take part. And so the idea for Stepping Stones was born.

It started with a very limited budget – just £100,000. It mushroomed, from an initial four weeks of desk-based work to a research process of over two-and-a-half years, involving three research, training, and review visits to Uganda. It stopped and started along the way, as we struggled to find new funds and because the enormity of the issues faced by the participants in the first workshop, in South West Uganda, took its toll on our spirits. Yet the generosity of everyone involved, with their time, their willingness to take part in a wholly new way of thinking about and working on these issues, won through. Together with the exceptional talents of the late Professor Rose Mbowa and her excellent team of former students who were the first facilitators of the workshop, as well as an extraordinary team of advisors all committed to the development of the programme, the training manual and accompanying workshop video was finally published in December 1995. The project has never looked back.

The process, from the outset, was designed as a collegiate venture, with multiple funding sources. Strategies for Hope, while the brainchild of Glen and Alison Williams, was at that time under the supportive umbrella of ActionAid. The first workshop was held in a Ugandan community where Redd Barna (who contributed most of the initial funds) was working (ActionAid et al., 1998). Other international donors contributed and soon became involved in rolling out Stepping Stones. While no explicit theoretical base to the programme was set out at the time, others have since written clearly about 'critical literacy', 'critical pedagogy', and 'scaffolded learning' (Stepping Stones, 2012a). These all connect closely with the participatory principles of shared learning which were, at that time, being developed through the Rapid Rural Appraisal (RRA) and Participatory Learning and Action (PLA) movement, spearheaded by Robert Chambers and colleagues at the Institute of Development Studies (IDS) and International Institute for Environment and Development (IIED), and in locations across Africa and Asia (Mascarenhas et al., 1991; Chambers, 1995). These participatory approaches established a clear and revolutionary (for development work) set of understandings about how people can change the way they (and we) think and behave over time (Chambers, 1995).

Stepping Stones offered an approach based on the principle that we are all struggling with some big universal questions in our lives, whoever we are and wherever we live in the world. Rather than parachuting in messages and solutions from other contexts and experiences, the idea was to support and enable communities to think through these universal issues in their own lives and in the context of their own experiences. This opportunity was offered through the creation of same-gender and same-age groups initially, allowing participants freedom and relative safety to express themselves and to think and talk about their lives in a way which enabled them to develop their own understanding about why we all behave as we do. The 18 sessions, each two to three hours long, allowed participants to work out alternative ways of communicating and taking decisions, 'rehearsing for reality' through role-plays, within the safety of the workshop setting (Stepping Stones, 2012b).

Growth and spread

The programme, piloted and developed with Rose Mbowa's team and the community in Uganda, has now been adapted, translated, and shared with communities in over 100 countries around the world (Salamander Trust, 2011). It has spread in multiple ways over two decades. ActionAid International used it in many of their country programmes, as did other agencies, notably Acord and Plan International. Acord, through the wonderful efforts of Angela Hajipateras, Denis Nduhuru, and colleagues, created *Implementing Stepping Stones*, an invaluable guide to adapting the material for different contexts (Acord, 2007). Over the years, we have gradually developed an international network of trainers (Salamander Trust, 2008) and/or programme managers (Stepping Stones, 2011) who use the material, and of others who continue to be interested in the programme and its spread.

More recently, as we realized that Stepping Stones continued not only to be in use but also to spread to new organizations and new communities across the world, we have developed a global 'community of practice'. This is accessed through our dedicated trilingual Stepping Stones website.[1] We have also launched a regular newsletter to share information between the members of our 1,000-plus database;[2] and, most recently, we have a Ning platform, a more community development-oriented version of Facebook.[3] This networking has been an inspiring recent development over the past three years, made possible by the way the material seems to have developed a life of its own through the work of the NGOs mentioned and also organically, through individuals as they move from one organization to another and as they hear about it from others. Thus, across the continents, we keep on learning about use of the material by organizations with whom we have had no direct contact. This is very exciting but also presents us with a huge challenge, since we would love to find a way of connecting with all the users and to learn more about their experiences. Yet to do so would demand a far greater investment in infrastructure than we can afford.[4]

Evaluating Stepping Stones

From the outset, we wanted to learn how organizations were using Stepping Stones. We included a quick review exercise with participants at the end of each session and also an evaluation questionnaire for organizations to fill in at the end. We also conducted a participatory review with participants from the original workshop in Uganda, 16 months after the programme had finished (Welbourn, 1999). This took place in a rural agricultural community with Protestants, Catholics, Muslims, and people of indigenous faith living

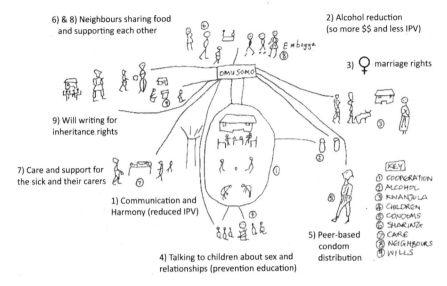

6) & 8) Neighbours sharing food and supporting each other

2) Alcohol reduction (so more $$ and less IPV)

3) ♀ marriage rights

9) Will writing for inheritance rights

7) Care and support for the sick and their carers

1) Communication and Harmony (reduced IPV)

5) Peer-based condom distribution

4) Talking to children about sex and relationships (prevention education)

KEY
① COOPERATION
② ALCOHOL
③ KWANJULA
④ CHILDREN
⑤ CONDOMS
⑥ SHARING
⑦ CARE
⑧ NEIGHBOURS
⑨ WILLS

Figure 13.1 Older women's group, Uganda, 16 months after the workshop
Note: *Omusomo* = workshop, *Kwanjula* = presentation, *Embogga* = cabbage

harmoniously together. Despite the relative harmony, HIV and AIDS-related illness and deaths had already deeply affected the community. During the review, members of the older women's peer group produced the diagram in Figure 13.1 (with the annotations in English written in afterwards for our benefit). This diagram, produced in late 1995, captures succinctly the breadth, depth, and interconnected complexity of HIV and related gender issues – not only for these women but for women around the world.

Amongst those undertaking Stepping Stones, gender-based violence was reported to have reduced through increased positive communication and improved relationships in the home. This had a knock-on effect of women feeling happier and of their children also feeling more content and able to play. Women elsewhere have also reported happier sex with their partners as a concomitant change (UNAIDS, 2010: 42). Women felt more supported by their neighbours in looking after their sick husbands. Although they were not, in 1994–5, talking openly about the HIV in their own homes, it was clear from the level of care for sick partners they were providing that AIDS-related illness and the physical and emotional burdens of care that go with it were very much a part of several women's lives. Women were also talking about the effects of their husbands' will-writing on their lives. This was an aspect of the programme which initially received heavy criticism from some NGO staff in other countries, since the exercise which promoted this response (called *The Long Journey*) was considered too morbid. However, property and inheritance rights for women are a major challenge, especially when a husband's relatives arrive to seize land, house, and possessions from his survivors (Strickland, 2004).

In Figure 13.1, the woman who reported that her husband had finally officially married her, by taking gifts as a sign of respect to her parents, was not just celebrating a party. Rather she was delighted that the workshop had supported her partner to formalize her rights in their relationship. The acceptance of condoms across the peer groups was another major break-through. Condoms had previously been rejected by older people. Yet here women were welcoming their new accessibility. The role of overuse of alcohol in relation to sexual and reproductive health and HIV had been addressed to only a very limited degree in most HIV work; yet here the women clearly flagged it up and reported that there had been a reduction in alcohol use in the community after the workshop. Finally the women reported their ability to overcome their embarrassment and talk with their children about sex and relationships. They explained how they had decided after the workshop that they could talk with their children in open, non-judgmental ways, just as they had learnt to discuss the many issues in the workshop. Here was a clear example of women, most of whom had very limited formal education, taking the initiative to apply new communication and relationship skills learnt from the workshop process, in order to communicate with their children.

Very similar issues have since been raised and discussed – and similar changes have taken place – in thousands of communities around the world.

Ultimately this diagram highlights how very limited and narrow in focus many previous 'behaviour change' interventions have been, when compared to the complex lived realities of people's lives.

The importance of involving men

The programme focuses very much on trying to support individuals, peers, and the wider community to understand *why* we behave as we do, rather than trying to apportion blame, which could also trigger potential recrimination. Thus, while gender-based violence is largely experienced by women as a result of male partners, the programme seeks to support *everyone* to understand *why* men behave as they do. Thus men also seem to have learnt a lot from the programme and feel positive about what they have managed to gain from new insights. From Fiji, for example, young men stated:

> Before Stepping Stones, even though I have known some of the girls in my village for my whole life, I never really talked with them or knew important things about them. I never really thought about getting to know them as they are girls and have their own secret stories. (UNAIDS, 2010)

Another young male Stepping Stones participant said, 'Stepping Stones has made the boys think about girls differently. I now don't always try to have sex with them' (ibid.).

Young men in Uganda after the original workshop reported:

> We used to blame young women, saying it was them who have brought HIV to our community. But now we have realised that we are all in this together and need to support one another. Now it's girls in our own community who have also gone through this programme whom we would like to marry in future, because now we understand each other much better. (Young man, Buwenda Village, Uganda, Alice Welbourn's personal notes, 1995)

Similarly, older men from different parts of the world have echoed the following story:

> Another couple Masautso and Loveness Nkhoma from Chisomo Support Group in T/A Mavwere's area in the same district says lessons learnt from Stepping Stones have revived their fading love. According to Loveness the husband (Masautso) used to refuse to use a condom saying it is his conjugal right. 'Lack of negotiating skills made me to accept the situation despite knowing that it was risky as we are both HIV positive,' says Loveness. Masautso acknowledges that Stepping Stones has helped him to understand the importance of condom use as well as respecting the sexual reproductive health rights of his wife. 'The project enlightened me on good sexual practices, couple communication and human rights' (Masautso). Today, happiness has returned in the Nkhoma's home courtesy of Stepping Stones and both can now afford a smile. (COWHLA, 2010)

'Proving effectiveness'

Despite the evidence of communities themselves, of facilitators, and of organizations implementing Stepping Stones, these (and other) participatory approaches and evaluations have regularly and repeatedly been dismissed as unproven and the data 'anecdotal'. Donors and academic researchers sought a more rigorous testing process and in 2006 ActionAid commissioned Tina Wallace to conduct a 'review of reviews' of Stepping Stones to date (see Stepping Stones, 2012b). This report collated the many reports written by evaluators from many different parts of the world, some long, some short, some rigorous, others less so. For the first time a picture emerged of the spread of the material and the extent of its effect to date. To give just one example:

> Almost every review and discussion paper reported an improvement in communication, usually between spouses or children and parents, as a result of the Stepping Stones training. This was seen as critically important in contexts where discussing sex is difficult yet essential in the fight against the spread of HIV & AIDS. This finding was very nearly universal. (Wallace, 2006: 21)

This particular finding was soon backed up further by the findings of a randomized control trial (RCT), conducted for the South African Medical Research Council by Jewkes et al. (2006, 2008) based on an adaptation of Stepping Stones for semi-urban South Africa (Jewkes and Cornwall, 1998). RCTs are very expensive and this RCT was only able to afford to run the Stepping Stones programme with the two younger peer groups rather than with all four peer groups, as originally recommended. It reported nonetheless a reduction in gender-based violence (GBV), less transactional sex, and less problem drinking and drug use amongst young men, as well as a 33 per cent reduction in the herpes simplex virus (HSV-2) for both young men and women.

However, the primary bio-medical marker, HIV, did not reduce significantly for either young men or young women. It could be argued that, since the normal pattern for HIV acquisition by younger women is through their having relationships with (and acquiring HIV from) older men before they, in turn, pass HIV on to younger men, that there was not yet a large enough number of young men with HIV in either the control arm or the intervention arm of the study for any intervention to manage to show a significant reduction in HIV. Whether or not this is the case, the fact that there was not a significant reduction in HIV amongst the male participants has led some to comment that this RCT produced a 'flat result' (Laga et al., 2012). This is a shame, because the other clear results that came out of the RCT – including reduced GBV, improved mental health of intervention arm participants, and fewer partners for males (Jewkes et al., 2006) – still stand and point to some significant changes going on, at least in part connected with the Stepping Stones programme.

Other work, by Devries et al. (2010) and others (GCWA, 2011), has subsequently established that increases in intimate partner violence (IPV) markedly increases women's vulnerability to HIV by a factor of 4–5 around the world. (Similarly, a review by Hale and Vazquez (2011) highlights the increased IPV experienced by women *with* HIV.) On the basis of the Jewkes RCT findings, the World Health Organisation (2007) and USAID (2010) have both identified Stepping Stones as a key community tool recognized to reduce GBV – and therefore, by proxy, a useful tool in the overall territory of community-based HIV prevention. While, as Wallace highlighted, an improvement in communication was 'very nearly universal' (2006: 22) from the many different reviews of Stepping Stones, it is the South African RCT which, being the gold standard in the eyes of donors and academics, has placed Stepping Stones in the WHO and USAID documents. Yet as Laga et al. have just published:

> Experimental designs will continue to have a place in the evaluation of specific well-defined components of prevention programs. But with 2 million new HIV infections a year, we cannot afford to dismiss potentially effective prevention programs simply because they can't easily be randomized or because they are 'too complex' to evaluate. Evidence-based HIV prevention is possible, but it must go beyond RCTs. (2012: 782)

Thus it is slowly being recognized by academic researchers what many in the NGO world have long felt: that RCTs, while they may be the best known method of testing new medications, have only limited efficacy in evaluating the messy realms of psychological and socio-economic behaviour change.

Stepping Stones is increasingly gaining attention from many key agencies as an approach that works to address gender-based violence – and thus, by extension – to reduce HIV risk. It is also being reported by many to reduce the risk of violence against women *with* HIV, as the quote below illustrates – although the work of the Coalition of Women Living with HIV/AIDS (COWLHA) has yet to be formally evaluated. Will we need to wait for another RCT to confirm this finding too?

> Flora Chingwalu is a 38 year old member and chairperson of Talandira support group. Flora had this to say about what the project has done for her: 'before the Stepping Stones training for our support group, my husband was forcing me to bear another child against my will by insisting on unprotected sex. This made our marriage reach a breaking point because we always argued over having another baby. But after we both attended the Stepping Stones training my husband began to understand that he does not need to force me to have another child against my wish because it is a form of gender based violence. As a result, my husband and I have agreed that we will not have any more kids in addition to the ones that we have. My husband and I are happily married again and we are enjoying a great sex life because we no longer argue.' (COWLHA, 2010: 7)

Going to scale – and going global

In the current climate, where HIV and gender-based violence are so widespread and have such a deep effect, scale-up of programmes is seen to be critical (UNAIDS, 2012). However, this is always a huge challenge for any programme – how to achieve scale-up without losing the quality of an intervention? Yet the Stepping Stones approach has been successfully taken to scale in a number of different contexts, including Malawi (where Stepping Stones is used by COWLHA in 18 districts now), the Gambia, India, and Ecuador. In Ecuador, it was introduced through Plan International, after they had heard about it from colleagues in East Africa. One Plan staff member then joined UNFPA and took on the wider promotion of the material. The Latin American adaptation, 'Paso a Paso', has been adopted by the Ministries of Education and Health for roll-out across schools in Ecuador (Bollinger, 2012). It has spread across the Central American region, with the support of Plan Las Americas, Ayuda en Acción, and other partners.

Meanwhile, in Fiji, Stepping Stones now forms part of the National Strategic Plan (UNAIDS, 2010). I believe it reached Fiji, because an Englishman and his Fijian wife lived in Malawi while he was working with ActionAid there.

They took the programme idea back to Fiji with them and asked trainers from Uganda and South Africa to help them to adapt it for the Pacific. Whatever the precise reason for its arrival in Fiji, it has now spread across the South Pacific Islands through the Regional HIV Programme (SPC, 2007). And the results reflect those found elsewhere over the years:

> 'My husband never cared about women's sicknesses. If I had a stomach ache and he wanted sex he would just have it. Now my husband tries to understand me as a woman. He talks to me more about women's sickness and if I don't feel like sex he is more understanding.'

> 'Even though I am married with four children, I didn't know much about sex and the different names and styles. After Stepping Stones and through talking with other women I have learnt a lot about sex. My sex life with my husband is now much better.' (UNAIDS, 2010)

There are hundreds of similar quotes from participants from widely differing regions. If well adapted and facilitated, Stepping Stones seems to work in similar ways in many diverse contexts, cultures, and groups. It can be scaled-up and continue to be effective.

There are times when we have managed to share Stepping Stones experiences in workshop settings. For instance, a rare opportunity arose when staff from civil society organizations, National AIDS Control Programmes, UN agencies, and networks of women with HIV from 16 countries across several regions of the world came together for a workshop in Istanbul in November 2011. This workshop focused on integrating strategies to address GBV and engage men and boys, while ensuring meaningful involvement of women and girls in National AIDS Control Programmes (Salamander Trust, 2011). There was an opportunity here to show a short summary video of how Stepping Stones works with men and boys, and the work of COWLHA, Malawi,[5] since its use of Stepping Stones in 18 districts met all the criteria of the workshop theme. In the words of one UN staff member:

> I think the real life examples of the changes we would like to see – the Stepping Stones video and the story from Malawi – were motivating and helped to ground the discussions. (Matthew Cogan, UNAIDS, email, December 2011)

Such workshops are extremely rare, however, and while this was deemed a success by all who attended, funding for follow-up is currently doubtful.

The significance of this experience

The long and experimental process of writing Stepping Stones was one which probably could not have happened had we been employees of a large organization. The trust and enthusiasm for creative innovation and flexibility which Strategies for Hope offered to the genesis of the programme was absolutely key in enabling the idea to develop. Large organizational structures often cannot allow the flexibility of experimentation and expansion from one modest concept to quite another over the course of three years.

Over the years we have also learnt that building alliances, forging cooperation, listening, and working together to bring change are critical and yet are often extremely hard to do – even harder to get funded. This has been a source of immense frustration. There has been a sense that, if only we had had better funding along the way, for example to conduct more acceptably rigorous evaluations earlier on, and to develop a wider cadre of good trainers and facilitators and more formal networks, we might have got to where we are sooner than the 17 years it has taken. It would also have been easier and better had people with HIV – especially women – not been sidelined from change processes, largely because of the stigma and discrimination we have faced, which have, for many, many years, forced most of us (myself included) to keep our status hidden from all but a very small circle of confidantes. It is also often interesting to see that large organizations sometimes struggle with the challenges to their hierarchical structures that working with Stepping Stones often throws up for participants and facilitators.

Yet, we have seen that if people feel a programme connects with their own experiences and works for them, they will pick it up, adapt it, and do their best to make it happen. What has been key to the programme's adaptation and spread is that one individual from within a country or region has identified with it and run with it. He or she has seen its potential in their own context, taken up the idea, and nurtured it to make it appropriate for their setting. While there are some 'foundation stones' that we ask all those who use the manual to maintain, there is also a lot of room for flexibility in local adaptation. It is not, therefore, a programme which has been *imposed* from outside, but is rather one that someone from within has decided to import and adapt. I think the successful expansion of the programme has been largely due to an immense sense of local ownership and pride in local achievements – often followed by a delight in being part of a global community of local practice.

As Amandine Bollinger wrote in her annual report of Stepping Stones activities for 2011–12, after a visit to Karnataka, India, where the use of Stepping Stones has now eliminated child marriage in communities where it has been used:

> Generally, the in-country teams are thrilled when we visit them. They're often not aware of the international dimension of the work. It makes them feel validated and part of something much bigger, much bigger than just the work they are doing locally (especially for participants at village level) – it's very motivational. Teams are eager to share what they are doing and what they've learnt. They often are aware of gaps in their knowledge and are really keen to find answers. Everyone likes to ask questions about other countries. (Salamander Trust, 2012)

The work of women's organizations, such as COWLHA in Malawi, and networks, such as our global Community of Practice, in promoting this approach are also a key element. These are often chronically underfunded and expend huge waves of creative energy in struggling just to exist. However much they have to struggle, their determination to keep going is immense, driven by their own personal experiences and an unwavering resolve to stick with and push an idea that works for them.

'Glocal' is a word I have recently learnt, linking, as it does, 'global' policies and issues with 'local' responses and practices. Perhaps this is what the spread of Stepping Stones has achieved. Perhaps Stepping Stones is 'glocalization' in practice. Perhaps this could *only* have happened as it has *without* our attempt to promote it, which might have made it feel something foreign, external, superficially imposed.

Concluding thoughts

This is not the history of Stepping Stones and the thousands who have been involved; rather it is a story of how a small initiative grew and became powerful through local ideas, local commitment, and local initiatives. Despite the lack of consistent and large funding, despite the many critiques of this 'messy' process by public health academics, donors, and the aid industry, the programme has been seen repeatedly, and in many different contexts, to change real women's lives for the better – and, by extension those of men, girls, and boys (and transgender people too). It could be argued that this account is biased, since it is written by the author of the original manual. Yet other, independent assessors have ranked Stepping Stones with a Gray II mark-up in relation to reduced GBV and gender-transformative processes (What Works for Women & Girls, 2012). As other contributors to this volume also show, the experiences of those most affected by an issue around the world – especially when they repeatedly sound so similar – should be respected by academics and donors alike (Reid et al., 2005). This story shows the power of participation and what people can do to change their own lives when given the space to work discuss, reflect, rehearse, and act together.

Participation, openness, willingness to learn about and embrace the complexity of our lives, rather than reducing them to oversimplistic linear models of behaviour change are hallmarks of involvement in this story at all levels: within the communities by using the manual and working through the issues; at the level of organizations by promoting this work; and at the global networking level by building the community of practice.

Meanwhile, as this chapter is being written, a new phase in the history of Stepping Stones is unfolding. We have received funds from Comic Relief to adapt Stepping Stones for use with children affected by HIV from as young as five years. Many are orphans and vulnerable. Many have been sexually abused and physically beaten, as well as being emotionally traumatized, especially by the loss of their mothers. Their grandmothers often feel totally overwhelmed by the catastrophic loss of the middle generation and ill-equipped to cope with bringing up such damaged young people. Ironically, it is clear that what would be best for these children would be their mothers still alive, safe, happy, and well (Welbourn et al., 2012).

Nevertheless, 19 years on from its first development, Stepping Stones seems to be as relevant and as urgently needed as ever. May it not take us[6] another 19 years to find the means to maximize its use around the world.

Notes

1. www.steppingstonesfeedback.org
2. Issues of the newsletter are available at <www.steppingstonesfeedback.org/index.php/page/News/gb>
3. http://steppingstonesfeedback.ning.com
4. We are indebted to the work of Amandine Bollinger, Nell Osborne, and Dan Fletcher for developing these e-communication platforms and moving forward with them.
5. http://vimeo.com/29733302
6. 'Us' includes long-term trainer, writer and Stepping Stones programmes adaptation adviser Gill Gordon as lead researcher, together with Florence Kilonzo, experienced Kenyan Stepping Stones trainer and co-author of 'Stepping Stones Plus', staff of PASADA in Dar es Salaam and children, their carers and service providers in Dar es Salaam.

References

Acord (2007) *Implementing Stepping Stones: A Practical and Strategic Guide for Implementers, Planners and Policy Makers*. London <www.acordinternational.org/silo/files/implementing-stepping-stones.pdf> [accessed June 2012].

ActionAid, Redd Barna, KAHCAE, AEGY (1998) *The teeth that are close together can bite the meat: a participatory review of Stepping Stones in two communities in Uganda*, SSTAP, ActionAid, London.

Bollinger, A. (2012) *Monitoring and Evaluating Stepping Stones Using the Outcome Mapping Tool*, Salamander Trust, London.

Chambers, R. (1995) 'Poverty and livelihoods: whose reality counts?', *Environment and Urbanization*, 7:1.

Coalition of Women Living with HIV/AIDS (COWHLA) (2010) *Fighting Gender Based Violence, Stigma and Discrimination Stepping Stones Way*, Lilongwe, Malawi. November 2010 [PDF] <www.cowlhamw.com/pdf/November%20 2010%20cowlha%20news%20update.pdf> [accessed June 2012].

Devries, K., Kishor, S., Johnson, H., Stöckl, H., Bacchus, L. J., Garcia-Moreno, C. and Watts, C. (2010) 'Intimate partner violence during pregnancy: analysis of prevalence data from 19 countries', *Reproductive Health Matters*, 18: 158–70.

Global Coalition on Women and AIDS (GCWA) (2011) 'Issue brief: stopping violence against women and girls for effective HIV responses', Global Coalition on Women and AIDS, Geneva.

Hale, F. and Vazquez, M. (2011) 'Violence against women living with HIV/ AIDS: a background paper', Development Connections, Washington, DC.

Jewkes, R. and Cornwall, A. (1998) *Stepping Stones: A Training Manual for Sexual and Reproductive Health, Communication and Relationship Skills: Adaptation for South Africa*, Medical Research Council and PPASA, Pretoria.

Jewkes, R., Nduna, M., Levin., J., Jama, N., Dunkle, K., Khuzwayo, N., Koss, M., Puren, A., Wood, K. and Duvvury, N. (2006) 'A cluster randomized-controlled trial to determine the effectiveness of Stepping Stones in preventing HIV infections and promoting safer sexual behaviour amongst youth in the rural Eastern Cape, South Africa: trial design, methods and baseline findings', *Tropical Medicine and International Health*, 11: 3–16.

Jewkes, R., Nduna, M., Levin, J., Jama, N., Dunkle, K., Puren, A. and Duvvury, N. (2008) 'Impact of Stepping Stones on incidence of HIV and HSV-2 and sexual behaviour in rural South Africa: cluster randomised controlled trial', *British Medical Journal*, 337: a506.

Laga, M., Rugg, D., Peersman, G. and Ainsworth, M. (2012) 'Evaluating HIV prevention effectiveness: the perfect as the enemy of the good', *AIDS*, 26: 779–83.

Mascarenhas, J., Shah, P., Joseph, S., Jayakaran, R., Devavaram, J., Ramachadran, V., Fernandez, A., Chambers, R. and Pretty, J. (eds) (1991) *RRA Notes 13: Proceedings of the February 1991 Bangalore PRA Trainers Workshop*, International Institute for Environment and Development, London.

Reid, K., Flowers, P., and Larkin, M. (2005) 'Exploring lived experience', *The Psychologist* 18: 20–23 <www.thepsychologist.org.uk/archive/archive_home.cfm?volumeID=18&editionID=114&ArticleID=798>.

Salamander Trust (2008) <www.salamandertrust.net/index.php/Resources/Video_Resources_3_-_Stepping_Stones_in_Uganda/> [accessed June 2012].

Salamander Trust (2011) *Integrating Strategies to Address Gender-Based Violence and Engage Men and Boys to Advance Gender Equality through National Strategic Plans on HIV and AIDS: Istanbul, Turkey 14–16 November 2011*, <www.salamandertrust.net/index.php/Projects/GBV_Workshop_Istanbul_Nov_2011/> [accessed June 2012].

Salamander Trust (2012) 'Stepping Stones annual report April 2011–March 2012' [PDF], <www.salamandertrust.net/resources/Stepping_Stones_Annual_Report_Final_March_2012.pdf> [Accessed June 2012]).

Secretariat of the Pacific Community (SPC) (2007), 'Sex and relationships: talking about taboo topics', *Secretariat of the Pacific Community, Public Health Programme: HIV & STI* [webpage] <www.spc.int/hiv/index.php?option=com_content&task=view&id=85&Itemid=88> [accessed June 2012].

Stepping Stones (2011) *Stepping Stones in India*, London <www.steppingstonesfeedback.org/resources/23/SS_Amandine_Bollinger_India_Aug2011.pdf> [accessed June 2012].

Stepping Stones (2012a) 'How does it work?', *Stepping Stones Training Package on Gender, Communication, and HIV* [webpage] <www.steppingstonesfeedback.org/index.php/About/How_does_it_work/gb> [accessed June 2012].

Stepping Stones (2012b) 'Stepping Stones resources', *Stepping Stones Training Package On Gender, Communication, and HIV* [webpage] <www.steppingstonesfeedback.org/index.php/page/Resources/gb?resourceid=7> [accessed June 2012].

Strickland, R. (2004) 'To have and to hold: women's property and inheritance rights in the context of HIV/AIDS in Sub-Saharan Africa', International

Center for Research on Women, <www.icrw.org/publications/have-and-hold-womens-property-and-inheritance-rights-context-hivaids-sub-saharan-africa> [accessed June 2012].

UNAIDS (2010) *Fiji – 2010 Country Progress Report*, UNAIDS, Geneva.

UNAIDS (2012) '30th meeting of the UNAIDS Programme Coordinating Board, Geneva, Switzerland, 5–7 June 2012', UNAIDS Thematic Segment Background paper [PDF] <www.unaids.org/en/media/unaids/contentassets/documents/pcb/2012/20120516_ThematicSegment_background_paper_en.pdf> [accessed June 2012].

USAID (2010) *Gender-Based Violence and HIV*. USAID, Arlington, VA [PDF] <www.aidstar-one.com//sites/default/files/AIDSTAR-One_Gender_Based_Violence_and_HIV_tech_brief.pdf> [accessed June 2012].

Wallace, T. (2006) *Evaluating Stepping Stones*, ActionAid, London.

Welbourn. A. (1995) *Stepping Stones: A Training Package in HIV/AIDS, Communication and Relationship Skills*, Strategies for Hope, London.

Welbourn. A. (1999) *Gender, Sex and HIV: How to Address Issues That No-One Wants to Hear about*, paper presented at the Geneva Symposium 'Tant qu'on a la Santé', January 1999 and published in the book of that name by DDC, UNESCO, and IUED.

Welbourn, A., Namiba, A., Foote, C., Paxton, S. & Dilmitis, S., 'In HIV prevention, protect the mothers: a message to the World Health Assembly 2012' [article], <www.rhrealitycheck.org/article/2012/05/22/let-them-eat-cake-enabling-mothers-to-protect-their-babies-from-hiv> [accessed June 2012].

What Works for Women & Girls (2012) 'Addressing violence against women' [webpage], <www.whatworksforwomen.org/chapters/21-Strengthening-the-Enabling-Environment/sections/59-Addressing-Violence-Against-Women/evidence#s-441>

Williams, G. (1989) *Strategies for Hope*, <www.stratshope.org/> [accessed June 2012].

World Health Organisation (2007) 'Changing men's behaviour can improve women's health', *Bulletin of the World Health Organisation*, 85: 501–68.

About the author

Alice Welbourn has worked on international gender and health issues for over 25 years. After completing a PhD at Cambridge University, she lived and worked in rural areas of Africa for several years, as an international development consultant. Diagnosed HIV positive in 1992, she wrote the 'Stepping Stones' training package on gender, HIV, communication, and relationship skills widely used across Africa, Asia, the Pacific, Latin America, and Eastern Europe. Alice was international chair of the International Community of Women Living with HIV/AIDS and on the Leadership Council of the Global Coalition on Women and AIDS. She is currently on the UNESCO Advisory Group for sex, relationships, and HIV education, Founding Director of the Salamander Trust, and co-founder and current chair of the SOPHIA Forum. In July 2007 she was honoured by the World YWCA for innovative leadership in the global response to HIV. She holds an Honorary University Fellowship at the Peninsula College of Medicine and Dentistry in England.

CHAPTER 14
Peace practice examined

Bridget Walker

Though linked since the 1967 encyclical Populorum Progressio *called development the 'new name for peace', development workers and peace practitioners have tended to follow different trajectories with different approaches. Peace is a process rather than a goal, collective effort over generations. Unlearning is as important as learning. Failure provides the material for reflection and fresh efforts. Congruence between the means and the ends is essential. This work is complex, continuing, sensitive, long term, and often slow. Peace-building frequently involves multiple actors and limited control over rapidly changing environments which can also provide space for experimentation, innovation, and room for risk-taking. This chapter draws on the work of the late Dekha Ibrahim Abdi in 'Linking Practice to Policy', a joint initiative of Responding to Conflict and the Coalition for Peace in Africa. The processes whereby traditional gender attitudes and behaviours were changed offer broad insights for development workers as well as peace practitioners.*

> Peace-building is not a fairy tale: there is no living happily ever after. The work of peace is long term, generation to generation; each face of conflict is different and needs different ways of addressing it. We are all contributing now and creating ways for others also to contribute.
> – Abdi (quoted in Francis et al., 2004)

This quotation comes from the late Dekha Ibrahim Abdi whose work in transforming conflict and building peace has been a model and inspiration in her own country of Kenya and internationally. From her experience she makes a sober assessment of the nature of violence and the need to take a long-term view. The protean quality of conflict requires flexibility and dynamism of response; there are no blueprints and success is fragile. This is a collective endeavour across generations.

Dekha was affected by violent conflict in her formative years and devoted much of her life to developing effective peace practice. Violent conflict, within and across national boundaries, has affected communities in many parts of Africa. These conflicts have often seemed intractable, extending over generations, resulting in displacement of people, destruction of lives and livelihoods, and degradation of the environment. Historical conflicts between different groups and across borders have become more deadly with the ready availability of arms and the existence of land mines. New conflicts have arisen.

http://dx.doi.org/10.3362/9781780447780/014

Yet wherever war is being waged there are also women and men working to tackle the violence, to create dialogue between warring parties, and to find pathways to peace. Their efforts frequently go unrecognized and unrecorded, so work on peace-building at community level can be undermined by policies which ignore these initiatives, and policies that lack the key elements necessary for effective development may be formulated.

> It is impossible for development to take place in areas of conflict. First, the insecurity puts off investors as no one would like to waste their resources and secondly, money meant for development projects is used to do rapid response or to carry out reconstruction in post conflict situations. (COPA, 2008)

Development and peace are interlinked. Forty years ago, in the papal encyclical *Populorum Progressio,* development was called the 'new name for peace'. To be authentic, the encyclical said, development must tackle not just material poverty but also issues of equity and discrimination; peace was defined as a process towards a more perfect form of justice. Since then a body of theory and practice has evolved in the fields of development and peace. There is considerable overlap but also different approaches and different models. Development hopes to achieve demonstrable positive outcomes; it is more difficult for peace-building to show that a negative outcome has been averted. The emphasis is on establishing processes and building relationships to create an environment which will enable and sustain development. As the quotation at the head of this paper suggests, this work is ongoing and does not have an endpoint. This account of peace-building practice is just one part of a broad spectrum, but it is hoped that the examples given here will offer insights which will be of interest to development workers as well as peace practitioners.

Linking practice to policy: a case study

This is an account of a particular programme with which Dekha Ibrahim Abdi was involved from the start and which she coordinated in the second and third phases. Called 'Linking Practice to Policy' it was a joint initiative of Responding to Conflict (RTC) and the Coalition for Peace in Africa (COPA).[1] The broad aims were to build linkages between practitioners and policymakers and to support and strengthen work which takes an integrated approach to conflict transformation and peace-building.

There were three phases to the programme. In the first phase video case studies were produced of peace-building initiatives in which COPA members had been involved in four African countries: Kenya, Somaliland, South Africa, and Uganda. A fifth video drew out the policy issues and recorded responses from decision-makers. This phase was followed by a 'learning year', revisiting the communities of the videos, holding workshops, and making connections with policymakers at different levels. The last phase built on the previous work, relating back to the original communities and undertaking extensive policy work at national and international level.

Phase 1: showing and sharing good practice

The first video in the series, *The Wajir Story*,[2] shows a community initiative in northern Kenya in which Dekha played a key role.

> In the early 1990s, a conflict between clans over water and livestock claimed 1,500 lives in Wajir. To this end, Dekha started a peace initiative with women from other clans. The initiative received negative perception and opposition from traditional leaders but this uplifted Dekha's spirit even more. She organised mediation talks between the warring clans. (Chege, 2011)

The Wajir Peace and Development Committee was formed and became an established structure, monitoring potential conflicts and responding when needed. This model went on to be developed and replicated elsewhere. The key features were inclusion, openness, linking of the local and the national, and mutual reflection. All the parties affected by a violent massacre in 1998 participated in a meeting in Nairobi in 1999. Just as in the Peace and Development Committees, women and young people, often on the margins of formal peace processes, had official representation. The meeting was open to others trying out the Wajir model, and there was a frank exchange of hopes and disappointments. In her account of the meeting Dekha wrote:

> People have the tendency to start an initiative and want quick results, and if things don't work well in two months then they give up and say it has failed. For me there is no failure in peace initiatives. If something is not working it is an invitation for further work, reflection and learning. Peacework needs some risk-taking and exploring sincerely and learning from our mistakes. (Abdi, 1999)

The Wajir Story presents a strong working model for conflict prevention. The case study from Uganda, *Gulu: The Struggle for Peace,* shows how even in ongoing conflict actions are possible, in this case the reintegration back into their communities of child soldiers, who had been both victims and perpetrators of violence. *Only Through Dialogue: The Somali Way to Peace* looks at the broad canvas of a disintegrating state, and how the northern part of Somalia was rebuilt from the bottom up, drawing on traditional methods of peace-building but including all stakeholders, both traditional and non-traditional actors. Inclusion, participation, openness, patience, and a willingness to take time were important in the process. Women had played a key role in the case studies from Kenya and Uganda. Ensuring that women were represented and their voices heard was a conscious feature of filming in Somaliland. The South African video *Pulling Together: Community Policing in the New South Africa* describes how one community has painfully rebuilt relationships and forged new roles for police officers and citizens in post-apartheid South Africa. The production of the videos was time-consuming and involved extensive consultation with the communities concerned. This process began building the relationships which took the next programme phase forward. The videos affirmed the peace-building efforts of the focal communities, and provided a vehicle for exploring their conflicts and finding new ways of dealing with them. The material challenges stereotypes of African situations, and of Muslim women.

Phase 2: a learning year

The video case studies were one part of a broader vision and provided foundation material for the next phase. Dekha became programme coordinator and, with a small steering group drawn from COPA members, designed the framework for a 'learning year'. This involved a series of workshops with many different actors drawn from the focal communities and beyond: elders and religious leaders, representatives of local government and the security sector, women and young people, and professionals such as lawyers and teachers. The learning workshops provided an opportunity to review the past and identify current challenges, to affirm traditional methods of conflict handling, and to recognize the value of extending the processes to include those traditionally not involved such as women and young men. The presentation of different peace-building initiatives offered new models. Links were made across borders, and between grass-roots communities and national policymakers. It was concluded that building peace requires commitment, courage, and a willingness to challenge government or other powerful interests.

Phase 3: finding a common theme

The work in the second phase led to the articulation of several key themes which were grouped under the general heading of human safety and security. There was engagement in policy work on cross-border conflict and advocacy on small arms both nationally, within Kenya, and at the regional level through IGAD and the African Union. At an international level COPA members took part in discussions hosted by UNIFEM on UN Resolution 1325 on women in peace building

Many of the activities described are concerned with making relationships within and across communities, capacity building, learning about peace theory and practice, and advocacy. At the same time Dekha and other COPA members also engaged directly in peace interventions close to home.

Lessons learned

This brief description does not do justice to a programme which was multi-layered and increasingly complex. In an evaluation of the work of COPA the external evaluators commented:

Our own assessment is that Linking Practice to Policy (LPP) as a project is clear in its objectives and strategic in its activities. Its conceptual clarity and sophistication give it greater impact than would otherwise be the case. The focal communities of its activities exhibit the impact of the involvement with LPP, in terms of the skills and confidence of practitioners and trainers, new and inclusive structures, the involvement of local leaders and administration in peace activities, and the capacity of the community to analyse conflicts and intervene. (Willams and Thomas, 2004)

From this summary account I would like to draw out some key features. Peace, as a concept, is not merely the absence of violence or war but an active, positive, and dynamic process. Building relationships is at the heart of this process; this takes time and continuity and consistency are important. In this way an enabling environment is created where risks can be taken with confidence, where old patterns of thought and action can be challenged, and failure can be acknowledged and regarded as an opportunity for learning.

Peace as a process: building relationships, taking time

Peace begins within ourselves. It is to be implemented within the family, in our meetings, in our work and leisure, in our own localities, and internationally. The task will never be done. Peace is a process to engage in, not a goal to be reached. (Bailey, 2009)

Underlying this work is a broad understanding of peace as a continuing process in which preventing and ending violence are essential but only initial steps at every level from the most personal family relationships to political engagement internationally. Conflict is inevitable; it is part of all work for change. The challenge is to acknowledge and transform conflicts as a foundation for peace building.

Building relationships is central to the process. The LPP programme began with four separate peace-building initiatives in different countries and contexts. There were strong relationships within each peace-building community and some links, through individual members, to the COPA network. The programme strengthened these links by bringing people together to exchange experience, skills, and learning and to develop strategies for action both on the ground and at policy level. Thematic connections were made and multiplied beyond the original focal communities.

This all took time. The LPP programme was active over a period of nine years. There was an iterative process of action and reflection with the focal communities and a consistency of approach. The key actors in Africa and at RTC accompanied the programme throughout the seven-year period following the production of the videos. The resources of people and time were consistently available. Money presented more of a challenge, with changing staff contacts and agendas in the funding agencies. It is difficult for many funding bodies to be responsive to changing situations, to accommodate risk and potential failure. During this time things went wrong at COPA and the secretariat broke down and ceased to function. Nevertheless, much of the programme work was able to continue, thanks in large part to the strength and connectedness of the LPP actors. The COPA membership undertook a 'clean-up' which involved dealing with the past and addressing the members' sense of hurt and distress about the failure as well as establishing a functioning secretariat once more. However, the memory of this failure lingered among some funders, who did not have the full history or continuity of connection.

Funders may also question the value of networks with their loose structures, broad aims, and flexible ways of working which bring inherent risks. Networks are a feature of peace-building communities, providing a space which is both protected and open equally to all members. Williams (2003) suggests that networks are well suited to bringing about change, as they can operate at different levels and with a range of actors. Their primary focus is not on rapid visible results but on making connections, building relationships, encouraging engagement, fostering learning, and exchanging knowledge and experience. They can provide space for experimentation and innovation – this includes risk-taking and being prepared to make mistakes. Individuals working in difficult and dangerous circumstances may be isolated. Phone calls, emails, and text messages from those in similar circumstances can provide advice and expertise and, importantly, support and solidarity.

Doing things differently

> Traditionally clan prestige and those who could shout the most were considered as capable of bringing change. But now nonviolence approach and persuasion can enable very notorious people to be changed. (Francis et al., 2004)

Working for peace means doing things differently both as individuals and collectively. Processes for discussing issues and reaching decisions need to be owned by all, not just those with social status or skilled in argumentation. Again this takes time. The dialogue process which led to the formation of Somaliland continued for months. These forms and processes can be challenging, taking the participants outside their comfort zones. In Wajir, police officers had to listen to criticism from the community; in Uganda, representatives from government and rebel forces engaged in heated exchanges. It is necessary to work collaboratively and allies may be found in unexpected places. Dekha, for example, said that she had found allies among ex-servicemen, religious leaders, and business people.

For individuals there are challenges and dangers. They may face mistrust from their own people and suspicion from the opposing side. It can be painful when one's assumptions and identity are subject to scrutiny. Personal support is needed and may come from different sources: colleagues in the peace-building networks, friends and family, or from faith and spiritual practice. As a devout Muslim, Dekha prepared herself for the pilgrimage to Mecca by going through a conscious process of forgiveness, which included forgiving her own government and its security institutions for past violence she had experienced. She said that, in doing so, she felt released from the burden of pain and anger that she had been carrying for more than 20 years.

There may be another hazard for individuals. In a speech given at a meeting of Asia Peacebuilders in Cambodia in 2010 Dekha said: 'Dealing with one's own ego is the biggest challenge, so that the personal does not clog but becomes a vital cog in the system.' Personal qualities play a powerful part in peace-building practice and the structures in which people work need to enable individuals to develop those qualities in ways that are collaborative rather than competitive. The LPP project was steered by a group of outstanding women and men, and their commitment, together with the drive and imagination of the coordinator, gave shape and coherence to what could have remained a set of valuable but disparate local activities unconnected to policy work at the national level. The LPP programme offered a model of connection, facilitation, and accompaniment. Accompaniment does not mean unquestioning support, but rather a relationship of critical solidarity, a space where there can be both dialogue and debate, challenge as well as exchange.

Doing things differently means not only learning different ways of working with different structures; it also involves unlearning. This does not mean doing away with what Maoism characterized as the four 'olds' – old culture, old customs, old habits, and old ways of thinking. It is more a matter of looking at them with fresh eyes. This may mean adaptation and letting go of patterns which have had negative outcomes in the past. Abdullahi Ina Irshat, a health worker from Wajir, commented on how his perceptions and practice had changed. He had been challenged by Dekha to attend a meeting about a clan conflict over grazing rights. This had seemed irrelevant to him. He had made a professional vow of compassion and also of neutrality, keeping his distance from the conflicts around. 'Saving lives and ameliorating suffering had been the hallmark of my career *not* mediating crazy kalashnikov-wielding clansmen' (Ina Irshat, 2011). He came to see that community engagement is essential in public health work and this involves understanding and working with community conflicts. He observed at first hand how the women of Wajir mediated the conflict and this led to a profound change of attitude:

> I had pitied women as lacking substantive influence in mediation and lacking leadership in a largely male dominated world. This blinded my horizon. I never imagined that three women; the late Dekha Ibrahim, Rukia Abdullahi and Madam Fatuma would have any clout and capacity to bring about peace to warring men. Little did I know I was going to be proved wrong by Dekha and the women of peace movement ... I also learnt, women are serious in their vision, and their solutions and are more compassionate than men. They have the patience and intellect

to mobilize and analyse impacts of pain and suffering in their midst. Women can be leaders and can be better leaders in their own styles. We need to acknowledge this, with no tinge of embarrassment as men, and reverse the centuries old stereo-type about women, falsely constructed in cultural-webs. (Ina Irshat, 2011)

When she received the Right Livelihoods Award, Dekha used the money for the foundation of a Peace University in Wajir. It is possibly unique in offering unlearning as well as learning in its prospectus.

Conclusion

Elsewhere in this book it has been argued that development aid as currently practised fails to understand and engage with the complex realities of the lives of poor and marginalized men and women. In this context it is worth noting that the majority of the references in this case study have been taken from original source material in unpublished reports in the archives of Responding to Conflict. There is a wealth of information in the 'grey' literature sitting in the files of many INGOs. Yet it can seem that these records are regarded as less authentic in some way. This raises questions about where such value judgments are made and by whom. It is the argument elsewhere in this book that the North has appropriated to itself so many of the drivers and processes of development. This may include the right to decide what information is valid.

Throughout the sector there is a managerial approach concerned with measuring performance, setting and meeting targets, and demonstrating achievement. This trend has been a challenge for peace practice too. These management tools and frameworks do not readily accommodate an under-standing of process and the dynamism of change. Conflict transformation needs support that is based on shared values, a long-term view, and readiness to be flexible and open to change and risk. There needs to be a relationship of mutual respect. Such relationships do exist, particularly with those funding bodies which have a specific mandate to address peace and conflict, and an institutional understanding that has been built over many years. However, the general trend towards a rational management paradigm is also evident.

In a private conversation with the author about the benefits from the work of a peace network, the representative of one funding agency said that within the agency, not least from the trustees, there is some scepticism as to the ultimate benefits that derive from this type of work. It is reasonable to expect positive outcomes but the phrase 'ultimate benefits' suggests something more final and attainable, rather like the statements of some development agencies about overcoming and ending poverty. Peace organizations have a view which encompasses memory from the past as well as a vision of a future that stretches ahead; they see the means as the end in the making.[3]

Perhaps it is time to do away with the logframes and the linearity of thinking of the past 30 years. C. Otto Scharmer (2011) suggests a holistic approach in a model for global development which uses language familiar to peace practice: an 'open mind, an open heart and an open will' are at the core of transformative change.

Notes

1. The Coalition for Peace in Africa is an African network of peace-builders whose purpose is to promote peace, justice, human rights, and development through capacity building, advocacy, research, and documentation (<www.copafrica.org>). Responding to Conflict is an independent peace-building organization that has worked since 1991 to support people and organizations in transforming violent conflict and building lasting peace.
2. *The Wajir Story* and other films in the series can be downloaded from <www.respond.org>.
3. Cf. Martin Luther King's frequently quoted observation that 'One day we must come to see that peace is not merely a distant goal we seek, but that it is a means by which we arrive at that goal. We must pursue peaceful ends by peaceful means.'

References

Abdi, D.I. (1999) Letter to QPS Africa Committee reporting on a grant, preserved in the author's papers.

Abdi, D.I. (2010) 'Transforming our woundedness for peace: voices from the frontline', keynote speech at the third meeting of Action Asia Peacebuilders, Action Asia. Available at: <www.opendemocracy.net/5050/dekha-ibrahim-abdi/transforming-our-woundedness-for-peace>

Bailey, S. (2009) 'Our peace testimony', in *Quaker Faith and Practice, Yearly Meeting of the Religious Society of Friends (Quakers) in Britain*, 4th edn, Quaker Peace and Service, London.

Chege, N. and Agencies (2011) 'Tribute to a warrior of peace', Standard Digital News [article] <www.standardmedia.co.ke/?articleID=2000042963&pageNo=1&story_title=> [accessed 2 November 2011].

Coalition for Peace in Africa (COPA) (2008) Report of the exchange visit between Kenyan and Ugandan women in Lira-Northern Uganda.

Francis, D., Leslie, E., et al. (2004) *COPA/RTC Partnership LPP Project: Mid-term Review*, Responding to Conflict, Birmingham, UK.

Ina Irshat, A. (2011) 'Keeping Dekha's dream alive', *Voice of Nomads*. Available at: <www.docstoc.com/docs/97980509/By-Ina-Irshat-abdullahi_irshat_hotmailcom-The-morning-sun-was-> [accessed 12 December 2011].

Scharmer, C.O. (2011) 'Leading from the emerging future, minds for change – future of global development', talk given at a ceremony to mark the 50th anniversary of the BMZ, Federal Ministry for Economic Co-operation and Development, 13 November, Berlin.

Williams, S. (2003) 'Thoughts on networks in conflict prevention', unpublished.

Williams, S. and Thomas, D. (2004) Coalition for Peace in Africa (COPA) Assessment/Evaluation Final report, unpublished.

About the author

Bridget Walker's background is in international development, primarily in the NGO sector. She has lived and worked in Cameroon and Sudan and travelled widely in Africa, Asia, and the Middle East. She was a member of the Gender and Development Unit (GADU) at Oxfam GB, and also worked on gender issues in humanitarian programmes. Most recently she worked at Responding to Conflict (RTC), an educational charity which provides training and skills development, and consultancy services in the fields of conflict assessment, conflict transformation strategies and methodologies, facilitation, and mediation. She had oversight of the Linking Practice to Policy Programme from joining RTC in 1999 to retirement in 2006. She remains an RTC Associate. She is a member of the editorial board of the Centre for Peace and Conflict Studies in Cambodia.

CHAPTER 15
I don't know ... and related thoughts

Ashish Shah

This chapter is about the three most important words I have learnt during the course of my engagement with 'development work' and sugarcane farming in Kenya over the past 10 years. It is a personal story and reflection on some of the many challenges, paradoxes, and hopes that I have encountered on the journey so far. It seeks to highlight the complex realities that we all encounter when we engage with social change. It emphasizes the importance of connecting with people's lives in ways that can improve our understanding and engagement with long-term change processes. It calls for greater perseverance, passion, hope, and fire to fight complex systems of marginalization and injustice.

The fresh 'idealist' and privileged graduate

At the end of August 2000, I had just completed a postgraduate degree in economics and social policy from the University of London. I was a privileged young man, with a middle-class upbringing, having had a mixture of family support and scholarships to complete my degrees, thousands of miles away from my home country, Kenya. Equipped with certificates embossed with the university insignia and the new 'knowledge' I had acquired, I felt equipped to go back home and make a contribution to the development of my country.

I was passionate about working with smallholder farmers in Kenya, and intrigued by the challenges and levels of poverty that they faced. Modules in development economics and agricultural economics had offered me a lens with which to understand and engage with the problems of rural poverty in my home country. My research had focused on the political economy of smallholder farming in Kenya. I was, to all intents and purposes, a member of the well-intentioned 'outsider' class. As Robert Chambers notes:

> We, these outsiders, have much in common. We are relatively well-off, literate, and mostly urban-based. Our children go to good schools. We carry no parasites, expect long life, and eat more than we need. We have been trained and educated. We read books and buy newspapers. People like us live in all countries of the world, belong to all nationalities, and work in all disciplines and professions. We are a class. (Chambers, 1993: 3)

http://dx.doi.org/10.3362/9781780447780/015

Encountering the 'poverty' of sugarcane farmers

I was drawn towards the sugarcane farming sector in Kenya. As an urban consumer of sugar with a sweet tooth, I was perplexed by how expensive Kenyan sugar was, and how frequently local shops and supermarkets were faced with sugar shortages. Poetic newspaper headlines such as the 'bitter sweet taste of Kenyan sugar' attempted to explain the woes facing the sector in Kenya. Some stories highlighted the fact that sugarcane farmers had not been paid their dues by the sugar mills for over two years, and this had led to an increase in farmer apathy and a decrease in production. Others highlighted the fact that Kenyan sugar on average was more expensive to produce than sugar grown in other more climatically favourable countries, and that the influx of cheap sugar, despite import controls, had led to deteriorating conditions for the Kenyan sugar industry, leaving farmers worse off and mills facing huge debts. Others managed to show the pathetic conditions under which sugarcane farmers and their families were struggling to survive. What was consistent in all these stories was the fact that sugarcane farmers in Kenya were experiencing increasing poverty and injustice as the sector neared the brink of collapse. I joined a group of largely urban researchers and activists who were genuinely concerned about the plight of sugarcane farmers in Kenya.

During the same period, after several internships with inspiring mentors, I found a vacancy with a British-based international NGO (INGO) to be based in their Western Kenya programme. The position looked exciting. Western Kenya was home to the majority of sugarcane farmers in the country, with up to six million people depending on the sugarcane farming economy directly and indirectly. The organization seemed to have a leadership that was flexible and encouraged young people to have space to think, and spend time in the field. It was also an organization that wanted to see action – action within the discourse of rights, to 'help poor and marginalized people fight against poverty and claim their rights'.

This was an opportunity to embrace the challenge of leaving my urban comforts and shift to a region where I could put my passion and perceived 'knowledge' to use. Armed with university degrees, enthusiasm, interest, and backed by a relatively progressive INGO with supportive leadership, I moved to Western Kenya with a key message drummed into my head: 'pick an issue, understand it, and make your mark fast'. That was how INGOs worked – you had to 'prove yourself' and 'make a mark'.

The plight of sugarcane farmers was going to be my issue, and I was going to play my part in helping to 'solve' the problem that sugarcane farmers faced. If I spent two years working on this 'issue', I imagined I would be able to achieve something and then move on to work on other things. It was all going to be that simple.

The 'problem' of sugarcane farming in Kenya

How difficult could it be to understand what was wrong with the sugar industry in Kenya? After all, it was simple economics. The problem seemed clear: it cost US$490 to produce a tonne of sugar in Kenya in 2001, and yet it was possible to import sugar from some of the Common Market for East and Southern Africa (COMESA) and South African Development Community (SADC) countries for anything up to US$290 per tonne cost insurance freight (CIF). As more imported sugar made its way into Kenya, it destabilized local production, and mills were unable to pay farmers. As one World Bank technocrat put it,

> Other reasons don't matter. The fact is that Kenya is an inefficient producer compared to most sugar producing countries. The markets need to be liberalised, and Kenya has to compete in the real world. If sugarcane farmers cannot produce and millers cannot mill sugar cheaply then they will have to switch to other crops where they have a comparative advantage. (World Bank Agriculture Consultant, personal communication, July 2001)

For many, particularly in the academic, private, donor, and government sectors, the solution and choice was simple: The sugar industry had to become more 'efficient' to compete with imported sugar. If that failed, Kenya would have to accept that it had no competitive advantage in producing sugar, and the sector would have to self-destruct. The only way the industry could become more efficient was for it to be 'shocked' into change, by facing competition from more efficient producers in the liberalized global markets.

For others, mostly within the NGO sectors, while the problem of inefficient sugar production was generally acknowledged, the solution and choice was also simple: protect the sugar industry from neoliberal tendencies to open up the markets, and prevent sugarcane farmers from being exploited by the risk of cheap imported sugar. Sugarcane farmers had a right to produce sugarcane if they so wanted. This position faced challenges: why should consumers in urban areas pay more for their sugar just to protect inefficient producers when sugar could be imported cheaply?

Despite these different positions, the fact remained that by 2001, sugarcane farmers were owed over Ksh 2 billion (equivalent to US$50 million in 2001) in delayed payments, were struggling with huge debts, and facing extreme hardship. I assumed that I had gained a basic understanding of the problem facing the sugar industry, as it seemed to fit neatly into my agricultural and development economics textbooks. But, driven by a sense of justice and equity, I adopted a slightly more nuanced stance: the Kenyan sugar industry was inefficient; so the challenge was to use the threat of liberalized sugar markets to help the industry become more efficient, using protectionist policies to improve the sector.

Keen to 'make a mark' I started having meetings and discussions with policy-makers, researchers, and head office staff in the INGO about a good entry point to tackle the 'sugar problem'. Suggestions ranged from 'feed into the campaign against inequalities in the World Trade Organisation (WTO), using stories of sugarcane farmers suffering' to 'introduce new varieties of sugarcane to improve yields', to the vague 'organize farmers to claim their rights'! And so for a couple of weeks we pontificated on the plight of the sugarcane farmer and imagined simplified solutions which would lead to some grand change.

I had the issue I was interested in; I thought I had understood the issue within two months and now felt ready to make some sort of mark. I was ready to draw up a logframe and plan of action that would see improved farmers' organizations claiming their rights and being paid their delayed payments as objectives, and a multitude of imagined indicators based on my limited understanding of the sugar industry in Kenya. Soon I was sitting opposite my country director telling him that I was raring to go.

It is scary how when one joins an organization, especially an INGO, the pressure to solve problems, and your own confidence in your knowledge (whether real or manufactured), can be so great that you actually forget the most basic common sense. Fortunately, I worked with a country director who was not only a gifted manager but a brilliant and inspiring mentor. He was worried I was jumping ahead of myself, and eased the pressure to make a mark. Instead he said: 'spend a few months just soaking up your understanding, and especially talk to the people who matter the most – the farmers'.

I don't think you understand the 'problem'

I must admit, I was a bit annoyed at the time. Here I was with youthful energy and ideas to run, and the country director wanted me to slow down. But I also knew he was right – in the time spent trying to 'understand' the sugar industry and plight of sugarcane farmers, I had not really interacted with farmers. What little interaction I had was in passing, or in small focus groups – consultations which could in no way be considered representative. Having access to the INGO four-wheel drive, I decided to 'drive around' the sugar belts in western Kenya and 'talk' to farmers.

The first month of driving around and 'talking' to farmers could be described as nothing short of rural development tourism, carrying with it all the perverse biases that Chambers (1983) describes. While I learnt a little bit more about the sugar sector with each trip, much of it was the same – sugarcane farmers had not been paid their dues, the mills were co-opted by the state in a patronage-based political economy, and the farmers' organizations seemed too divided and politicized to challenge the state. It was not until the fifth week that I bumped into, what I thought at that time, a rather arrogant farmer.

His name was Ochieng. He was in his early sixties and had been growing sugarcane all his life. I met him quite by chance at a local village centre where I was 'interviewing and surveying' a few farmers. He stood in the background, silently observing the conversation, sometimes rolling his eyes and smiling when I tried to ask questions. As I wound up my questions and was about to board the INGO four-wheel drive back home, he walked up to me and asked: 'So you want to help sugarcane farmers do you?' in a rather sarcastic way. I looked at him, a bit irritated as it had been a long day, and affirmed that I wanted to help farmers organize themselves so they could fight for their delayed payments, while also helping the industry become more efficient so it could compete against cheaper imported sugar.

He laughed at me, implying that I had no understanding of the sugar industry at all, let alone any idea what farming entailed with any crop. He said

> I don't think you have ever farmed before in your life. You don't know what it is like to grow sugarcane or any other crop. You are just a little boy from Nairobi, who has studied in university and who is now working for an NGO driving a big car pretending he knows what he is talking about! I don't have time for people like you.

I was about to cry. So far all the farmers I had talked to had been so polite to me, giving me their time, and here was this man pricking whatever pride I had, and essentially snubbing me. 'What do you want me to do?' I asked trying to hold myself together. He said,

> I want to challenge you. I am going to set aside a quarter acre of land on my farm, and I want you to come and stay with me and grow sugarcane on your own. If you can't stay with me, I want you to at least try and farm and you can go home and sleep comfortably wherever you live. But I want you to try and farm. After that, I will feel comfortable talking to you. Until then, I don't want to waste my time with you.

Of all the farmers I had met so far, this one both irritated and inspired me. 'How long would I have to farm for?' I asked. 'Until the first ratoon appears,' he replied. I stared at him blankly, and agreed to the challenge to maintain my pride, despite the fact that I had no idea what a ratoon was. That was the first moment it hit me. Three words kept bouncing in my head and knotting my stomach ... I don't know! And these three words were going to provoke me over and over again as I sought to try and 'understand' better the sugar problem that I once thought I knew.

Over the next nine months I found myself farming sugarcane and trying to balance my job at the same time, engaging with farmers, activists, academics, policy-makers, and just about anyone who had anything to say about sugarcane farming in order to construct a better understanding of the sugar problem. Some nights I would spend on the farm, other nights when I longed for a comfy bed I would go back home. Every morning, especially in the first few months when planting cane was done, I would be on the farm at the crack of dawn. I did not know you could get such painful blisters from holding a hoe. I did not know how expensive it was for a tractor to plough the land and how tough the land was to plough with oxen. I did not know how difficult it was to acquire seed-cane for planting or that farmers were indebted to the mills after being overcharged for the supply of overpriced fertilizer inputs. I did not know how the quality of soil had been degrading over the years, making each harvest harder, or that rents were being extracted from farmers, whether it was for cane cutting or cane collection. I did not realize how difficult it was to get from one part of the village to another when it had rained (without the luxury of an INGO four-wheel drive). I did not know that farmers were trapped in a cycle of unending debt to mills and yet were forced to sell their cane at cheap prices for cash to middlemen. I did not know that the road infrastructure was so bad that much cane got wasted during transportation; that it was so difficult for farmers to switch to other crops because they were trapped in cycles of debt; or the extent of hunger on the farms. I did not know that farmers were selling off the fertilizer they were given in exchange for cash to meet basic needs like school fees, health, and food costs, or that so many children from sugarcane farming families had dropped out of school to take up manual work as cane cutters. I did not know that when farmers took their cane to be weighed, the mills would under-declare the weight of the cane or that farmers did not have access to new varieties of cane that could help reduce the maturing period.

There was so much I did not know: how much power the mills had over the farmers given the fact that most mills were government-owned; how the mills had become conduits to finance the system of political patronage especially during peak election years; that the national sugarcane growers' association was fragmented along ethnic lines and marred by ineffective leadership that had not held elections for over 10 years. I was unaware how heterogeneous and polarized different local farmers' groupings were and how difficult the notion of 'organizing' farmers really was. I did not know that the mills did not pay farmers for the many by-products from sugarcane, or that the impact of having over two years' worth of delayed payments was the ironic fact that many farmers could not afford to buy the sugar produced from their cane.

I also did not know that when the World Bank economists talked of inefficiencies in the sugar sector, these inefficiencies were a result of a complex political economy and not simple price differences. I did not know that some key ministries in Kenya had taken a conscious decision to let the industry die, nor that politicians had formed alliances with importation cartels. There is far more I did not know that I restrict sharing due to word constraints. There is much that I still do not know!

What I do know now, however, it that a ratoon is the shoot of a sugarcane plant, which can be harvested in Kenya up to four times before having to replant the sugarcane. What I learnt from farmer Ochieng was the lesson of humility. I appreciated better what Chambers (1983) has been reiterating for the past three decades:

> The village is the centre, you are peripheral ... the micro level is again and again out of focus; and when in focus it is seen from a distance, through the urban professional's telescope. To understand rural poverty

better, and to judge better what to do, outsiders, of whatever persuasion, have to see things from the other end. (Chambers, 1983:46)

We come into the development world equipped with some knowledge, reflecting our own biases and positionality. We try and offer ourselves and others a simplified understanding of the challenges, yet the reality of those living in poverty, faced with marginalization and injustice, is far more complex. The systems that keep sugarcane farmers trapped in perpetual poverty are a mixture of historical, economic, social, and political relations at different levels (local, national, or international). Instead of my initial linear, static, and simplified understanding of the 'problem facing the sugar industry', my understanding shifted (and continues to shift on a daily basis) to accept and embrace a much more complex and dynamic picture of the realities facing sugarcane farmers and the sugar industry in general.

I still don't think you understand the 'problem'!

After more than a year, I began to regain confidence that I had a better under-standing of the challenges than when I first started; but I had another valuable lesson to learn. One morning I was walking from my little 'experimental' farm to a farmers' meeting when I bumped into a young, energetic lady in her mid-forties, also a sugarcane farmer. Her name was Linda.

As we got chatting, she asked me what I thought of what was happening in the sugar sector. I proudly gave her a speed version of my understanding of the different complexities facing the sector, and saw in her the same bemused look I had seen in farmer Ochieng when I first met him. For some reason I had been expecting a 'pat on my back' for having made the effort to understand the sugar industry better. Instead I got a 'slap on the wrist'. She told me that I had no idea how big the problem was. I looked at her bewildered and asked, 'Why do you say that? I have spent so long trying to understand this sector, I have spoken to so many people, and I have blisters on my hands to prove that I have genuinely tried to understand what is going wrong. How can you say that?'

She answered simply: 'Everything you talk about is from a man's viewpoint… . I don't think you understand what it means to be a woman sugarcane farmer.' Defensive juices poured through my veins. How could she say I did not understand what women sugarcane farmers were going through? I thought I was 'gender sensitive'. I had spoken to women farmers often. I had put myself forward for several gender trainings within my organization. I knew the difference between WID, WAD, and GAD[1] and could appreciate the conceptualizations of patriarchy and their implications. Surely I was a gender-sensitive man and development worker. I had always included the words 'and women' in all my analysis. I had always tried to make sure I talked to women, and questioned when farmer groupings consisted only of men. How could she say that? But I knew she was serious. She genuinely thought that I had no clue about what it meant to be a woman sugarcane farmer. I asked her to explain.

'I don't think you will understand if I explain. I want you to come and live with me for a week, not longer than that, and I want you to try and live like a woman sugarcane farmer,' she said. What was it with her and Ochieng, who thought that only when I was immersed in their situation would I understand? Again my ego and pride took over and I accepted the challenge.

I had attended numerous gender training workshops; I had even attended feminist trainings where I had been the only man, and in all these settings I felt I had come out with a better understanding of gender and feminism. Yet they failed to achieve what Linda managed to achieve by making me live her experience for only a week. She was right. As a man, as a privileged NGO worker, as an economist, an urbanite, whatever hat I wore, I had failed to see and understand what she as a woman sugarcane farmer was going through. The understanding I had developed of the sugar industry became even more complex. Again I realized 'I don't know and if I thought I knew, I didn't understand!'

I did not understand how difficult, if not impossible, it was for women sugarcane farmers to claim payments compared to their male counterparts, for a multitude of reasons. I did not understand the actual workload involved for women engaged in the multiple roles forced onto them by society, coupled with the expectation to be a good sugarcane farmer. I did not understand the level of abuse and exploitation that women faced at all levels of the farming process, or the impact of cultural practices and women's vulnerability in areas of their life that they should control – be it their bodies or their land. I did not understand the extent of violence against women and its psychological, social, economic, and political impact on them. I did not know about the internal organizing structures of women cane farmers, how different these were to the formal organizing structures for most of the male farmers, or that women were trying to introduce complexity into mono-crop sugarcane farming systems to counter the growing hunger periods.

I realize the difference between attending a gender training and actually understanding and trying to empathize with the different world that women live in. As men, as people with different positions of power (whether we are men or women), as people from biased professions, as outsiders, even when we make significant efforts to try to understand a problem or context, we are always only getting a partial picture. While we will never fully grasp the realities experienced by women, as men, and as people who want to do good development work, we owe it to ourselves to break out of our comfort zones and try to experience reality from the perspectives of those we say we work for.

So what? What are the implications of this complexity and messiness for our work in development?

It is not the place of this chapter to tell the story of the various changing processes and struggles that have been underway in the sugar sector, for this has been documented and is still evolving (Harding, 2005). But there are some general reflections on complexity and its encounter with current development practice that this chapter seeks to highlight.

Where you start from matters

Our work in development could benefit greatly if we started from the premise that 'we don't know'. This is a scary premise because at some level it challenges our own sense of self-confidence, and the tendency to feel that we know things in simplified reductionist form, because we convince ourselves that only when we know can we act. But to know, especially in development, means to accept that what we know is very little. The knowledge we hold as truth, and the attitudes, beliefs, and principles we carry with us, are a function of our position and place in society. By opening ourselves up to the premise that 'we don't know', we actually find that we can know more, empathize more, understand more, and only then are we able to act.

There are several weak points in our current form of development practice that prevent us from engaging with this starting premise. To start with, engaging with and trying to understand the complexity of sugarcane farming in Kenya immediately shifted an attitude in my own head – the belief that you can effect significant change within a two- or three-year period. The sheer complexity of the systems that keep sugarcane farmers poor, excluded, and marginalized in Kenya implies that for farmers and many of us involved in change processes, the time required to dismantle such systems of deprivation will be measured in decades, not in short programme or project cycles. It also implies that there may not always be one clear-cut strategy to address complex systems of deprivation. To highlight this we attempted to simulate the systems of deprivation that trapped sugarcane farmers in Kenya. Using causal loop analysis, and based on what we had understood so far about the sugar industry, we found that there were at least 33,000 possible strategies of action to dismantle this system of deprivation, from dealing with cheating at the weighbridge to taxing farmers more fairly. If we added an additional layer of complexity reflecting the different conditions facing women sugarcane farmers, the number of possible strategies rose to 56,000. What this implies is that one could generate a minimum of 56,000 logframes or strategies for the 'problem of sugarcane farming in Kenya', and even then we may still not get our strategy right given that complex systems change over time and with every 'intervention.'

It requires an internal shift to commit to change processes over such a long period of time, particularly one that can embrace multiple permutations of action. As we grow, as we change jobs and career, as we have relationships, as we start families – can we truly commit ourselves to long-term causes? We as outsiders have the ability to choose when and how to engage, whereas the sugarcane farmers do not have the same luxury. Can donors and NGOs accept that change is going to take decades, and will involve engaging with complex and evolving realities which we cannot necessarily plan for? Can we accept that given how complex and messy sugarcane farmers' realities are at all levels, we will inevitably make mistakes, we will have to strategize against a constantly emerging understanding? But we will also have to be persistent and committed to a long-term process of change to help dismantle a complex system that perpetuates injustice and poverty, no matter where we are located.

Our problem is our failure to articulate the complexity of the system that we promise to change. We allow ourselves to get sucked into the game of false articulation of simplified problems and impact because we want to impress donors. The more important starting premise of our work is the complex system of poverty and injustice that we claim to be able to dismantle.

Mentorship and learning of the heart matters

I appreciate now, more than ever, the role that mentors have played in encouraging and supporting long and reflective engagement with sugarcane farmers. As the tendency towards managerialism increases, the development sector is losing the important qualities of 'mentorship'. As new recruits joining the development sector, we are expected to make our mark and the mark is usually made by being able to secure a donor grant or a high visibility campaign that may get the NGO's name in a national newspaper. It is becoming increasingly rare to meet country directors who encourage their staff to take time in the field, to engage with local realities, to start building empathy and understanding complexity. It is rare to find field staff who are valued and listened to by organizational hierarchies, and this lack of value and listening is passed on in our interactions (or lack of them) with the communities we claim to work with.

Significantly the current development aid system revolves around paper reports and paper understandings of poverty and change, which fail to engage with an important aspect of understanding. I asked farmer Ochieng why he did not just tell me all the problems that he was facing when I first met him – why did he make me farm, toil, and go through the pain of blistering my hands? He replied: 'It is not about understanding in the mind, it is about understanding in the heart.' We no longer talk about the heart or the soul, or passion or fire, in our development discourse. We have become comfortable with reports, indicators, results, and efficiency. How do we find a balance between mind and heart? How do we find a balance between management and mentorship?

Gender trainings are not enough

Amidst all these internal practices that prevent us from engaging with complexity, perhaps the most detrimental is the fact that, in the end, apart from a few gender trainings conducted in organizations, there really is very little incentive to encourage us to truly understand, truly empathize with, and truly act in ways that can change the power balance which oppresses women. One of my regrets is that I met Linda too late. Prior to meeting Linda we had been involved with the sugar campaign to institute a new law in the sugar sector that gave farmers a much bigger say in how their industry was being managed, and removed the manipulative powers of political patronage that had been instrumental in destroying the sugar industry in Kenya. At that time, had we known that women had different organizational structures and known how to access these structures, and had sugarcane farmers such as Linda had a genuine say in the crafting of the new law, so many of the inequalities facing women sugarcane farmers could have been addressed legally, including the most immediate priority of claiming payments for sugarcane from land which was registered in the name of their husbands. How can we build systems that can provoke all of us, but especially men, into engaging, empathizing with, and understanding the complex realities of women?

It's time to get 'real' about impact

If our starting point is the premise 'I don't know', then what does this mean for our understanding of 'impact' in our current world of results-based management? In the context of sugarcane farmers, if our end vision is to see farmers free from poverty and oppression, impact actually means dismantling the entire system within which farmers are trapped. Simply addressing one part of a system and claiming impact is a fallacy. While our work in the sugar sector has seen some changes in addressing levels of political patronage, we are also clear that this has not resulted in significant impact for sugarcane farmers since the systems of injustice exist at many levels.

The challenge is how to move on from tackling one part of the system to another, without losing sight of the big picture. This calls for a new honesty in terms of how we measure impact and a new humility. There is no magic bullet when it comes to measuring processes of social change. The current preoccupation with randomized control trials (RCTs) must be tempered with the fact that when we engage with complexity, the complex reality faced by one farmer is always going to be different from the complex reality of another. In a situation where it is possible to have over 56,000 different permutations of a single farmer's problems, we must ask, what can you randomize and control for? This does not negate the usefulness of RCTs, but does call for caution about how much truth we can derive from them, and what use we make of them. Whatever methodology we use to measure impact, perhaps the most important point is that if methods for measuring impact or social change do not build in strong elements of reflection, they will fail to engage with the original premise of 'I don't know'.

Hope or despair? Complexity implies hope and fire

There have been moments while working with the problem of sugar in Kenya when the sheer magnitude of complexity has left us despairing and overwhelmed. The point of this chapter is not to nurture a feeling of how impossible it is to plan any kind of intervention at all, because we do not truly ever know. On the contrary, by bringing complexity to the fore I want to nurture hope and fire amongst us. We owe it to ourselves, our privileges, and future generations to persevere and engage with complex systems of injustice. We have a choice either to nurture a cynicism and hopelessness that leaves us resigned and apathetic or to embrace complexity and engage with realities reflectively, yet proactively.

It has been 10 years since many of us joined an existing struggle to change the sugar sector in Kenya. Farmers have had their delayed payments cleared, political control of the sugar industry has reduced drastically, and an industry that could have died in 2001 is still surviving. Much more needs to be done, and we make no claims about success or impact. What we do know is that each time we feel like giving up it is the same complexity that keeps the fire burning within us, encouraging us to take small incremental steps, based on growing understanding.

Conclusion

There is nothing new that this chapter brings to development discourse. As Robert Chambers has noted:

> Social change flows from individual actions. By changing what they do, people move societies in new directions and themselves change. Big simple solutions are tempting but full of risks. For most outsiders, most of the time, the soundest and best way forward is through innumerable small steps and tiny pushes, putting the last first not once but again and again and again. (Chambers, 1983: 217)

Change is complex, not linear. Change is messy, not straightforward. Change requires mentorship as much as it requires management. Change requires more time than we often assume. Change requires constant reflexivity, strategizing, participation, and feedback. Change for women requires more than a couple of gender trainings. Change requires building empathy and reconnecting with the people that matter. Change requires knowing that 'we don't know'.

Note

1. Women in development, women and development, gender and development.

References

Chambers, R. (1983) *Rural Development – Putting the Last First*, Longman, London.

Harding, D. (2005) 'The Sugar Campaign for Change (SUCAM) Kenya: an inside history of success and continuing struggle', *Critical Stories of Change*, Action Aid International, Johannesburg [PDF] <www.actionaidusa.org/sites/files/actionaid/sucam_0.pdf>.

About the author

Ashish Shah is a Kenyan citizen, currently completing his doctorate at Oxford University. His doctoral research looks at how citizens gain voice beyond procedural processes such as the vote and elections. It compares experiences of democracy and voice in Rwanda and Malawi. It builds on his earlier research into 'hidden democracy' in Rwanda, notably 'Ubudehe', one of Rwanda's home-grown development strategies. An economist by training, Ash has spent the past 12 years on agricultural reform in Kenya especially the sugar Industry; he is a volunteer with the Sugar Campaign for Change (SUCAM). He is also actively involved in governance and constitutional reform processes in Kenya. He has 10 years of local and regional experience with two international NGOs. His deep concern is how NGOs and donors can improve their accountability to the citizens they claim to work for and engage with the complexity of change in a more holistic way.

CHAPTER 16

Apolitical stories of sanitation and suffering women

Deepa Joshi

This chapter reviews developmental sanitation policies and interventions to argue that the sector depoliticizes gendered complexities in relation to sanitation. Sanitation is a complex social construct related to basic concepts of hygiene and socially appropriate 'cleanliness'. Many sanitation tasks are gendered and unquestioningly considered women's responsibilities. Indeed women's needs for greater privacy, modesty and safety are ground realities as are the fact that women disproportionately experience these constraints and disproportionately remain responsible for sanitation tasks at home. Offering faeces-related, health-only, women-centric, apolitical, cookie-cutter solutions is indicative of a conscious and convenient ignoring of gendered realities around sanitation. Such solutions claim to be gender-focused, but actually reiterate entrenched inequalities by gender.

> We are told that the little girl is ashamed of urinating in a squatting position with her bottom uncovered – but whence comes this shame?
> – Simone de Beauvoir (1949)

Sanitation is said to be the Cinderella of the water sector – poorly performing and tenaciously resistant to achieving the sectoral goals of 'hygiene health'. Whatever may constrain the meeting of 'sanitation' targets, the sector is said to be gender-focused. Indeed some gender experts argue that the reason sanitation as a development sector lags behind is 'partly because they are female rather than male priorities' (Sijbesma, 2008: 360). There are few sanitation programmes that do not mention gender (meaning women), and few initiatives that do not claim gender success in having provided poor women with the security and privacy of toilets as well as the education and awareness on the improved hygiene needed to achieve family wellness and child survival. More recently, sanitation interventions are said to *even* address the formerly hushed *special menstruation* needs of women.

It is ironic, then, that sanitation projects and interventions are also occasionally but regularly critiqued for their *inattention* to women's *special* sanitation needs. I refer, as an example, to a recent report detailing the indignity, insecurity, and sexual violence of urban poor women resulting from

http://dx.doi.org/10.3362/9781780447780/016

a lack of access to appropriate sanitation (Amnesty International, 2010). In presenting these polarized arguments about whether gender is addressed in sanitation programmes, I argue that an apolitical positioning of gender and a persisting and deliberate misinterpretation of gender cuts across the spectrum of positions. This, as I explain, stems from classic flaws of the developmental simplification and depoliticization of sanitation, as well as of 'gender' in relation to sanitation.

Sanitation policies are centred around health concerns relating to faeces disposal and hand-washing. While technically logical, the promotion of low-cost toilets and hygiene behaviour as 'safe or appropriate sanitation' is reflective of 'obscure engineering and public health concerns which are far-removed from local level needs and socio-cultural practices' (Mehta, 2007: 1). Sanitation as experienced by all, including the poor, is, in addition to its health aspects, a complex social construct, driven by universal personal desires of feeling or being clean and/or achieving culturally symbolic notions of cleanliness. The maintaining of the decorum of socially appropriate sanitation activities are tasks mostly gender-assigned to women. The coupling of sanitation (as toilet use) to women's special need for privacy during defecation not only ignores the diverse range of socially and culturally imposed (sanitation) burdens on women; it also reinforces popular imagery around women and sanitation, thereby reiterating, rather than reducing, structural relations of inequalities by gender.

In this chapter I argue that sanitation is not only about health; it is, to the contrary, a deeply 'social' construct, where a complex of socio-cultural local realities determines perceptions and practices around sanitation; sanitation issues *are* rooted as de Beauvoir identified in 'biological politics' (1949). This is precisely why sanitation must not be mistaken as a 'women's issue'; addressing women's needs for greater privacy, modesty, and safety mask the core realities around why women disproportionately experience these constraints. Building on these observations, I argue that offering faeces-related, health-only, women-centric, apolitical, 'cookie-cutter' solutions to the complex reality of a lack of sanitation for the poor is what makes for the rhetoric of developmental sanitation goals.

The first half of this chapter discusses the limitations of restricting the definition of sanitation to excreta disposal and hygiene health. Later, I examine the rhetoric of sanitation as a women's issue, which only serves to reiterate entrenched gender inequalities.

The developmental politics of interpreting sanitation as toilets and insisting that the poor pay

There are some fundamental concerns relating to the politics of sanitation. The first area of concern is, as Jørgensen (2008: 1) notes, 'sanitation' being deliberately narrowed down to mean 'human excreta disposal, even though other interpretations and implications of the term' are acknowledged (though rarely acted upon) by key sanitation agencies and actors. Evans (2005: 6) agrees the term 'basic sanitation' implies 'not indulging in semantic nit-picking and in explicitly recognizing that access is access – to any means of safe excreta disposal'. She further clarifies, 'linked to hand washing, safe excreta disposal will yield large [health] benefits' (ibid.). The overriding 'efficiency' agenda in development tends to selectively recognize quantifiable parameters, such as hygiene health, identified as *important* by 'expert others' (Jodha, 1988). This agenda dominates even though (sanitation) experts themselves stress that sanitation 'is as much as about seeing from the outside, from the scientific observer [health] point of view as it is about understanding the insider [emotion, social, anthropological], the people's point of view' (Curtis and Biran, 2001: 75).

Sanitation statistics quantify the significant health impacts of the safe disposal of human faeces and hand-washing after contact with faeces, which are considered twice as effective in reducing diarrhoea as improving the availability of water and its quality. In contrast, there are few measures of the inconvenience or indignity created by the failure to meet other needs constituting appropriate sanitation. Seventy-year-old Margaret Wangui, an elderly grandmother living in the Maili Saba slum in Kenya, eloquently summarizes what sanitation implies to her:

> Clean toilets; not having to lift raw sewage [from rapidly filling pit latrines] and dump it into the Mwengenye River [which we also use for bathing and cleaning]; bathing spaces with warm water for us [elderly] and the young children; water to clean clothes and homes; roads [outside my home] that are not always filled with [human and animal] wastes; roads, homes and toilets that don't flood in the rainy months – that is what I think is appropriate. (Joshi et al., 2011: 106)

The mismatch between what expert others and those who lack services regard as 'appropriate' sanitation results in the indignities of having to accept that being poor means having to make do and not being able to be or feel clean even though this is the most basic of human needs with social and cultural implications. Additionally, there are enormous burdens on women, like Mrs Wangui above, who struggle with 'keeping the home and [grand]children clean', 'in situations where there is a near complete lack of access to any kind of sanitation services' (Allen et al., 2006). These very visible dilemmas are consistently ignored by expert outsiders who insist that sanitation simply means 'access to [any] toilets and washing hands after defecation'. And yet, even if one were to hypothetically assume that toilets or safe faeces disposal alone constitute sanitation, Penner (2010) asks, 'Who decides what is appropriate? And when is [toilet] provision good enough, [humanely] dignified enough?'

The second area of concern relates to a growing emphasis on the discourse that public funds for sanitation are scarce and therefore need to be prudently targeted in order to make investments efficient. Advocates of this approach argue that the practice of 'supplying [providing] sanitation must stop ... (and) make way for marketing incentives and mechanisms to stimulate user demand

---

Box 16.1 A sanitation ladder

The Joint Monitoring Program of the WHO and UNICEF ranks the range of sanitation services as rungs on a ladder. At the bottom of the ladder are those who lack any kind of sanitation facility and still resort to open defecation. The first rung of the ladder refers to various kinds of traditional systems, such as pits for disposal of excreta. Thereafter come *improved* latrines — comprising SanPlat, VIP latrines, and basic pits with slabs — all of which ensure a hygienic separation of excreta from the immediate living environment. The final rung of the ladder is the flush toilet, which may be connected either to a septic tank or to a water-borne sewer network. Each successive rung of the ladder represents a higher unit cost but a correspondingly lower level of health risk. The top two rungs of the ladder are recognized as *improved* (or *safe/appropriate*) *sanitation* for purposes of measuring progress toward the MDG target (Morella et al., 2009).

---

for sanitation' (Evans, 2005: 17–25). In other words, the un-served and under-served need to start paying for their (health-enhancing) toilets. And scarce public resources are to be directed to creating 'excreta-toilet-hand-washing' awareness to stimulate demand and support markets for 'safe sanitation' infrastructure and facilities (ibid.). It is argued that the currently-excluded-from-safe-sanitation are unaware of health–faeces links but when made sufficiently aware, will 'climb the sanitation ladder' (see Box 16.1) transitioning from defecating in the open to investing in and using an improved (safe) design of toilet and washing hands with soap after defecation. Having done so, the reformed will then stimulate and/or coerce others into adopting these practices. This, in summary, is the current developmental sanitation agenda.

Toilets and indignity – health or comfort and convenience?

The policy of 'promoting' self-investments by the currently under- or un-served is justified by claiming that the 'poor already finance their sanitation ... in terms of time, energy, dignity, health' and 'creative financing systems can ... turn

---

Box 16.2 Slum latrines

In crowded urban slums in Nairobi, completely de-networked from the urban sewage systems, the 'provided' options are community latrines, where communities pay to use the toilets. The fees include the cost of periodic vacuum lifting of the sewage by private entrepreneurs. The poorest, who cannot pay or are unwilling to pay, dig their own shallow pit latrines: small holes in the ground covered with corrugated tin or wooden planks with a squat-hole. The stench from the numerous shallow pit latrines permeates the surroundings, and the pits, being shallow, need to be emptied frequently, manually. The faeces, still raw, are carried in buckets and dumped into the nearby river. Those who do not have even this option defecate in the open or in a plastic bag that they throw away when no one is around or in the dark, resulting in what is popularly known as the 'flying latrine'. Fifty-year-old Bernard Mutitso, living in Kibera, speaks of the additional 'defecating and urinating in the narrow alleys when it's dark – creating an awful odour'. In his perception, should this de-humanizing trend not be reversed?

---

these losses around and fulfill basic human rights' (Sijbesma et al., 2008: 1). The popular talk is of '*full cost recovery* even when it is clear that many services cannot reach the periphery without subsidies, nor were they ever expected to do so' (Black, 2002: 81).

Sixty-year-old Gul Bano living in the Beguntila slum in Dhaka City pays to use the communal toilet, which, as she describes, 'During the monsoon ... is a slush of water and faeces. It is so dirty that I lose my appetite. If only one could breathe calmly and not have to hold one's breath while defecating'. In the same slum, a male blind beggar Kuddoz says it's impossible to go there to defecate; if he does, he ends up all soiled around his feet (Joshi et al., 2011: 105). Contrary to popular notions about a low demand for toilets, there is significant evidence that as far as possible, the poor, like all others, prefer not to defecate and urinate in the open. In informal settlements in Nairobi the poorest households opt to build and share latrines, even in the most constraining circumstances, compensating their neighbours or landlords through help in construction or cleaning activities when they cannot pay (see Box 16.2). Users acknowledge the social and health gains of decent and functioning toilets.

However, sanitation designs considered appropriate for the poor are either not accessible or often simply not good enough to be endurably used. That the poorest make do with indecent toilets is indicative of a serious compromise around human dignity in the planning and providing for sanitation. There are few who question the ethics of transferring the costs for such sanitation to the poor given that most not-poor have their waste disposal services heavily subsidized.

Even if the poorest were able to cough up finance for toilets, there is robust empirical evidence about the complexities of poverty, particularly urban poverty and the related land-tenure insecurity, that constrains infrastructure investment in locations where settlements are demarcated administratively as illegal. Consequently, far from a laddered access to improved sanitation, the bottom rung of sanitation risks becoming permanent for poor communities as 'infrastructure gets cemented in at the lowest levels' (Bond, 2002).

Apolitical conceptualizations of sanitation and gender

In this section I discuss how women burdened by additional veils of a socially and sexually imposed need for privacy experience the inappropriateness of what is promoted as 'appropriate sanitation'. There are two issues here: first, still focusing on toilets, the promotion of sanitation as a woman's sector, and toilets as disproportionately addressing women's special needs for privacy, seems hardly to be the case in reality. As illustrated in the Amnesty report (2010), the transfer of responsibilities for finding space for, investing in, and managing toilets – to the excluded themselves – makes it difficult for the poorest, but particularly for women, to access toilets whether sanitary or otherwise. Second, contrary to popular rhetoric, the sector reiterates and reinforces gender divides by continuing to emphasize women's 'special' need for privacy. De Beauvoir (1949) wrote of how young girls across different cultures grow up learning to feel ashamed of their bodies, and how a parallel notion of shame and a need to hide their bodies is not socially instilled in men. While the sector shies away from challenging the socially instilled negativity around women's sex and sexuality, it reiterates the need for women's greater privacy – ironically only in relation to defecation – ignoring parallel notions of shame that apply to activities like bathing or managing menstrual hygiene. It also makes 'normative assumptions about women's nurturing [cleaning, child hygiene care] roles, thereby actively reinforcing and deepening gender divides ... through a feminization of [sanitation] responsibilities and obligations' (Molyneux, 2007: 231). But because there are few health gains related to these tasks, they are not sanitation priorities or concerns (Jenkins and Sugden, 2006).

Toilets for women?

Driven by the need to maximize efficiency above all, stand-alone (not connected to sewage networks), low-cost toilets designed for the poor are prone to stench and/or overflow, demanding high levels of cleaning and maintenance – usually by women (see Box 16.3).

In urban poor settings, improved facilities are also often far from home, opened and closed at fixed hours and accessible only by payment, hence often inaccessible to women because of their poverty and/or demanding domestic workloads:

> The main hindrances are the costs involved ... How can you afford to pay KSH 5 (0.064 US$) each and every time a child and yourself uses the toilets?
>
> Most women report having to walk at least 300m from their home to use the available 'improved' latrines. Access is especially unsafe and particularly at night ... Men equally face the threat of violence, but women are at increased risk of sexual violence. (Amnesty International, 2010: 18–21)

Abrahams et al. (2006: 753) write that 'improved toilets' when provided in public spaces are hardly accessible to women. Their research describes adolescent girl students speaking of the fear of using toilets in schools where

---

Box 16.3 The Maili Saba Slum

In the Maili Saba slum in Nairobi, Grace Wanjiku, a single mother with six children, shares a latrine with several tenants living on the landlord's plot. Her children use the latrine as well, and Grace spends considerable time trying to clean it before the children use it. Without adequate water it is incredibly difficult to clean the platform of rough wooden planks which covers the pit. (Joshi et al., 2011)

girls were often harassed by boy students, expelled male students, and school administrators. A security guard admitted he 'kicked open doors in the girls toilet ... to catch them smoking. Or he would lock the toilet to threaten the smokers'. Abrahams et al. report that coercion is often internalized by the females, not reported or under-reported because of past experiences 'that nothing much got done'.

The Amnesty Report (2010: 22; 38) mentions similar fears experienced by women:

> 'I did not report the incident (a near rape averted by some others coming to the rescue) because one of the men who was well known told me if I reported it to official authorities ... they would look for and deal with me.' ... Nearly all victims of violence had not reported ... to the police ... They stated their fears of being stigmatized by their family and neighbors; their distrust of the system; the frustration of others who had attempted to seek justice; the cost, time and unlikelihood of being provided justice; negative attitudes of authorities ... to their illegality and social insignificance.

In such complex social landscapes, a toilet at home might be depicted as eliminating risks, 'of women having to go out to defecate; of fears of men hiding and watching and molesting women' (Bapat and Agarwal, 2003: 74). Yet O'Reilly (2010: 53–4) describes the complex gender-space relations that influence the fact that 'while having an individual household latrine may eliminate men's concerns about providing safety for women, for women themselves, the provision of toilets at home does not easily eradicate 'gendered, social conventions around women's modesty'. Presenting examples of patriarchal cultures in North India, O'Reilly explains how the social segregation of adolescent daughters and other sexually active women from men of the same family highlights the myth of their safety and privacy at home. These examples draw attention to the politics of biology in relation to sanitation and stress the need for reordering local social constructs around masculinity, including the masculine mapping, monitoring, and control of the female body and movement. Yet, no sanitation projects, no matter how steeped in their intention to addressing gender, reflect on these issues.

Instead gender in developmental sanitation translates simply into instru-mentalist approaches: 'women targeted as the primary users of latrines ... having the greatest incentive to keep systems functioning ... where sanitation [read toilets] is assumed to lower women's insecurity risks ... and enable women to achieve family wellness and child survival' (O'Reilly, 2010: 47). While sanitation projects reach their toilet-use targets by harnessing women's uncompensated contributions, these processes are claimed to lead to women's empowerment; 'through the provision of latrines women would become empowered in terms of "finding their voices", participating in public women's meetings, and moving from house to house in order to proselytize about latrines' (ibid: 51). This is what is identified as the 'gender success in sanitation projects': 'women are (the) main actors in sanitation, and engaging women in sanitation will ensure 100 percent coverage, improved practice and the sustainability of upkeep and use' (Islam et al., 2000: 379).

Sanitation needs beyond defecation: reinforcing gendered sanitation responsibilities

A persistent ignoring of other essential, gendered sanitation tasks compounds this irony. From an ethnographic perspective, there are clear divides around men and women's sanitation responsibilities. In Bangladesh, men identified providing *'tel-saban'* (hair-oil, soap, a proxy for sanitation implements), investing in sanitation infrastructure, and/or upholding the dignity and privacy of (their) women as their 'sanitation' responsibilities (Joshi et al., 2011; O'Reilly, 2010). Women identified a longer list of tasks as their daily responsibilities: cleaning the house, cleaning the garden, washing utensils, washing clothes, washing and watering animals, disposing of children's faeces and cleaning the children, cleaning the toilet, collecting water for bathing, performing a ritual cleansing (purification), etc. (Islam et al., 2000).

Poverty or circumstantial realities (for example, in slum settings) seem to relieve men, and quite easily too, of their gendered responsibilities in providing sanitation services and needs. Unfortunately, women's sanitation responsibilities are less easy to let go. Even in harsh urban settings, good women are considered those who diligently keep the house clean, provide clean clothes for the family, keep their children clean, and perform their personal sanitation needs in private dignity. *Good women* also uphold and maintain the local decorum on cultural aspects of cleanliness. Ignoring how women perform these diverse sanitation burdens in compelling situations, and/or differentiating faeces-health from culture, leaves little space or scope to challenge entrenched disparities by gender in relation to sanitation.

Cultural notions of sanitation as opposed to health in sanitation

Notions of appropriate sanitation are derived from basic human needs and influenced by religious beliefs, local culture, individual needs and preferences, as well as by what is seen and learnt from the media and from one another. In other words, sanitation as experienced and desired includes facilities and services that provide for personal privacy and dignity and ensure a clean and healthy living environment both at home and in the neighbourhood of users. Here I discuss socialized feelings of 'disgust and dirt', which influence what is practised as sanitation – a complex of basic 'feel-good' as well as 'must-do' sanitation issues required by religious and/ or cultural needs. While women defecate, wash, and bathe (as do men), they are also required to ensure household cleanliness as well as managing menstruation, post-childbirth hygiene, and ritualistic needs. Yet, not only are these other 'non-health' sanitation issues ignored, they are persistently reiterated as women's responsibilities.

Dirt, disgust, and sanitation

Looking clean is a universal basic need, deeply influenced by cultural notions of personal and environmental sanitation; however, these notions are not as straightforward as technically defined sanitation-health arguments. Mary Douglas's (1996) analysis of hygiene, culture, and pollution explains why looking and feeling clean is far more important socially, especially to the poor, than defecating safely. The stigma of 'looking dirty is the most visible stamp of poverty, which is explicitly or otherwise expressed to the poor by the "not poor ... not dirty" others' (McKean, 2009, in Joshi et al., 2011: 102).

The indignity of lack of access to clean water to bathe and wash clothes in, as well as the inability to pay for water and cleaning materials, impacts both men and women, especially the young (see Box 16.4). Physical attractiveness, social acceptance, and aspiring to look like the 'not poor' are high aspirational priorities for adolescents, both girls and boys. Young and unmarried girls working in the garment factories in Bangladesh take great care to look and smell clean – even in the most constraining of circumstances. And there are others who need to smell and look clean for a living. Joshi et al. (2005) reported on young female sex workers who live on the pavement and can only rent toilet and bathing facilities in nearby dwellings.

Box 16.4 Bathing in Beguntila

Young girls in Beguntila slum in Dhaka explain how they struggle every day to bathe: 'We bathe in the dirty pond, with our clothes on. Then we go home, change our clothes and then come back to wash the "changed" clothes. This is so difficult when we are bleeding (menstruating)'. There are several accounts of the inconvenience of dealing with menstruation in the absence of adequate facilities. 'Where will we wash [rags used for menstrual flows], where will we [be able to] dry them?' report women in crowded slums in New Delhi. (Garg et al., 2001: 21)

'I feel unwell when I am not clean, yet it's an enormous effort to stay clean on the streets' says Marium, a 55-year-old woman who lives on the streets in Dhaka. Water, toilets, and bathing spaces require building relationships with those who can provide access, yet this does not guarantee full access. 'I have a rapport with the guards of the sports stadium. As an old woman – I am allowed to fill my container with water for drinking. I often lie and take a quick shower under the tap, with my clothes on, and pretend I got wet in filling my pot. I would like to take the time to bathe but that would be too much to ask.' Marium has strict rules for her daughter-in-law to forge such social networks around sanitation needs. 'I will not allow my daughter-in-law to go to the stadium. The guards will harass her for a "relationship".' Many urban poor women in Dhaka city reported taking up lower-paying domestic household help jobs, just because it offered the possibility of convenience and dignity in meeting personal hygiene needs: 'We can bathe in the privacy of the bathrooms where we wash clothes – with clean water and soap'. (Joshi et al., 2011: 103)

In South Asia across Hindu and Islamic cultures, secretions issuing from the peripheral extremities of the human body, faeces, blood, semen, urine, etc., are considered polluted and the body itself acquires a temporary pollution or impurity during the act of excretion, during sexual intercourse, and for women after childbirth, menstruation, etc. Sanitation as socially and locally conceived requires a ritualistic cleansing of the body (Joshi et al., 2005). These social notions around pollution determine, for example, why it is so crucial to take a ritualistic bath after sexual intercourse; this is considered more important locally than washing hands after defecation. Ritual cleansing or *wuzu* is required for Muslim women and men after defecation, as is bathing after sex and/or after menstruation. Cultural assumptions around 'filth' and the need for cleaning vary by age. Curtis et al. (1991) report that faeces of very young, unweaned children is considered to be less or not polluting, hence less unclean. It is this belief that influences many mothers to ignore hygiene lessons around faeces when dealing with very young children. While women and men both acquire temporary bodily pollution after sexual intercourse, women reported they had to find and store water for bathing, for both themselves and their husbands; this is a woman's task (Joshi et al., 2005). Women have additional cleansing needs during and after menstruation and childbirth and are often responsible for finding this water.

> Women in the Lingojigudem squatter settlement in Hyderabad city reported helping each other by providing a bucket of water [by each household] to women to meet ritualistic cleaning requirements post child-birth; as well as water to manage basic post-natal water needs. For a vast majority of urban poor women, adequate water, hygiene and privacy during childbirth and menstruation are a luxury. (Joshi et al., 2011: 104)

Age, class, disability, religion, ethnicity, and spatial variations in access to services and facilities all play some role in determining which women are more or less vulnerable. Crowded urban settings offer higher risks to women especially because of the lack of a social cohesion, and of legal recognition of the community by authorities; the dominance of religious intolerance and of stigma affect women's ability to talk about such issues in tight-knit settled rural locations. While all of these needs are ignored in the delivery and promotion of sanitation, it is ironic that sanitation is still referred to as a women's sector.

The apolitical positioning of 'women's special sanitation needs'

While the more mundane feminized tasks of cleaning the home, cleaning clothes, cleaning children, etc. are by-and-large ignored, menstruation, an 'ultimate feminine' specificity, is quite popular in recent sanitation discourse. However, as Lahiri-Dutt and Nair (n.d.) argue, the focus on menstruation serves only to highlight an intriguing anthropology. Social and religious taboos around menstruation, women's lack of knowledge around menstrual hygiene, or in some cases, even 'associating the connotations of disgust around menstruation with women's core identity and subjectivity ... [means] that menstruation is a metaphor for women's real and symbolic absence, marginalization, fragile status ... and misrepresentation' (Kerkham 2003: 279). Lahiri-Dutt and Nair (n.d.) show that identifying menstruation as a symptom of women's greater vulnerability leads to the relative ignoring of menstruation as a 'normal' biological process and the practical 'need for sanitation investments and action' (Bharadwaj and Patkar, 2004: 1). Women face enormous constraints in managing menstrual hygiene, but these have less to do with the 'social and traditional taboos' around menstruation, or women's lack of knowledge about it, than the striking inattention to the subject as a component of basic sanitation and hygiene. Addressing menstrual hygiene requires that sanitation services and facilities routinely and unquestionably pay attention to, invest in, and provide for sanitation facilities that enable women to deal with their cyclic menstruation, rather than explore and present exotic stories of how women deal with menstruation in the absence of appropriate services (Lahiri-Dutt and Nair, n.d.).

The 2010 Amnesty report contains stories of women's indignity and insecurity. The report is important in its pointing out the disproportionate challenges to women as an outcome of inappropriate defecation and other sanitation (bathing, washing) facilities. Yet this report is acutely apolitical. First, it pays little attention to Kenyan policies relating to informal settlements and fails to acknowledge that in Kenya, as in many other countries, there is a stark official silence on the legal and basic rights of the urban poor living in 'illegal settlements', i.e., the lack of a secure tenure. All slums are, therefore, officially illegal and the government – local and national – is not legally bound to provide basic services in these locations. What makes the difference in terms of access to basic services in different slums in Nairobi are twists of fate in the form of occasional attention from primarily non-governmental organizations. In the light of this political reality, many recommendations made in the report, albeit well intentioned, are unrealistic and barely applicable to these illegal settings: for example, the recommendation that landlords (themselves illegal) be forced to construct toilets/bathrooms in the vicinity of each household; subsistence be provided to enable toilet/ bathroom constructions; increased level of street-lighting; provision of '*equal* protection to those living in informal settlements'; or even increased policing (Amnesty International, 2010: 43–4).

In assuming that these recommended measures will be technically feasible and politically prioritized in areas long-existing but enduringly ignored as 'illegal', this report is a fine example of the apolitical nature of discourses on sanitation.

In relation to gender, the report, on the one hand, tends to eulogize women's caring, nurturing *sanitation* roles, and on the other, reiterates women's greater sexual vulnerability by accepting and validating an easily tampered-with 'modesty' for women. Indeed, women's greater vulnerability is stressed or even blamed for the possible impacts or consequences on 'women's productive capabilities and a consequential impoverishment of their families and communities' (ibid. 5). Such sweeping generalizations have enormous social and political consequences in revalidating entrenched gendered inequalities.

Conclusion

It is evident that sanitation is not a simple health issue limited to the safe disposal of faeces and hand-washing. On the contrary, appropriate sanitation is derived from basic human needs, influenced by the need for privacy, comfort, and dignity, and by religious beliefs and local cultures. These multiple aspects of sanitation intertwine and influence the health and social connotations of appropriate sanitation.

Ignoring this complex reality and providing only health hygiene translates into significant indignity for the poor. They speak of an enormous prejudice. Such work fails to address the basic human aspects of privacy, safety, comfort, and convenience in the design and promotion of toilet facilities for the poor, and stopping sanitation interventions at that point is unacceptable. Sanitation, if it is to be appropriate, especially for a disenfranchised poor, will need to expand beyond the promotion of 'any access to excreta disposal facilities'. Unfortunately, these are not currently the criteria that define the provision of sanitation for the majority of the poor. While the benefits of hygienic excreta disposal facilities are important, of course, not paying attention to other essential non-health needs is unethical and serves to continue the persisting sanitation gap. Above all, it continues to entrench gendered fractures relating to sanitation responsibilities at the household level.

Acknowledging and addressing holistic sanitation needs will not readily translate to 'empowering' women. Empowering women would require taking strategic steps that enable women and men to acknowledge and address gendered inequities that tie women to sanitation roles and responsibilities, and reduce the persisting greater shame and the oft too easily tampered-with dignity relating to female biology. It is important, then, to prioritize women's sanitation needs and responsibilities but also, while consciously refraining from stereotyping women, their feminine vulnerabilities and negativities, to engage in transforming unequal gendered sanitation responsibilities

References

Abrahams, N., Mathews, S., and Ramela, P. (2006) 'Intersections of sanitation, sexual coercion and girls' safety in schools', *Tropical Medicine and International Health* 11: 751–6.
Allen, A., Davila, J. and Hofmann, P. (2006) 'The peri-urban water poor: citizens or consumers?' *Environment and Urbanization* 18 (2): 333–51.

Amnesty International (2010) *Insecurity and Indignity – Women's experiences in the slums of Nairobi, Kenya*, Amnesty International, London.

Bapat, M. and Agarwal, I. (2003) 'Our needs, our priorities; women & men from the slums in Mumbai and Pune talk about their needs for water and sanitation', *Environment and Urbanisation* 15: 71–86.

Bharadwaj, S., and Patkar, A. (2004) *Menstrual Hygiene and Management in Developing Countries: Taking Stock*, Junction Social, Mumbai, Social Development Consultants, [DOC] <www.wsp.org/wsp/Hygiene-Sanitation-Water-Toolkit/Resources/Readings/Bharadwai-2004-Menstrual.doc>.

Black, M. (2002) The No-Nonsense Guide to International Development, New Internationalist Publications, in association with Verso, London.

Bond, P. (2002) *Unsustainable South Africa: Environment, Development and Social Protest*, University of Natal Press, Scottsville, South Africa.

Curtis, V., and Biran, A. (2001) 'Dirt, disgust, and disease: is hygiene in our genes?', *Perspectives in Biology and Medicine* 44: 17–31.

Curtis, V., Voncken, N. and Singh, S. (1991) 'Dirt and disgust: a Darwinian perspective on hygiene', *Medische Antropologie* 11: 143–58.

De Beauvoir, S. (1949) *The Second Sex*, David Campbell Publishers, London (1993).

Douglas, M. (1996) *Purity and Danger: An Analysis of the Concepts of Pollution and Taboo*, Routledge and Kegan Paul, London.

Evans, B. (2005) *Securing Sanitation – The Compelling Case to Address the Crisis*, Stockholm International Water Institute and the World Health Organization, Stockholm.

Garg, S., Sharma, N., and Sahay, R. (2001) 'Socio-cultural aspects of menstruation in an urban slum in Delhi, India', *Reproductive Health Matters* 9: 16–25.

Islam, Z., Akter, N., Hossain, M. Z., and Barnett, T. (2000) *Women's Approach to Rural Sanitation*, 26th WEDC International Conference, Dhaka, Bangladesh: 379–81.

Jenkins, M. and Sugden, S. (2006) 'Rethinking sanitation: lessons and innovation for sustainability and success in the new millennium', Human Development Report 2006, Human Development Report Office, Occasional Paper, UNDP.

Jodha, N.S (1988) 'Poverty debate in India: a minority view', *Economic and Political Weekly* 23 (45–47): 2421–8.

Joshi, D., Morgan, J. and Fawcett, B. (2005) 'Sanitation for the urban poor: whose choice, theirs or ours?', unpublished research report [PDF] <www.dfid.gov.uk/r4d/PDF/Outputs/Water/R8028-FTR.pdf>.

Joshi, D., Fawcett, B, and Mannan, F. (2011) 'Health, hygiene and appropriate sanitation: experiences and perceptions of the urban poor', *Environment and Urbanization* 23: 91–111 <http://dx.doi.org/10.1177/0956247811398602>.

Jørgensen, D. (2008) 'Putting dirt in its place: review of Campkin, Ben; Cox, Rosie, eds., *Dirt: New Geographies of Cleanliness and Contamination*', H-Water, H-Net Reviews [article] <www.h-net.org/reviews/showrev.php?id=14597>.

Kerkham, P. (2003) 'Menstruation – the gap in the text?', *Psychoanalytic Psychotherapy* 17: 279–99.

Lahiri-Dutt, K., and Nair, A. (undated) 'Women, menstruation and water: avoiding biological essentialism in development', unpublished.

Mehta, L. (2007) *Liquid dynamics*, STEPS Briefing 6 from L. Mehta, F. Marshall, S. Movik, A. Stirling, E. Shah, A. Smith and J. Thompson (2007), *Liquid Dynamics: Challenges for Sustainability in Water and Sanitation*, STEPS Working Paper 6, STEPS Centre, Brighton.

Molynuex, M. (2007) 'The chimera of success: gender ennui and the changed international policy environment', in A. Cornwall, E. Harrison and A. Whitehead (eds), *Feminisms in Development: Contradictions, Contestations and Challenges*, pp. 227–40, Zed Books, London and New York.

Morella, E., Foster, V. and Banerjee, S. G. (2009) 'Climbing the ladder: the state of sanitation in Sub Saharan Africa', Africa Infrastructure Country Diagnostic Background Paper 13 (Phase I), World Bank, Washington, DC.

O'Reilly, K. (2010) 'Combining sanitation and women's participation in water supply: An example from Rajasthan', *Development in Practice* 20: 45–56.

Penner, B. (2010) 'Flush with inequality: sanitation in South Africa', *Places: Design Observer* [webpage] <http://places.designobserver.com/entry.html?entry=21619>.

Sijbesma, C. (2008) 'Sanitation and hygiene in South Asia: progress and challenges', Summary paper of the South Asian Sanitation & Hygiene Practitioners' Workshop organized by IRC, WaterAid and BRAC in Rajendrapur, Bangladesh, 29–31 January.

Sijbesma, C., Diaz, C. Fonsec, C., and Pezon, C. (2008) 'Financing Sanitation in Poor Urban Areas', IRC Symposium: Sanitation for the Urban Poor: Partnerships and Governance, Delft, 19–21 November.

About the author

Deepa Joshi is interested in the gendered impacts of development interventions. She has worked in South and South-east Africa, and Latin America, managing programmes, conducting policy research, and leading local research capacity building. She is interested in analysing the drivers and processes of policy reforms, understanding how policies evolve within different institutional cultures and structures, and the hierarchies of knowledge and power which shape practice in these institutional spaces.

CHAPTER 17
Postscript

Tina Wallace

Standing back in time and space from the hurly-burly and demands of getting a book together with multiple authors, it feels possible to reflect on the core issues, as well as to look back over my experiences through decades of working in development, much of it with international NGOs. It feels important to also look forward. I am sitting on a small island hung between Africa, the Middle East, and Europe, feeling the different pace of life, the deeply different history, the legacy of different cultures as well as centuries of being conquered and subservient yet sensing through it all a pride and independence of spirit. As a relatively new member of the EU, Brussels feels far away; the gulf between the language and policies there and daily life on this rocky island is stark. Many new EU requirements make little or no sense and are poorly understood; yet decisions taken far away by bureaucrats, bankers, PR staff, and others have huge repercussions here.

It is a timely reminder of the often vast and growing gulf between the policies and thinking around 'development' – aspects of which are so well analysed in Part I, 'A perfect storm' – and the realities of people's lives, their hopes and fears, their opportunities and constraints, their thoughts, ideas, and feelings. These realities, especially those of the most marginal, forgotten women and girls – whose aspirations are still rarely voiced and even more rarely heard by aid bureaucracies – are well described and articulated in Part II. The chapters here highlight the need to 'change the conversations' among aid professionals, especially in the NGO sector, to enable a better response to the needs of those in whose name they work.

Some authors attempt to explain and understand what drives the growing gap between the rhetoric, procedures, and claims of aid – especially but not only of INGOs – and the realities of those experiencing the painful, arduous, limiting demands of deep poverty. Upon reflection there seem to be many drivers: one is the shift in funding sources accompanied by growing demands for measurable evidence of short-term gains. Another is the growing role of private-sector norms, evident in INGO boardrooms, in communications and marketing departments, in companies regulating INGO applications for large government funding and organizing the evaluations for them. A third is undoubtedly the competition between INGOs for funding and influence, which appears to have shifted them away from portraying themselves as

http://dx.doi.org/10.3362/9781780447780/017

supporters of development towards taking centre stage, so that their role now is one of engineering change and delivering results; this edges out the voice and role of their partners, of the women and men they work with.

Whatever discussions take place in private within INGOs, the public face and language of many of these organizations has become more focused on understandings of change based on linear models of cause and effect, models that make a virtue of simplifying the complex as captured in the KPMG strapline, 'cutting through complexity'. Yet the causes of poverty are multiple, interrelated, complex, and hard to shift; gains in one area – e.g., preventing measles – can so easily be overturned by a poor harvest. Addressing poverty requires actions on multiple levels including large-scale government (and private sector) investment on infrastructure, public health measures, and agricultural extension that reach whole populations and address specific barriers to change. Much else is needed, though, to move people out of poverty and to address their deep inequalities, especially gender inequality; it keeps many women from accessing resources even when they become available, silences their voice and participation through violence and lack of education and of confidence, and prevents the addressing of legal, religious, and cultural barriers that have for so long kept women as second-class citizens. These are the ongoing concerns of international, national, and community-based non-government organizations; work on these areas is critical to leverage real change for women and girls, as demonstrated in several chapters. It is also to support such work that the public donates.

The role of the third sector, as it undergoes current changes, is increasingly being questioned by some; it is not now unusual to hear people working in development talk of the irrelevance or even death of the third sector. Some feel that the increased blurring of boundaries between the public, private, and third sector is positive and means that all energy and resources are focused on delivering 'aid'; everyone is 'hoeing the same row'. For them, issues of power differences, how agendas are set and by whom, seem to evaporate in the new 'partnerships' with government and private-sector agencies. In the process, however, others observe that partnerships with NGOs, CBOs, and communities diminish because they lack the power to demand rigid systems of accountability – or often, indeed, any accountability – and they wield no power through funding or setting agendas.

This book does not share the view that the third sector is no longer relevant and I, along with most of the authors in this book, support the need for a non-government sector, in UK and in development, which is able to work and talk differently. Here INGOs that have more resources and power than many other civil society organizations need to take a lead. There are multiple roles for NGOs and space for wide diversity, including, for example, speaking out against injustice, enabling those most marginalized and excluded to find their voice, working alongside them with respect, giving them dignity, and tailoring support to the local realities in which they live. When I started out with INGOs in the 1980s the watchwords in many agencies were the need for independence of voice, the importance of autonomy and independence, partnership and playing the roles of supporter, accompanier and pilot light for those struggling for their rights. There was – as now – huge diversity; while some focused on services, others on speaking out, and others on working welfare and emergency hand-outs, there was a passion in many INGOs for their work and a strong political commitment to the need for transformatory change. While much NGO literature still uses concepts of passion and commitment, as the book illustrates, the lived realities of those working with and for them and on the receiving end of many of their programmes can be very different. There has always been much to challenge, question, and learn in INGOs about what works, and what is defined as important, and previously there was space within them to argue and debate. However, in contrast, many currently working in INGOs have concerns that they cannot raise their voices outside, and even sometimes within, the organizations they work for. Many who spoke out behind closed doors felt unable to write about their experiences here. Even some who have written feel nervous about what repercussions there may be and how hard they will be hit by any debate generated.

The debates I was engaged in then took place between gender programme staff in government and those in INGOs, and within INGOs; they were focused on issues such as how to enable women to find their voice, what kind of agriculture worked best for communities living in arid lands, and how to find ways to better understand local realities and work with them. There were huge challenges and many flaws, especially around the lack of concern with women in development, and little understanding of issues of gender inequality as drivers of poverty and marginalization. Gender staff had a difficult time raising challenging issues, and experienced many kinds of marginalization and exclusion. Even so, many open roundtables were held with gender staff in aid agencies, both donor and INGO, to think through how to work together on these development challenges.

Such debates can be much more difficult now when, for example, private companies stand between many in the INGO sector and government donors. When INGOs and government do meet, concerns often focus on the condi-tionalities of aid and more instrumentalist agendas. The outsourced agencies themselves have limited room for manoeuvre or judgement, because they are working to tight government contracts; this seriously limits what individual INGOs can challenge and discuss. The 'straightjacket' of much funding has been made even tighter recently by conditions demanding that milestones be met (whatever the local realities) and if they are not, funding can be withdrawn. Reports must be scored by the outsourced contractors in many cases, and must meet benchmarks defined by them or again money will not be released. This structure squeezes the room for debate, and these conditions are not conducive to good development practice. By playing different roles with different responsibilities and accountabilities to government and the private agencies, how can the sector work more coherently and with a collective voice, to regain legitimacy and authority as a third sector? In a world dominated by manuals and formats and written in opaque language not based on development practice, there is an urgent need to find new ways of ensuring that partners and the women and men they work with have a voice.

Instead, the focus is likely to be less on issues of partnership or participation than on grant compliance, and how best to tell a success story of aid. One outside observer from a UK Foundation described the multiple and highly bureaucratic strictures placed on development staff in INGOs as the 'lilliputization' of the sector, where proficiency at documentation within tight formats dominates, and rewards are closely related to raising and accounting for funds in prescribed ways. Earlier research in *The Aid Chain* showed how many development staff now feel they have become administrators and are no longer development workers; high staff turnovers would indicate quite deep levels of dissatisfaction in some agencies. In the field offices and the partner organizations the constraints imposed on them through the current aid systems were also explored and several of the chapters in this book show how these have deepened over time. Current ways of working are profoundly changing the relationships around aid, and not, according to many observers, for the better.

Indeed, even during the past year of writing the book, new approaches, manuals, and requirements have further entrenched the focus on documentation and quantitative evidence. For example, evaluation manuals written for DfID by private-sector consultants focus on value for money, added value, validating theories of change to assess how well they align with donor theories of change, and much more in the same vein; all such are frequently accompanied by long glossaries of terms to be applied, terms more usually associated with measuring profit and loss. While broader development debates certainly still go on within NGOs, the space for these is squeezed by the constantly escalating donor requirements and the need to produce 'currently sanctioned' forms of evidence. The demand for these kinds of evidence increases despite the emergence of critiques (e.g., from the National Audit Office, UN, USAID, and others referred to in this book) about the time needed for much current data collection, the relative emptiness of the numbers collected, and the need for more detailed understandings of what is being done, with whom and to what end. There are growing – but still largely muted - concerns about how evidence is defined in contexts where numbers are hard to access because populations are not known, the cost of baselines is high, and follow-up data are often not of the same populations. When 25 small and medium INGOs in a workshop in 2010 were asked whether their figures were reliable, none could hand-on-heart say they were.

According to those who contributed to this book, and from my own experience, this all matters because, in order to support real change for the most disadvantaged, especially women, the work requires strong relationships to be built and power dynamics addressed. The work needs to be understood and approached differently. Women, and men, need to be listened to, their sensitivities and dignity respected, and their wide differences rooted in diverse historical and cultural contexts understood and addressed. Sometimes women need protection from those who threaten them, while others need confidence and skills-building or recognition of who and what they are in order to release their energies. Sometimes they need recognition and funding support to enable them to do what they know needs doing. It is in meeting these context-specific needs that development workers, partners, and CBOs from the non-government sector play or can play a critical role. Addressing inequality requires addressing multiple issues; change does not follow simple interventions, will take time, and will be erratic and incremental. Yet understanding complexity, engaging with uncertainty, learning as you go, listening, and working contextually, which this book argues are essential elements in addressing gender inequality, are often characterized as negative, backward-looking, and over-complicated in the new 'can do' world of targets, rollout, reach, promises, and demonstrations of success.

The questions now are rarely 'Is the work working?', 'Why did the approach fail to deliver what was expected?', or 'Why was the experience patchy across regions?', and are far more likely to be 'Have we met the targets?', 'Can we show we did what we promised?', and 'Is the story of our effectiveness well told?' These approaches can so easily silence resistance and critical analysis; in many agencies, annual reports no longer carry accounts of challenges, assumptions that did not hold up, or analysis of failure. Failure has become a dirty word. In this context, raising concerns and asking questions is very difficult. Yet the dangers of ignoring what has been learned, what has gone wrong, and why, are well illustrated in this book. The push to show success, to be taken seriously, to be part of the policymaking takes risks with the essential ability to take time to listen, to build good working relations across cultures, and to analyse the limitations and also the potential of the role of NGOs.

There is a need, perhaps more than ever during the current economic crisis and political shifts in Europe and the USA, for genuine independence and at times for dissent, and for an open critique of dominant paradigms. This book suggests the critical importance of INGOs remaining distinct from, and in creative tension with, other organizations. The rhetoric of rights and equality for women is in common use now, and focused solutions are proposed to bring short-term change; however, the work to address the challenges that keep women from realizing these rights is often poorly funded and the barriers for women remain firmly in place. These issues and constraints need to be challenged in multiple ways and at multiple levels.

I have been asked recently how this book will change things. Having written over the past 25 years about trends that have subsequently deepened and taken a stronger hold on INGOs and those they relate to, I am under no illusions. There are no grand expectations of a book changing the minds of those who maintain that the current procedures and systems norms are professional and appropriate and will deliver real change for the poor, or those who suspect that the concept of civil society and a distinctive NGO sector within it is outmoded or dead. For those that see the core issues as accountability to taxpayers, the need to prove how effectively and efficiently they are delivering change for others, and defining current evaluation methodologies as transparent and accountable, this book will do nothing except perhaps bring a wry smile to their faces.

This book is written for those staff within donor agencies, within NGOs in the North and the South, and those within the academic world who feel uneasy about the dominant trends. It is hoped that knowing others are questioning and even rejecting some current practices in development will enable those who sense things are not right to feel it is worthwhile raising their voices. It is for those who believe that what is done matters more than what is said or claimed, that practice trumps rhetoric, and that time and resources need to be redirected back to working alongside poor women and men and away from the intense focus on systems, manuals, and formats. It is for those who share the concern of Onora O'Neill in her Reith Lectures (BBC, 2002, lecture 3) where she noted, 'Central planning may have failed in the Soviet Union but it is alive and well in Britain today'; it is planning where you dream a future, plan for it, and then show it has been delivered. The tight control of staff in the Soviet model undermined trust and respect for their skills, limited the judgment and creative energy of staff, and led to false reporting to show that what had been promised had been achieved. She warned how corrosive such trends are proving within UK institutions; this book argues that development aid is no exception.

This book draws on the thinking and work rooted in many disciplines, including feminism, post-colonial literature, complexity theory, management studies, and development practice, and concludes that what is needed for development is often undermined by current ways of working, systems, and priorities. Those sharing some of the unease or experiences of the authors might, perhaps, be able to find and articulate resistance or alternatives. It might enable some to re-envisage 'the poor' in Africa, Asia, Latin America, and the Middle East as citizens of their own countries, and as subjects of their own development. The issue of accepting sovereign nation states might seem a strange one to be raising 50–100 years after independence from colonial rule for most of these countries. The current 'feel' of development, however, with DfID projects and reports displaying the Union flag and prominent agency logos, and increasing claims that what has changed for the better has occurred as a result of agency interventions, recalls a colonial heritage. It feels timely to remind development actors, ourselves included, about the importance of respecting 'the other', the need for humility, and recognizing the limits of agency and roles, points so well made by several writers in this volume.

This book highlights what is being lost or ignored in much current development work in INGOs and those they fund, organizations where a detailed, nuanced, and context-relevant approach might most be expected. It raises questions about the roles and purpose of NGOs, where their legitimacy lies, who they represent, and their relationship to wider civil society organizations and movements. Those roles are diverse, complex, evolving, and changing. But much is being lost by the race to join 'the mainstream', to be conduits for government and institutional funding, to increase reach and influence, and to form partnerships with the powerful. This book argues that key characteristics and values are being undermined in the race for survival in a harsh economic climate, in which organizations are starting to collapse for lack of funds.

Several challenges seem critical for the future work by INGOs, their staff and partners around the world if the focus is to remain on addressing inequality, especially gender inequality, promoting justice, and combatting the multiple causes and effects of poverty.

In relation to gender equality, for example, gender staff have argued for a focus on women and girls. The current fashionable interest is, however, often a travesty of what is needed, offering instead easy answers which are measurable and marketable. Such approaches risk undermining years of work experience by and for women who know that the issues perpetuating gender inequality are interrelated, culturally and politically supported, and rooted in relations of power. Understanding complexity, engaging with uncertainty, learning as you go, listening, working contextually, which the book argues are essential, are often characterized as overcomplicated in the new 'can do' world of targets, promises, and proving success. This world needs confronting through building on recent debates around gender mainstreaming and the transformation and political agendas of gender equality. The debates could be taken up by agencies that espouse gender equality rather than left to often marginalized gender staff.

The dangers of ignoring both what has been learned and the knowledge, theory, and practice of development have been well illustrated. It feels important now for NGOs to revisit their own development practice and explore together as a sector how far this practice is being supported or distorted by current funding requirements. Questions such as whether there is a need to redress the balance between the power wielded by agencies in the North – funders, boards, private-sector contractors regulating grant management – and those in the South – partners, staff, local organizations, women, and men – need discussing.

More particularly there is work to be done in challenging the current language and systems in place for managing development. We need to interrogate the value and relevance of the concepts dominating donor accountability in meeting the needs and rights of the poor. New manuals and processes are tumbling in, arbitrated by private-sector companies used to the language and norms of that sector. Can INGOs debate the relevance and usefulness of such approaches, and the methodologies used? These require critical analysis to see how robust they are (the reliance on statistical data collected from contexts where data collection is often problematic for example) and whether they do indeed lead to greater transparency. At the moment many quantitative methods appear to be followed and given a status denied to other more qualitative ways of learning, including listening to the poor. Is that status justified and what is actually being learned from current rounds of reviews and evaluations using these methods? What might work better to ensure accountability to the poor as well as the powerful, and show what, how, and why change is actually happening on the ground? Are there ways to find space for such debates?

It will be important to understand better how aid-flows are changing, which organizations are receiving government aid money, and to do what. In common with the rest of the UK, development aid has seen a sharp rise in funding for the private sector through outsourcing a wide range of functions, as auditors, grant managers, project managers, assessors, and evaluators, as well as writing core manuals and guidelines for development practice. This is only now becoming an issue for debate and it will be essential to be clear what the implications will be of having private-sector companies becoming the arbiters of what is and what is not good development, and what constitutes valid evidence. Will there come a time when INGO work fails to fit the set requirements, resulting in evaluation and learning work being permanently outsourced? To what extent is the privatization of aid a reality, and what is needed to address the implications?

Perhaps one overall core challenge arises from this book: how can the organizations in the sector find a more coherent voice about what they stand for, what their bottom lines are, what they will do to raise funds and account for them, and what do they feel is a step too far? Fundamentally, who are they to align themselves with? Raising questions, challenging, openly disagreeing with a particular version of events or way of working has never been easy, but it is essential in order to explore the distinct role, purpose, and value of a third sector going into the future. Those writing here believe in the value and multiple roles for organizations working with and representing civil society, but, in order to find that coherent voice and the best ways of working, the challenges need to be openly discussed, and criticisms and questions allowed. The calls for humility, for openness and learning, for respect for the other, for more complex and open ways of understanding the world seem good starting points for such discussions.

About the author

Tina Wallace has worked in development for over 30 years, as a teacher and researcher in the UK and Africa and with international NGOs. Her PhD was from Makerere University in Kampala; she taught for many years in Nigeria. She has extensive experience of field-based work in Africa and the Middle East (some in Asia), in both research and development practice. She has worked in INGOs such as Oxfam and World University Service, more recently working as a freelancer with a wide range of UK and African NGOs, especially on issues around gender, strategy, monitoring, and learning. She works from a gender perspective, recognizing inequality in gender relations as a driver for poverty and injustice.

Index

.